TORAH LITERATURE
OF QUALITY

DESIGNER WORLD

נפלאות הבורא

ഔ ൠ

Rabbi Avrohom Katz (Tuvia Cohen)

Distributed in Europe by:
J Lehman Hebrew Booksellers
20 Cambridge Terrace
Gateshead / Tyne & Wear
NE8 1RP / England

Distributed Worldwide:
Feldheim Publishers Ltd
POB 35002
Jerusalem, Israel

COPYRIGHT
©
1994
by Rabbi Avrohom Katz and GJBS

All rights reserved. No part of this book may be reproduced without written permission from the copyright holders, apart from a reviewer who quotes short passages as a review written for newspapers or magazines

---

Published by:
GJBS
35-37 Gladstone Terrace
Gateshead, Tyne & Wear
NE8 4HE
ENGLAND

Designed and Typeset by **TOPIC** *TOrah Publication Centre, Gateshead, +91 477 6809*

plates by Frank, Jerusalem

Printed in Israel

RABBI B. RAKOW
RAV OF GATESHEAD
138 WHITEHALL ROAD,
GATESHEAD   NE8   1TP
Tyne & Wear
TEL. 0632-773012

בצלאל בהרה"ג ר' יום טוב ליפמאן ראקאוו
אב"ד דנייטסהעד

Gateshead Talmudical College

Principal Rabbi Z. Cohen
Rosh Hayeshiva Rabbi A. Gurwicz

בס״ד

בס״ד

It is with very special joy that I write these few lines of appreciation on the unique work of a very beloved Talmid whose friendship I have cherished for over 25 years.

בעל מדות and ירא שמים, בן תורה is renowned as a הרי״ר אברהם טוביה הכהן כ״ץ שליט״א טובות. But most outstanding is his אמונה - which is what this book is all about.

The chapters of this book do not just contain clever comparisons in parable form, but they are דברים היוצאים מן הלב - sincere words emanating from a pure heart, designed to enter the heart and strengthen the reader's awareness of הקב״ה in all his surroundings.

This ספר is an updated שער הבחינה, expanding on the theme begun by the בעל חובות הלבבות, and continued through the years up till our times by such גדולים as the חזון איש in his ספר חיי עולם and the Steipler זצ״ל in his קונטרס אמונה ובטחון.

The author of this work has his own original approach, and although his style is sometimes light, one is never diverted from the central theme of the book which is to make the reader - at the end of each chapter - gasp in astonishment and exclaim over and over again - נפלאות הבורא! נפלאות הבורא!

זכה המחבר שליט״א להיות ממזכי הרבים הגדולים בדורנו על ידי שעוריו המתוקים בכמה מוסדות בעירנו וכמה מקומות במדינתנו - ועכשיו זיכנו השי״ת להרחיב גבולו על ידי ספר נפלא זה שיגיע בעזה״י לכל קצווי תבל ותתרבה הדעת והאמונה בעולם - אשרי חלקו!

ויהי רצון שיפוצו מעייינותיו חוצה ויראה ברכה בעמלו כל הימים

ממני הכו״ח באה״ר

[signature]

מתתיהו חיים סלומון

JEWISH TEACHERS' TRAINING COLLEGE

Founded by: Mr A. KOHN

FOR TEACHERS IN DAY SCHOOLS, HEBREW CLASSES AND NURSERY - SCHOOLS

Principal: Rabbi M. MILLER

50, BEWICK ROAD
GATESHEAD NE8 4DQ
Telephone: 091-477 2620
091-477 1566

ב"ה

It gives me considerable satisfaction to write a few words of approbation with regard to the book, "Designer World" — נפלאות הבורא — compiled by Rabbi A Katz who has been a most successful lecturer at the Gateshead Jewish Teachers' Training College for several years.

Rabbi Katz is endowed with an unusual gift both in the written and spoken word to demonstrate the incontrovertible wonders in the universe at large and in the personal human physique, thus accomplishing the dual function of שאו מרום עיניכם וראו מי ברא אלה —"Raise your eyes to the heavens and contemplate, 'Who created all this?'" (Yeshayoh, 40:26) and מבשרי אחזה אלוק — "And from my own flesh I can perceive my Creator" (Job 19:26) in its positive sense.

Rabbi Katz's writings are infused with both wit and erudition and his style fascinates the reader. He has been a regular contributor to the "Yated Ne'eman" and the present volume is a compilation of those articles.

The book is an invaluable source from which the reader will derive an appreciation of the wondrous world of the Creator and it will undoubtedly strengthen his Emunah. It is a path trodden by אברהם אבינו and commended to us by so many of our גדולים; in particular, חובות הלבבות, רמב"ם and חזון איש.

In seeking to emulate their illustrious example, albeit in a modern context and idiom, Rabbi Katz has provided the reader with a wealth of material from which he can attain greater awareness of the גדלות הבורא.

I profoundly hope that "Designer World" will reach the minds and hearts of a wide public to accomplish the purpose for which it was written.

Rabbi M Miller
Principal, Gateshead J T T C

Dedicated to The Memory of

My Mother
Mrs. Claire Rachel Katz ע״ה

*a woman of valour, the crown of her family,
whose kindliness and noble principles
made her beloved to all who knew her.*

Passed away 24th Iyar 5739

My Father-in-law
Mr. Avrohom Pinchos Kind ז״ל

*who in every facet of his life
personified love of Hashem and love
of Klal Yisroel.*

Passed away 28th Adar Sheni 5744

My Brother
Yitzchok Efraim Katz ז״ל

*who, in his short life, demonstrated kindness,
strength of character and love of Torah,
that remain an inspiration to this day.*

Passed away 11th Elul 5723

ॐ ACKNOWLEDGEMENTS ॐ

When the time comes to give thought to thanks, one particular feeling predominates. 'How can I repay *Hashem* for all his kindness to me?' (*Tehillim* 116).

How can I begin to give thanks to *Hashem* for all the multitude of kindnesses which have been bestowed upon me? How can one detail particular benefits, when all of life is an endless chain of benefits. '... for Your miracles that are with us every day, and for Your wonders and favours in every season...' (*Amidah*).

Again, to use the words of *Tefillah* — although it is true that 'Were our mouth as full of song as the sea, and our tongue as full of joyous song as its multitude of waves, ...we still could not thank You sufficiently...' (*Nishmas Kol Chai*) — there is nevertheless an obligation to express gratitude to the best of our ability.

If this particular book 'Designer World' is a series of observations pinpointing specific details of the wonders of G-d's Creation - then I too would like to pinpoint areas of specific gratitude.

First and foremost my dear parents — my father Mr Arnold Katz and להבדיל בין חיים לחיים my mother Mrs Rachel Katz ה"ע, who together constantly nourished and sustained me with every form of support and encouragement possible. No words would do justice to the debt of gratitude that I owe them. May *Hashem Yisborach* grant my dear father many years of good health and happiness עד מאה ועשרים שנה, reaping the *Nachas* that he so richly deserves.

The town of Gateshead is blessed with a *Kehillah* rich in *Talmidei Chachomim*, and Institutions of Torah. In particular, it has the great merit to be led by a *Rov* of wisdom and renown, Rabbi B Rakow שליט"א, whose encouragement has benefited me in so many ways. I offer my thanks to *Hashem* for my good fortune in being able to live in this town, and draw so abundantly from the fertile Torah-rich atmosphere that prevails. In particular, the profoundest debt of gratitude is due to Gateshead Yeshiva — its revered *Roshei Yeshiva* and *Rabbonim* שליט"א, from whose association I gained my formative Jewish education, inspiration and spiritual development and much more, for close to thirty years.

My interest in the wonders of Creation was kindled by Rabbi Avigdor Miller שליט״א, and I am sure that I am one amongst thousands who have benefited from his unique approach in *Avodas Hashem*. May *Hashem Yisborach* give him good health and lengthy years to continue his *Avodas Hakodesh*, disseminating knowledge and love of *Hashem* throughout the world.

It was my good friend Dr Michoel Cope who formulated the idea to teach the wonders of Creation as a subject; and Rabbi Dovid Bowden, Principal of the Gateshead Jewish High School who provided me with the opportunity to transfer a simmering interest into a solid subject taught within a school framework. I am immensely grateful to them both for their constant encouragement, both in my teaching of this subject, and transposing 'Oral Law' into 'Written Law'. Without them 'Designer World' would have remained an inspired, but purely embryonic idea.

For the detailed medical knowledge required for many of the articles, I was fortunate to have access to the Gateshead Jewish Community's three wonderful doctors, Dr Selwyn Bolel, Dr Michoel Cope and Dr Shlomoh Rutenberg. My sincere thanks are extended to them for their valuable input. The allegory of the Moon landing in the introduction was taken from a lecture on 'Design in Creation' given by Dr Zvi Inbal, of the *Arachim* organisation. The ideas so lucidly formulated by Dr Inbal did much to lay the foundation for the theme that runs throughout this book.

The articles from which 'Designer World' is formulated have all appeared in *Yated Ne'eman*. I would like to express my gratitude to the Editorial staff of that worthy paper for permission to reprint those articles in book form. In particular I would like to articulate my sincere gratitude to Rabbi Bezalel Rappaport for his constant co-operation and cheerful encouragement in the ongoing publication of those articles.

And now to the book! Once again, 'good things happen through good people'. Divine Providence sent along Rabbi Nesanel Lieberman, Principal of the Gateshead Jewish Boarding School, who, with characteristic flair and foresight, undertook the formidable task of producing and publishing the book. Together with Rabbi Dovid Kornhauser, they have spared neither time, effort nor expense in producing a book which is both technically and aesthetically pleasing. The credit of the finished product is theirs, and to them both I express the most sincere thanks.

The photographs, which serve to enhance as well as to illustrate the book, are the products of three exceptionally talented photographers, Moshe Aharon Ruskin of Gateshead, and Michael Braham & Mike Poloway, both of Manchester. I would like to express my sincere appreciation for their willingness to share in the idealism that motivated this venture, and for their valuable time and expertise. The diagrams have been drawn by the extremely talented pen of Shlomoh Zeiger of New York.

Last but not least, I would like to express — something that words cannot express — to members of my family, none of whom wish to be mentioned by name, but whose encouragement, forbearance, tolerance and good humour, made it possible to devote the time to this work. They seek no greater reward or *Nachas* than that the book should provide a vehicle to spread the Name of *Hashem* in the world.

May *Hashem Yisborach* grant them that *Nachas*, in good health and happiness, עד מאה ועשרים שנה.

Elul 5754

❦ CONTENTS ❧

	Designer World *Introduction* 1
Chapter 1	The Peach Tree *Seed Dispersal* 7
Chapter 2	A Piece of Liver *Liver* 14
Chapter 3	The Listening Ear *Ear and Hearing* 20
Chapter 4	The Perfect Jig-Saw *Teeth* 24
Chapter 5	Food For Thought *Swallowing* 34
Chapter 6	The Car Wash *Digestion* 40
Chapter 7	Defence Forces *Bombadier Beetle and Adrenalin* 47
Chapter 8	My Good Friend *Heart* 54
Chapter 9	A Breath of Fresh Air *Lungs* 61

Chapter 10	Ayin Tovah I *Sight* 66
Chapter 11	Ayin Tovah II *Sight* 73
Chapter 12	Flight *Birds* 80
Chapter 13	Computer Speak *Brain and Voice* 87
Chapter 14	"Computer — Speak!" *Voice* 95
Chapter 15	Take A Look At A Leaf *Photosynthesis* 102
Chapter 16	The Crane *Arm and Hand* 110
Chapter 17	The Eight-Legged Wonder *Spider* 117
Chapter 18	A Master of Good Taste *Tongue* 124
Chapter 19	The Phenomenal Filter *Kidneys* 131
Chapter 20	The Most Modern Building *Bones* 138
Chapter 21	A Balanced View *Sense of Balance* 144

Chapter 22	Radar Patrol *Bats and Echolocation* 151
Chapter 23	The Thermostat *Temperature Control* 158
Chapter 24	Invisible Mending *Healing of Wounds* 165
Chapter 25	The Space Capsule *Eggs* 172
Chapter 26	Memories *Memory* 179
Chapter 27	The Suit of Armour *Skin* 187
Chapter 28	Current affairs *Electric Eel* 195
Chapter 29	'By Your Blood You Shall Live' *Blood* 202
Chapter 30	Counter-Espionage *Fighting Germs* 209
Chapter 31	The Queen of Fruits *Grapes* 216
Chapter 32	Long May She Rain *Rain* 223
Chapter 33	Underneath The Arches *Feet and Walking* 230

Chapter 34	The Real Facts *Nerve Transmission* 237
Chapter 35	Small is Beautiful *Insects* 244
Chapter 36	Heaven Scent *Sense of Smell* 251
Chapter 37	Biggest is Best *Elephants* 258
Chapter 38	Wonder of Wonders *Birth* 265
Chapter 39	A Joint Effort *Synovial Fluid* 272
Chapter 40	Strike a Light *Firefly* 279
Chapter 41	The Complete Medicine *Garlic* 285
Chapter 42	The Greatest Lift of All *Muscles* 292
Chapter 43	The Conductor *Pituitary Gland* 299

DESIGNER WORLD

Introduction

Imagine the following scene. The year is 1969, and the Apollo 11 space-craft manned by American astronauts is approaching the moon's surface. History is about to be made, and hundreds of millions of viewers down on earth are excitedly glued to their television sets. Slowly, the command module comes to rest on the barren moonscape. The door of the space-craft opens, and the television cameras strategically positioned on the side of the craft focus on the cumbersome form of Captain Neil Armstrong as he painstakingly descends the ladder. The very first human moon-booted foot is ready to tread the moon's surface. At that precise moment, the television cameras focus on something totally unexpected. There, lying on the moon, just where Capt. Armstrong's foot is about to tread, lies an empty bottle. There is no mistake. Hundreds of millions of viewers catch their breath. Not only is it a bottle, it is a vodka bottle!

What do you think would be the reaction of all those who witnessed this scene? "The Russians beat us to it." Bitter disappointment and incredulity would sweep America like wind through a cornfield.

Now imagine that immediately afterwards, the President of America appears on television, and makes the following pronouncement.

"Fellow Americans. I want you to know that no Russians have ever set foot on the moon. As for the vodka bottle that you saw, I have the following explanation. Everyone knows that the basic ingredients of glass are sand, silica and heat. All those ingredients exist on the moon. I would like to suggest that a stray meteorite struck the surface of the moon, generating great heat, which combined with the resident sand and silica to form a blob of glass. The fact that the glass was in the shape of a vodka bottle is just pure coincidence. Long live America!"

It is doubtful whether even the most fervently patriotic American would accept that explanation. And with good reason. Examine a glass bottle, and look for features of design. It has a flat base, giving it stability. It is round in shape, enabling it to be held in the hand. There are no sharp corners or edges, ensuring safety of usage.

It is hollow and transparent, has no flavour or aroma, making it ideal to store food. It has an opening at the top, so that the liquid can be poured out. There is a screw-top cover, allowing the user the luxury of not having to finish the contents at once. In short, every single aspect of the glass bottle demonstrates purpose, and there is not a single molecule in the bottle which is not in its correct place and serving a positive function. When that level of design is apparent, the human mind will not accept that the object in question is the result of an accident. It can be said to be axiomatic that where there is design, there is a designer. Sorry Mr President, we cannot accept your explanation!

It was this self-same axiom that was utilised by *Avrohom Ovinu* on his own voyage of discovery that convinced him of the existence of a Creator. The Rambam (*Hilchos Avodas Kochavim 1:3*) writes, "When this giant among men was weaned, he began to cast his mind about by day and by night, wondering how it was possible for the earth to operate without a Director". The diligence and dedication of his intellect led him to the inescapable conclusion that where there is plan and purpose, there must be Intelligence.

Should one think that *Avrohom*'s example need not be emulated by our generation, the *Rambam* quite clearly informs us of our duty. (*Hilchos Yesodei Hatorah* 2:1-2) "The Almighty has commanded us to love and fear Him; as it says, 'You should love *Hashem* your God' and '*Hashem* your God you should fear.' What is the method by which one can come to love and fear Him? When one reflects on His deeds and His great and wonderful Creation, and discerns and discovers the limitless wisdom contained therein — immediately he is gripped by admiration and love for the Creator..."

It is obvious that the more detail one knows, the more one admires the Designer. Can you imagine waking up on your birthday to discover that your rich uncle has sent you a huge parcel, which is sitting outside your front door. With great excitement you run outside to discover an enormous wooden crate, beautifully wrapped. Eagerly removing the wrapping you discover a metal box. You notice that the box has four doors, which open to reveal comfortable-looking seats. "How very generous of Uncle," you think, "to send me a little metal house that I can sit in during the summer months. He really is thoughtful." Just then, a friend passes by and asks you when you received your new car!

"A car?" you ask, "What is a car?" Patiently, your friend begins to explain that the metal box you are sitting in can move, take you anywhere in the country, and has limitless refinements and luxuries. It will warm you in the winter, and cool you in summer, there is a radio and a cassette, with which you can listen to *shiurim* whilst you drive, the seats are adjustable, and the rear windows are heated, there is power steering and a digital clock, central locking and a fog lamp... The more amazing details you learn about your new car, the more your admiration and gratitude for your uncle grows and grows.

To go to the countryside, stare blankly at the fields and the cows, and declare: "Aah, *Niflaos Haboreh!*" is a level of recognition akin to describing a car as a metal box with seats. To probe and discover the details of the millions of components which make up our own bodies and the world that we live in, is to gain a real appreciation of the beautiful car that we have been given, and enables us to admire and be grateful to the Creator on a much deeper level.

It is with this in mind that this book has been written. Originally appearing as fortnightly articles in the English edition of the *Yated Ne'eman* under the pen-name Tuvia Cohen, the motive has been quite simply to walk in the footsteps of *Avrohom Ovinu*, to observe the wonders of the Creation, discover the purpose and design inherent in the created world and gain a new awareness (and love, and fear) of the Creator. The approach is not new. It was advocated by the *Rambam*, expounded at length by the *Chovos Halvovos* in *Sha'ar Habechinoh*, emulated by the *Chazon Ish* in his *Emunoh u'Bitochon*, expanded by the *Steipler Rov* in Chaye Olam, and in our own day given wide publicity and popularity by the prolific pen of Rabbi Avigdor Miller of America.

The reader will find that the message in each chapter is essentially the same, and no apologies are made for that. The Creator has created millions of examples of design, each different in some aspect, to enable everyone to find the essential kernel of truth somewhere. There are those who are fascinated by the human body as a phenomenal machine, others will be impressed by wonders in the animal world, whilst others will find inspiration in examples of design in the world of plants. There is no limit in the opportunities to discover the wisdom of the Creator, and there is no easier or more enjoyable occupation!

Each chapter has a structure of trying to discover plan and purpose in some familiar manufactured article, and then to see how that very same design exists in a much more sophisticated form in some aspect of the Creation. The conclusion is always the same (and for that reason the reader is advised against attempting to swallow all the contents in one helping). Where there is plan, purpose and design, you will find Intelligence and a Designer.

'Designer World' is a small sample of the myriad *Nifla'os Haboreh*, wonders of creation, that exist in our world. Its purpose is to stimulate the reader to think of the world that is him, and the world around him, in a novel manner, and to see design wherever he looks. It is a humble attempt to walk in the footsteps of *Avrohom Ovinu*, and to emulate the great example set by so many of our eminent scholars. If it is successful in activating the mind of just one person to think, probe, and discover the greatness of the Creator, and by so doing increase his level of belief in and love for our Creator (and even if that one person is the writer), then all the hours of effort will have been worthwhile. It is my earnest prayer that in some small way, 'Designer World' will spread the recognition of, and love for *Hashem Yisborach* in this, His world.

1

༄ THE PEACH TREE ༅

A Story of Survival

The situation was desperate. The family was huddled together, and the enemy was closing in. Survival! The children had to escape, to survive, to guarantee the continuity of their own special unit. No nearby hiding place was acceptable — the dangers were too great. The only chance was, somehow, to despatch the children as far as possible in the hope that there, at a distance, they would find the peace and security so essential for the perpetuation of their dear family. This story had a happy ending.

The parents managed to find safe havens for their offspring, far from the threatening adversaries, and there they settled and flourished, and produced families of their own.

It sounds realistic enough. But imagine that the problem recounted above did not concern people, but instead a lower form of life — a peach tree. The parental trees had a problem — how to guarantee the survival of their children. If they would drop their seeds in the close vicinity of their own boughs, the competition of limited nutrients and water would prevent them from germinating. There was only one option. They had to, somehow, ensure that their offspring travelled far away, and in distance would lie the possibility of survival.

That sounds fine on paper, but how can you send your children far away when your feet are firmly rooted to the ground? Again, imagination is required. Imagine that we are now attending the annual conference of Peach trees. This problem, the paramount and overriding concern of survival, is the main item on the agenda. The problem cannot be shelved or adjourned. It must be solved, and now! The chairman is eagerly awaiting suggestions, and they have to be practical! If the suggestions are unworkable, for even one generation, that would spell the end of peach trees for evermore. At this critical juncture, what would **you** suggest?

One sagacious and wizened tree, widely respected for his wisdom, raised a gnarled branch and requested permission to speak.

"Since we ourselves are immobile, and are therefore severely restricted, may I humbly suggest that we devise a plan whereby we use members of the human race to act on our behalf. They have legs, and could do the job for us. My plan, although daring, even preposterous, is as follows. We have to tempt the humans into taking our precious seeds away with them. We should therefore cover the seeds with a most delicious package, which is attractive in every possible way, to guarantee its desirability. This package, which we shall call fruit, should have a pleasant, eye-catching colour, perhaps yellow, tinged with red and orange. The skin should be velvety and unblemished, and delicate aromas should further enhance its attractiveness. The flesh of the fruit should be edible to humans, and juicy, so that it may be eaten raw. Above all, it should have a pleasing taste, so that his first taste should not be his last. If we can achieve all these objectives, then we can be sure that the unsuspecting humans will clamour to take away our beloved children, clothed in fruit, to safety."

He paused, and waited for the inevitable question. He did not have long to wait.

"That is all very well, O wise peach tree, — but when humans will carry away our children to consume the fruit, the seeds, our precious offspring, will be digested along with the fruit!"

The old tree smiled patiently.

"You are correct, but your fears are unfounded."

His eyes then flashed with fiery inspiration.

"If we send away one seed covered with fruit, that is an only child — and an only child has to be protected. We cannot take chances. What I propose, is to encapsulate the seed with an impenetrable casing that will withstand the sharpest and strongest teeth that humans possess. People might be able to bite off their own thumbs, but when they bite on one of our steely seed protectors, they will break their teeth in the attempt!"

Then with rising excitement and in a flourishing climax, he cried:

"When people will come to this rock-hard casing, which, by the way, will be tasteless, colourless, rough and rigid, they will throw it away in disgust. Our children will then be where they need to be, on the ground, ready to take root, and grow into the next generation. Our objective will then have been achieved."

The wise tree swayed with emotion, whilst waves of admiration and applause swept through the branch members. But, above the tumult, one dissenting voice rang out.

"Call yourself wise? You will have achieved nothing — our little children, encased in their protective cage, will surely be impris-

A wealth of wisdom in an everyday peach

oned for life. If the protection is so strong, how will they, the fragile little seeds, manage to escape to germinate! Their protection will be their tomb!"

Standing erect once again, the wise tree approached the podium and said:

"Dear friends, have no fear. This also has been thought of. The protective casing will be designed with a seam running along its length, which will be bounded with powerful adhesive. Not even a metal hammer will be able to crack it. However, when the case falls to the ground, there in the soil will be provided a special enzyme which will dissolve the glue and allow our precious seed the means to exit to freedom, and life."

It is said that truth is stranger than fiction — and so it is. For in the above analogy lies the truth. The tree — in this case the peach — must spread its seeds, and it does so in the cunning way described. In so doing, it demonstrates amazing knowledge. It has a cognizance of the crowded conditions around it and the need to scatter its seeds. It knows that humans have eyes that can detect colour, have a sense of smell, a sense of touch, and the ability to differentiate between a variety of tastes. It is also aware, amazingly, which tastes appeal to his taste, and thus chooses sweet rather than sour. It understands that humans have hands that can carry, have teeth that bite, and most astounding of all, knows precisely the strength of his teeth and the limit of his biting capacity. It also possesses the know-how to manufacture superglue and its solvents.

Yet, the tree has learned nothing, sees nothing and knows nothing. The tree is a super chemist capable of producing a wonderfully delectable package simply from soil, sunshine and rain. If we had to produce anything from these ingredients the result would be nothing but sunbaked mud. We, with our advanced intelligence, can produce nothing, yet the peach tree, which has never learnt anything, produces the goods. Imagine if at the convention, the suggestion is aired: "We cannot think of anything just now, but give us a few million years and we will try to perfect some system!" Sorry, it has to be present and perfect from the very beginning, otherwise there will never be a second generation.

Logic shouts loud and clear that the Master Designer who fashioned man with the ability to see, smell and taste, was also responsible for the magnificent design of the peach tree and all its friends, together with the superglue solvent which lies patiently and humbly in the soil, awaiting its Divinely appointed task.

The same pattern of design appears in so many trees. All fruits with a single seed, protect their *Ben Yochid* with the hard shell. Whenever you eat a plum, date, cherry or apricot, and throw the inedible stone to the ground, please pause to admire the design. On the other hand, fruits which produce multiple seeds, the melon, tomato, apple and pomegranate, can afford to be less concerned about the absolute survival of each individual. Their seeds are covered with a slippery substance and are eaten, but some will survive their harrowing journey through the digestive system and when they eventually fall on to receptive soil, they will live to produce a fresh tree.

Look around, and you will see the manifold examples of Design in the varied methods that plants utilise to spread their seeds. Isn't the Velcro fastener a wonderful invention? So simple and effective, just tiny hooks gripping tangled looped fibres. The idea emanates from certain seeds, such as burdock, which have rows of hooks to grip the coat of passing animals. They may be carried many kilometres before they are brushed off by the undergrowth, then grow into new plants. There is a squirting cucumber that bursts open to shoot its seeds like bullets from a gun, and they travel as fast as a hundred kilometres per hour. The familiar coconuts float away from their parent trees on ocean currents, drifting for several months and travelling for up to two thousand kilometres before reaching dry land. Special fibres around the seeds help the coconut to float. There are parachutes from the dandelion, flying kites from the Chinese lantern plant; — the list goes on and on, and the evidence grows and grows.

Who was it who taught the burdock to grow hooks, the cucumber to produce explosives that can shoot its seeds (without destroying them in the explosion)? Who instructed the coconut to thoughtfully provide its *Kinderlech* with rubber rings to help them float, and the humble dandelion the intricate laws of aerodynamics? And remember, it all had to be absolutely perfect from the very start, otherwise there would be nothing at all for us to see. To see, and think. To think, and with great excitement, testify

מה גדלו מעשיך ה' כולם בחכמה עשית

2

℘ A PIECE OF LIVER ℘

If you take the train from Gateshead to London, you are travelling southwards. Ten minutes after the journey has begun, look out of the window on the left hand-side, and you will see a chemical factory. It is very definitely a chemical factory, and could never be mistaken for anything else. There are valves which belch steam, smoke stacks which disgorge fumes, with conduits, storage tanks, and pipes running, seemingly haphazardly, in all directions. Fork lift trucks and plastic barrels lay scattered around, and an

The sprawling complex of a Chemical Factory, just a small part of your liver.

eerie dehumanised atmosphere pervades as the metal and plastic hisses and wheezes, with unrecognisable liquids frothing and boiling. White-coated technicians are the only indication that you are indeed still on planet earth, and not trapped in a science-fiction nightmare. Knowing nothing about the place, or how it works, you still have the confidence of the uninitiated that presumably, "They know what they are doing, and it is all perfectly safe." Then the train passes, and it is gone.

When you go to the butcher's shop, you can buy liver. It is nutritious, rich in Vitamin B, and, relative to other cuts of meat, reasonably priced. After *kashering*, it can be fried, boiled and then, a firm favourite in Jewish homes, chopped, mixed with egg, and eaten at *Shabbos* lunchtime.

The intriguing question is: What is the connection between the complex chemical factory, and the shapeless, dark-red slippery chunk of liver lying on the kitchen unit? The amazing answer is that the liver puts the chemical factory to shame in terms of capability and efficiency. The human liver performs more than **five hundred** important jobs, and a very large chemical plant covering many acres would have to be built to perform the simpler of these jobs. The more difficult ones could not be done at all! An enzyme is a substance which allows two other substances to react, very much like a *Shadchan*. Each enzyme is enormously complicated and a wonder in itself. The liver modestly produces more than **one thousand** different enzymes!

Imagine you had to design a machine weighing one and a half kilos that could produce one thousand different chemicals and perform five hundred enormously complicated jobs. And your life depends on it. Where would you begin? Remember that the raw materials available to build this machine are boiled potatoes, toast and cream cake! How valuable such a machine would be and how we would treasure it. Are we not therefore fortunate? We have this wonder-machine, working silently and efficiently, constantly attesting to the wisdom of its Designer. Before we chop it up and consume it, let us pause for a moment and study some of the vital jobs that it performs.

As the winter months approach, people's thoughts turn to heating. In an age of Central Heating and the luxury of warmth in every room, it is hard to remember the toil and trouble involved in preparing a coal fire each dark and cold morning. Now, with a flick of a switch and a twist of a dial, warmth radiates from the pipes. In this sophisticated system, the most important component, and the one on which all the others depend, is the boiler. Whether fuelled by gas, electricity or oil, the boiler heats the water which is then pumped around the house, spreading its beneficial comfort. We do not take the boiler for granted. We choose it carefully, maintain it regularly and recognise its pivotal function.

Now let us look at ourselves. Our bodies are warm, and need to remain warm. Because of the great many chemical changes that take place in the liver, many of them release energy in the form of heat. As the blood flows through the liver it is warmed up, and then spreads through the circulatory system maintaining body temperature. So there you have it — long, long before central heating boilers were thought of, each human being was thoughtfully supplied by the Creator with his own private C.H. Boiler, guaranteeing his body heat, and fuelled by nothing grander than potatoes, toast and cake.

When you drink a cup of coffee or tea, you do not consider it a dangerous pastime. Yet without the liver it could be worse than dangerous. Coffee and tea contain caffeine, which act as a stimulant. If you would shoot this drug into the vessels leading **out** of the liver, leading to the heart, the poor man would not live for long. Fortunately, they come through the liver's **entrance** vessels and the six to ten seconds that it takes to pass through the liver gives plenty of time to extract the potential poison. Plenty of time! Imagine a conveyor belt carrying metal containers. You are standing behind the conveyor belt, and as each metal box passes before you, it stops, for ten seconds. Each metal box is a bomb. Your job is to defuse the bomb and render it completely harmless. You have just ten seconds. After that it will move inexorably onwards to a crowded room, and then..! Is ten seconds a long time? Yet our liver, the great de-toxifyer, performs its life-saving task silently and efficiently, just as the Designer intended.

Every housewife knows that the liver requires special attention to *kasher* it. It contains so much blood that only strong direct heat can satisfactorily extract it. Why is it so full of blood? Again, we witness a miracle of design. Approximately one litre of blood flows through it every minute. Much of it comes from a special vein which transports the blood from the stomach and intestine. All the food which has been absorbed into the bloodstream from the stomach and intestine is taken to the liver in this vein and is processed before it reaches the heart and the rest of the body. Protein fragments that are made from meat, could be as deadly as cyanide if they got into the bloodstream. The liver changes them from amino acids to harmless human protein. If there is a surplus that the body does not need, the liver changes it into urea and passes it along to the kidneys for exit. The liver itself is composed of masses of small cells and the whole organ is riddled with narrow passages and blood vessels which give it its soft spongy texture.

A factory which never closes, or goes on holiday, but remains vigilant, purifying, cleansing and producing the vital ingredients that keep us alive.

If anyone is unfortunate enough to spring a leak in their car radiator, they know that it will drip away until not one drop remains. If a person cuts his finger, blood will flow for a few seconds, but then it will gradually stop. The reason for this life-saving phenomenon (which is not logical, and does not occur in central-heating radiators and leaking kettles) is that the blood contains ingredients which make it clot on contact with air. Whilst remembering this miracle, bear in mind the equally great miracle of the blood not coagulating whilst circulating in the body, thanks to the presence of anti-coagulants. One of the vital ingredients in the clotting process, PROTHROMBIN, is produced in the liver.

Who told the liver to produce this wonder protein? If it 'just developed' how did we survive the aeons that it took to develop? "Try not to panic. We hope to perfect the clotting agent in about 40 million years. Just try to hang on until then!" Logic shouts that this phenomenal ability to automatically mend leaks must have been present from the start, otherwise we would not be here to speak about it.

Silently, efficiently, this amazing little machine does its work. It stores vitamins, making liver itself such a valuable asset in one's diet. It stores iron from broken up blood cells, conserving them for use over and over again in new red-blood cells. The list seems endless. The liver produces antibodies that protect us from disease. It carefully monitors the blood passing through it, maintaining the concentration and composition of its vital components. It breaks down alcohol, a potentially lethal substance into harmless carbon dioxide and water. If the liver performs five hundred different jobs, then we have barely succeeded in lifting the lid, and the humble liver cooking in the pot is not so humble after all!

The *Loshon Hakodesh* for liver is כבד. Honour is כבוד. Heavy is כבד. The connection is not a coincidence. The Designer of the heaviest organ in our body—the liver—is deserving of the greatest honour.

מה רבו מעשיך ה' כולם בחכמה עשית

3

෨ THE LISTENING EAR ෬

Have you ever thought what your great-great grand father would think if he came to your house? The revered gentleman, who lived in the last century, is coming to tour your place of abode, and to observe your modern life-style. He would stop in front of a white cabinet standing on the floor, and ask you what it was.

"Why," you would reply, "that is our fridge."

Observing his puzzled look, you would explain how this wonderful invention keeps your food cold and fresh, and the smaller cupboard on the top keeps food frozen. He would scarcely believe you as you described your miniature North Pole which can keep *cholent* and *kugel* fresh as a daisy for months.

Another little box would be the microwave. His eyes would stare in disbelief as you related how a meal can be cooked in a few short minutes. Noticing the absence of a kitchen hearth and blazing fire, he would ask you how you keep warm. Again you would show him a box — this time a Central Heating boiler, which, and this he would find difficult to accept, would heat the home at the mere flick of a switch. No wood, no coal, no cinders, no mess — and you can even regulate the temperature to your individual comfort.

Stopping in front of a small rectangular box, he would ask what it was, already anticipating a mind-boggling answer.

"That," you would announce, "is our radio. If you twist a button, it speaks."

If he had a sense of humour, he would then burst out laughing.

"A talking box — who has ever heard of such wonders!"

Patiently you would explain how transmitters send out signals (just try explaining that!) which are invisible, and can travel hundreds, even thousands of miles. The little box receives the signals as they fly through the air, converts them back into sound, and that is what you hear.

Your poor *elter Zeide* will by now be absolutely astonished. And just think — you have not yet shown him the telephone, ("Would

"A talking box – who has ever heard of such wonders!"

you like to speak to anyone, anywhere in the world?") the washing machine, or the car outside the front door!

If the radio would greatly impress him, it would be because the concept of sending out a spoken message in the form of invisible signals which can retain their individuality over extensive distances, and be collected and converted back into meaningful sounds is so phenomenal, as to sound almost impossible. What an amazing world you live in!

"My dear *elter Zeide*," you would gently explain, "This little box is nothing new. You have one just like it, and not only one, but even two!"

In response to his request to kindly explain yourself, you would begin to describe the wonders and intricate design of the human ear. The ear is a remarkable machine, containing advanced technology, which is capable of receiving waves of sound which travel invisibly through the air, and even through solid objects (Can you hear the noise of traffic through a closed window, or your neighbours' arguments through the dividing wall?). The little machine, having received the signals, then sends them to the brain, (the main computer) where they are converted back into meaningful sound. Instead of taking a tour of your home, let us rather take a closer look at this extraordinary little wonder-box, strategically positioned on either side of your head.

Of all the limbs of the body, perhaps the ear has the most weird and wonderful shape. Its whirls and curls are asymmetrical, and seem to demand an explanation. Their function is to gather sound waves as they travel through the air, and it is because of their shape that they are superb. The story is told of an architect who once designed a prison in the shape of a human ear. By positioning himself in the very centre of this most unusual structure, the chief warder was able to hear every sound and conversation spoken in the entire prison. It worked!

The sound wave (air on the move) then enters a twisting and winding channel before reaching the eardrum. The twists and the turns, like all components of a complicated structure, are not haphazard, nor are the hairs which line the tunnel or the impressive avenue of wax factories along the route. In a designed machine, everything has purpose. If the ear canal was quite straight, any young child could too easily and inquisitively poke in a potentially damaging instrument. These twists and turns protect the delicate inner components, and give the air a chance to warm up before meeting the eardrum. What consideration!

The profusion of hairs and the four thousand wax glands act like a fly-paper trap for insects, dust and other irritants. The wax guards against infection, particularly when swimming in dirty water. Imagine a long road, and on either side, stretching as far as the eye could see, factory after factory producing wax candles. What a hive of activity, what a vast quantity of raw materials, oils, fats, electricity and transport would be required. What a huge industrial project it would be, — yet we have four thousand individual factories in a one-inch canal on either side of our head, faithfully producing wax, day after day, without rest, respite or appreciation! Most people would not have the tiniest clue how to produce a wax candle, yet their ears do possess that knowledge. Who taught them?

Then we meet the eardrum — a tough, tightly stretched piece of skin, about half an inch across. No water can penetrate, which explains why we don't fill up with water whilst swimming! When sound-bearing air-waves strike the eardrum, they set it vibrating, like a stick striking a drum. The sensitivity of the eardrum is such, that even a whisper from across the room can set it vibrating. If you could observe it, hoping to see it shake, you would be most disappointed. As it vibrates, it moves just **one billionth of a centimetre**! That incredible minutest of minute movements is sufficient to set up a chain reaction of events that gives us recognisable sounds.

Behind the eardrum, in the area called the middle ear, live three tiny bones, the smallest bones in the body. They are popularly known as the anvil, hammer and stirrup because of their distinctive shape, and they are delicately hinged together. In response to the tiny vibration of the eardrum, they in turn vibrate, amplifying the vibrations until they are something like thirty times stronger. The stronger vibrations are then passed on to the inner ear via the oval window, attached to the stirrup. The positioning of these three tiny bones is crucial, and, like the minute mechanism of a wristwatch, any slight deviation would render the whole machine ineffective.

We have now arrived at the most impressive and amazing section of our tour — the inner ear. This section is a fortress-like cavern, hollowed out of the hardest bone on the body, and filled with a watery fluid. The major component is a snail-shaped coil called the cochlea, whose twisting interior is studded with thousands of microscopic hair-like nerve cells. In response to the vibrations passed through the oval window, the tiny hairs wave in the fluid, like seaweed in a tidal current. This waving incredibly generates a minute wisp of electricity that feeds into the auditory nerve (which is the thickness of a pencil lead and contains more than 30,000 electrical circuits) which in turn leads to the brain just three quarters of an inch away. Different hairs respond to different keys, so we have middle C hairs and B Flat Major hairs. In all, thousands of different

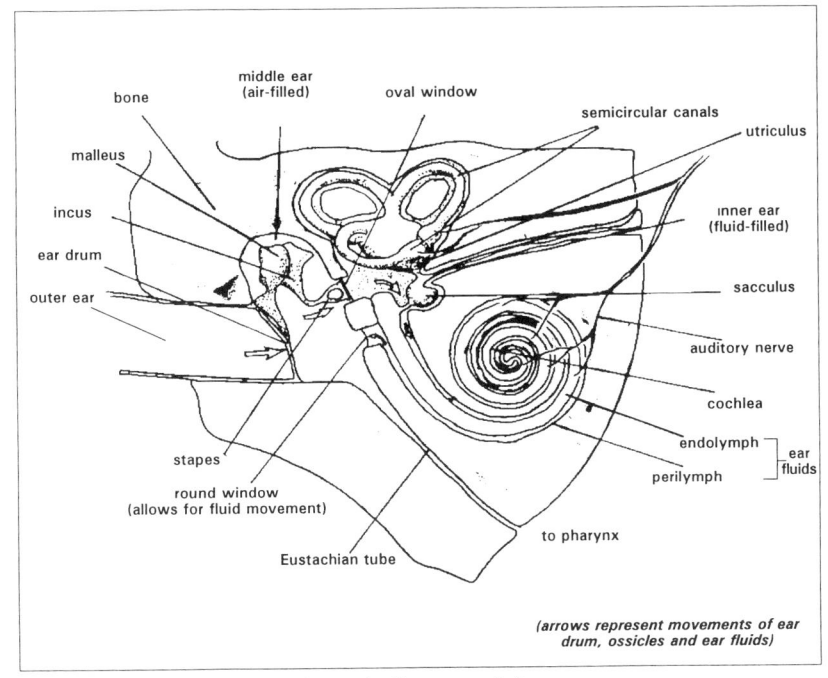

Schematic diagram of the ear.

messages pour simultaneously into the brain, which then unscrambles the flood of data and hands down its verdict — the alarm clock is ringing.

As if this were insufficient, every sound received by the brain is carefully stored away in the memory bank for future reference. A voice, a message, a distinctive sound, once heard is always recognised when heard again. Can you conjure up in your mind the sound of rain on a tin roof, rustling leaves, the blast of the *Shofar*? There you have it!

How is it possible for the eardrum, tiny bones and drifting fluid to transmit not only one sound, but many different sounds, all at the same time? At any one instant, you can hear someone talking to you, the ticking of a clock, a door closing and the telephone ringing. All the sounds are different, and all are transmitted. Even the vibrations of the eardrum, a seemingly simple mechanism, are thus seen to be enormously complex. Add to that the many sophisticated refinements that the system possesses, — one, to block out unwanted background sounds, another to reduce the level of damaging volumes as they crash through the ear, yet another to repair the eardrum should it become perforated — and we see that even at the simplest level, the mechanism of the ear — not much larger than a hazelnut — is a masterpiece of design and planning.

If *elter Zeide* would be impressed by the fridge and radio, we in turn can be grateful for two such beautiful machines, and cognizant of the One Who made them.

Shlomo Hamelech said it all:

"אזן שומעת ועין רואה — ה' עשה גם שניהם. (משלי כ-יב)

"*The listening ear, and the eye that sees,* השי"ת *made them both*"

4

ಎ THE PERFECT JIG-SAW ಎ

In England, there is a consumer magazine which appears each month. Each issue reports on the results of vigorous tests to which various commodities have been put, together with the magazine's recommendation for the best buy. One month, there was a feature on jigsaws. "Jigsaws," you ask. "What major decisions are involved in buying a jigsaw to keep children occupied? Has consumerism reached such a sophisticated level that we need to have a report on various standards of cardboard and plastic to determine which pattern, picture and texture should be chosen for junior's leisure?"

A jig-saw is also a hand-held machine with a sharp knife protruding vertically downwards, and is used for precision cutting. The magazine compared various models of jig-saws, noting their refinements, motor speed and price. It then listed fourteen different types of blade which can be acquired as optional extras. One blade has tiny teeth, useful for cutting metal with a special attachment which emits oil to act as a lubricant. Another has large teeth, to achieve greater cutting power, whilst yet another blade has no teeth at all, just a plain metal knife, ideally suited for cutting floor tiles. The most ex-

A Swiss Army knife. Ten blades individually designed for ten functions.

pensive blade is coated with carbon on both sides to enable the saw to cut through ceramic surfaces. Each blade is tailor made and designed for its specific task. After reading the article, you will be convinced that the jig-saw is a vital component in the handyman's armoury, and any one person owning all fourteen varieties of blade is a fortunate man indeed.

The fact is, that had you never heard of the celebrated jig-saw, there would be no cause for worry, for you are already the proud possessor of thirty two highly specialised, sophisticated cutting tools, called teeth. Teeth come in various shapes and sizes, and have many important and highly specialised functions.

It is always of interest to see how *Loshon Hakodesh*, the original language, describes the essence of every object. Since every human being is endowed with two sets of teeth, it is not surprising that they should be called שינים, implying two!

When a person is born, he has fifty-two teeth buried in his gums. Remarkably, although a baby arrives with all his limbs in position, from toe nails to eyelashes, he comes into the world with no visible teeth. This can hardly be an accidental omission, and the reason is clearly because a baby's face is shaped for nursing, and not for chewing. For the first six months of his life he does not require teeth, so he has none!

In a world of design, every facet of life deserves examination in order to see the wonder and wisdom of each component. The first baby teeth arrive at about six months, when the lower two incisors begin to push their way upward. By the time baby is two years old, he is the prowd owner of twenty beautiful little teeth. The appearance of each tooth is felt by the young child, and the effects are heard by all members of the family, usually at 3.30 a.m. Just think what it would be like if all twenty teeth appeared simultaneously, and it is indeed an immense kindness that their appearance is staggered. A precise and hidden time clock regulates the time when each diminutive tooth should begin its journey through the gum.

The first permanent teeth, the molars, make their appearance at the back of the six year-old child's mouth, allowing him to chew with the greatest of ease. Gradually, the baby teeth loosen and fall out, making room for all the permanent teeth. Have you ever seen a baby tooth when it falls out? It does not seem to have any roots, just the plain little tooth which drops out! It is a remarkable fact that the tooth did have a root, but the roots of the milk teeth are absorbed by the body, thus loosening them sufficiently to fall out. Absorbed by the body! Who has ever heard of such a thing! Try an experiment. Take twenty screws of varying lengths from your tool box and put them into your pocket. Leave them for six months and see if they become absorbed into your trousers! The most that they will do is to rub a hole in your pocket, but they will not become absorbed, not in six months or in six years. Yet the body knows exactly how to absorb a tooth root. Just another example of efficiency and planning, which staggers the imagination.

The actual structure of the tooth is a brilliant piece of engineering. Do you remember kitchen sinks and pots made of enamel? It was a hard and resilient material which could withstand decades of wear and tear. The part of the tooth that protrudes from the gum is coated with this same enamel. Enamel, or calcium phosphate, is comprised of tiny rods which look rather like pencils standing on end. One hundred of the tiny rods would fill the width of one hair! The enamel coating has two important qualities. It is tough enough to endure the ferocious and constant pressure of chewing; and also it contains no nerve endings, and so is insensitive to pain. Try to imagine the consequences if teeth did indeed have nerve endings on their outer surface, as most of the body has. Chewing would be agony, and brushing the teeth would be absolute torture!

Beneath the enamel is a layer of hard ivory-like dentine, related to bone, and it is here that tooth sensitivity begins. In the centre of the tooth is a soft area called the pulp cavity, containing nerves and blood vessels. Tiny channels containing extensions of living cells run out from the pulp cavity into the dentine, making it so sensitive. The whole structure sits in a tailor-made socket in the jaw, anchored by a hard material called cement. Just think, our teeth are quite literally cemented into our jaw. Without that firm anchor, it would be impossible for the iron-hard teeth to sit firmly in soft gums. Try attaching a screw to a jelly sweet! Our teeth would flap around like leaves in an autumn wind, and would be incapable either of biting or chewing. So we have cement, produced by and provided for by the same Master Designer who designed the teeth in the first place.

Just to complete the picture, attached to the cement are tough fibres which run into the jaw bone. These fibres hold the teeth in its socket, but they permit it to move very slightly, and cushion it from excessive jarring when it hits something hard. Just like a steel bridge has the ability to expand and sway slightly despite its tensile strength, so the teeth are designed in a similar way.

The most exciting aspect of examining any new machine, be it a computer, a car or a digital watch, is to discover all the refinements that the designers have incorporated into the new model, and see how every button activates a different process, yet all are co-ordinated to form an integral working unit. So it is with us. Examine the refinements of the teeth and get excited! The molars at the back are heavy-duty grinders and require firm anchoring, so they have been

32 / Designer World

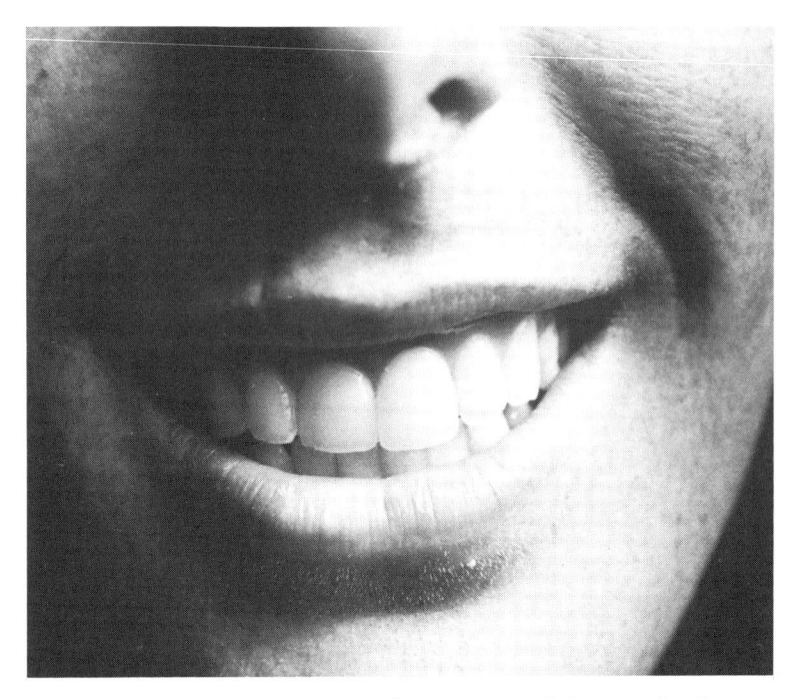

Good reason to smile - he's the happy owner of the most dazzling toolbox ever designed!

provided with two roots each. The cutting teeth at the front, the incisors, which perform the less rigorous biting and cutting are sufficiently firm with a single root. All our teeth, both front and back, would be as useless as clothes flapping on a washing line without powerful muscles to raise the lower jaw against the upper jaw and provide an iron grip. Behold — they are there!

Animals have differing needs, and have been kindly provided with different teeth. A lion which needs to quickly despatch a zebra or antelope for its dinner has two enormous dagger-like canines on its top jaw with another two on its lower jaw, carefully positioned to enable the king of animals to actually close its mouth! The docile sheep, who eats nothing more exciting than grass, requires no teeth for biting, and so it has no top front-teeth at all. Instead, it has a hard pad. The lower incisors (front teeth) meet the hard pad and pull the grass, producing the characteristic ripping sound of sheep grazing rather than the sound of cutting. Its back teeth are designed with raised enamel ridges which grind the grass as the jaws move from side to side. Dogs, which love to gnaw meat from the bone, have been provided with extra large cheek-teeth on either side of their mouth, which as they slide past each other, scrape their dinner off the bone. Their back teeth fit together like two interlocking sections and effortlessly crush hard material, such as bone.

In a world of kindness, we humans have been given the ability to enjoy our food. Without teeth, we could not bite, and food would have to swallowed whole, resembling the snake to whom everything tastes of dust. Besides their chief purpose, which is to enable us to eat, they have other functions too. Teeth help us speak and articulate words; they give shape to our mouth and face. White teeth, when revealed as part of a friendly face, cheer people up and demonstrate pleasure (*Kesuvos 111b*).

The editor of the consumer magazine, when researching the most efficient and cost-effective jig-saws, missed the obvious. He merely had to look in the mirror, smile, and there he would have seen the most dazzling array of the cheapest, most efficient biting, sawing, grinding, chewing, talking, pleasure-giving instruments ever designed. His very own teeth!

5

ಸಾ FOOD FOR THOUGHT ಅ

You cannot fool a car. If you put orange juice in the petrol tank, it will not take you too far. Which is a great shame; with petrol at sky-high prices, it would be an enormous advantage to be able to fuel a car with less expensive materials than this oil-based derivative. Why not convert the engine so that it can run on potato peels? Would it not be wonderful if, before embarking on a long journey, you could fill the tank with all your kitchen waste and left-overs? It would revolutionise the cost of travel and be a major advance for mankind.

In the field of motor travel it has not yet happened, but in the human being, it has. In order to keep our engines working we too require fuel, yet the fuel that we ingest would make a car's hair stand on end. From *cholent* to chips, pretzels to paprika, meat balls to mushrooms — we cheerfully partake of a vast range of foods and expect them to fuel our bodies without difficulties or complications. It is a sign of the wonder of our bodies that we are rarely disappointed, and the whole process deserves a closer look.

Placing food in one's mouth brings it in contact with the teeth. The teeth chop the food into small pieces, thus increasing its surface area. This is a major benefit when the food eventually enters the intestine, as the various enzymes which are produced can then have the maximum effect.

As soon as the food enters the mouth, a strange thing happens. Suddenly, without warning or noise, the mouth floods with a liquid. This liquid, saliva, is produced by six glands which are housed in the cheeks and in the floor of the mouth. Just think — in the enclosed area of one mouth are six separate factories producing a wonder fluid. They work noiselessly, tirelessly and efficiently, producing one and a half litres of saliva each day. This saliva, although not accorded too much honour, benefits us in a host of ways. It contains mucus, which makes the food slippery so that it slides easily down the throat when swallowed. Swallowing a piece of dry food, such as a digestive biscuit, without first moistening it with saliva, can be a painful experience. It also contains a chemical called amylase, which acts on starch, breaking it down into a type of sugar called maltose. If you chew a piece of bread long enough you can actually taste the sweetness as the maltose is formed. Saliva also contains a chemical which kills many germs, preventing them entering into the stomach. And we thought that saliva was just water!

Apart from these functions, the saliva keeps the mouth moist, serves as a solvent for the molecules that stimulate the taste buds (with a dry mouth you can taste very little), aids speech by allowing the lips and tongue to move freely, and keeps the mouth and teeth clean. Just thinking of food makes the mouth water. That just could not happen without a plumbing system to transport the precious liquid from the six hidden factories to the mouth's surface. If the central heating system in a house has to be perfectly designed and fitted in order to work efficiently, with all its pipes in the correct place, and pumps working in co-ordination, then the pipes and ducts which empty the saliva into the mouth at six separate locations, are no less well designed and perfectly co-ordinated. One duct actually cuts through a muscle — without impairing its function — to open into the mouth. Without our being aware of it, and certainly with no intellectual input from ourselves, they faithfully supply the complex fluid to perform its manifold functions.

The food is now ready to commence its journey; and it needs to be swallowed. The 'simple' act of swallowing is a symphony of co-ordinated activity, conducted by nerves, and executed by intricate muscles. The tongue (a muscular wonder) manoeuvres the food to the back of the throat by squeezing against the hard top palate. (If you stick your tongue out, or open your mouth wide, as you do in the dentist's chair, you cannot swallow). The tongue humps up, gives a push, and the food is on its way down.

Now comes a situation which could be extremely dangerous. If the food dropped into the windpipe, violent choking would result!

*Orange Juice would be so much cheaper,
but only 4 star petrol will do.*

However, and for this we cannot be sufficiently grateful, a brilliant mechanism operates. A specially designed valve, called the Epiglottis, perfectly covers the windpipe, causing the food to slide safely into the ten-inch long food pipe. Besides this, another valve, called the Uvula, which is the little red finger hanging from the roof of the mouth, rises and shuts off the passage to the nostrils. If it failed to do so, soup would drip out of our nose! If you laugh whilst swallowing, laughing, like talking, opens the epiglottis, and you nearly always feel a very painful sensation (choking) as crumbs of food or drops of liquid enter the opened windpipe. Therefore, the rule is —

when you eat, don't talk! When praising *Hashem Yisborach* for *"Your miracles that are with us every day"* it is worth remembering this perfectly co-ordinated and vital function called swallowing — in which flaps and valves are opening and shutting, allowing us to eat in safety. Here is a complex system, on which one's life depends, which must be perfect from the first moment of life. How can such a system have developed 'by chance'? How were the countless generations surviving whilst the Uvula and Epiglottis were desperately attempting to perfect themselves?

"Hang on, don't choke yet, we hope to get the Epiglottis working in ten million years....!"

Now that the nourishment has reach the food pipe, (OESOPHAGUS) it needs to descend to the food reservoir, the stomach. If it just dropped into the stomach, by gravity, it would be mighty painful. When suppliers of beer deliver their barrels of precious liquid to hotels, and have to drop them into the basement, they cannot simply drop them onto the concrete floor. Instead, they fall comfortably onto a foam mattress — an efficient system. The design of the food pipe is even more efficient. It does not drop at all. As it enters the food pipe, a gentle muscular contraction forms behind the particle of food, propelling it gently downwards (or upwards if you stand on your head) at the rate of four centimetres per second. Thus it takes about six seconds for solid food to descend. Even then, the food cannot just rush into the stomach, because at the stomach's entrance there is a valve-like muscle that allows the food in only as fast as the stomach can comfortably handle it.

There is further design in the difference between the food pipe and windpipe. If you place your finger just below your Adam's Apple, you can feel your windpipe (TRACHEA), and that is situated just in front of the food pipe. The windpipe has to be kept open at all times in order to allow air to pass freely to and from the lungs. To keep it open, the wind pipe is stiffened by rings of gristle. These rings are like a pile of C's which face towards the centre of the neck, so that the open end of the 'C' is next to the food pipe. Why are the rings not completely round, like the letter 'O'? The answer is, in order to allow the food pipe room to expand as the food passes down. Just think. If the food pipe could not expand, swallowing a large particle of food could block the pipe and be severely hazardous. It must expand to allow everything safe passage. If the windpipe, which needs to be rigid for its own purposes, would press against the food pipe, there would be no room for expansion. Fortunately, the 'C' shaped rings of the windpipe have their opening adjacent to the food pipe, giving it its life-saving room for expansion.

"ועל נסיך שבכל יום עמנו..."

Inside the stomach, we find its wall thick and muscular, with numerous holes through which the gastric juices, produced by the gastric glands, arrive. These gastric glands produce large amounts of hydrochloric acid. The acid helps to kill germs whilst at the same time providing ideal conditions for the enzyme PEPSIN, also contained in the gastric juices, to work on protein. The question arises. Since the stomach digests protein, why does it not digest itself? After all, if you eat cow's stomach, it will be efficiently digested, so why not your own? The answer is another miracle. The wall of the stomach 'produces' large amounts of mucus which coat the stomach lining, and protects it from damage by the acid.

So many wonders, so much design — and the story is only beginning...

6

ಎ THE CAR WASH ಲ

Car owners love them. Some children are terrified of them. They use enormous amounts of water, but perform a magnificent job. They have made plastic buckets and big sponges redundant. They are the highly popular, effort-saving mechanised car-washes. You drive in, carefully position yourself, drop in a coin, and quickly close your windows. In a second, the silent sulking monstrosity springs to life, and with a whirring of brushes and clanking of chains, advances inexorably towards its victim. Enclosed in the security of his vehicle, the owner stares in mesmerised fascination as the Thing envelops him in a darkened world of hissing jets, beating bristles, and foaming liquid. He stares transfixed as the Monster moves to the back of the car, pauses for breath, then proceeds from the rear to beat its vehicular client into cleanliness. Slowly it moves along, now ejecting hot water, then emitting shampoo, and then cold water to dissipate the lather, finally wiping the perspiring car down with an enormous rotating cloth. The massive machine retreats, a green light signals a cessation of hostilities, and the proud sparkling shining and rejuvenated car is ready to face the traffic once again.

Just washing the car – a monstrous machine in co-ordinated action.

The wonder of the car wash is not so much the fact that such a ponderous machine can work at all, but the fascination of seeing everything happen in a particular and precise sequence. First the hot water, then the shampoo, cold water and then a wax finish — rather like washing your hair! If the order would be reversed, the result would be a frothy sticky mess. Presumably, a world without a car wash would still function. We would just have to re-acquire a bucket and a sponge and get our hands wet. Nothing worse should happen to anyone. But think of a machine that has to produce highly-specialised liquids and chemicals, where the sequence is not just a matter of convenience and practicality, but a matter of life itself, and the result is not merely fascination that such a machine exists, but a definite and grateful respect for the machine and its designer. Enter the digestive system!

The food that we ate has been ground by the teeth, coated with saliva, has negotiated the hazardous route to the food pipe, and carefully lowered to the storage reservoir. It is safely in the stomach. The stomach is not simply a receptacle to hold the food, it has important functions to perform, all of which make life so much more pleasant.

The stomach lining, which looks rather like folds of glistening velvet, contains some thirty-five million glands which secrete about six pints of gastric juice per day — mainly hydrochloric acid. If you would be brave enough to pour acid onto your carpet at the rate of six pints per day, very soon you would have neither carpet nor floorboards, yet the stomach wall remains cheerfully impervious to the relentless attack of the corrosive acid, thanks to the tough mucus lining that protects it. Certain situations — stress, worry or overwork — can increase acid production to the extent that the gastric juices eat into the stomach lining, making it raw and painful. Perhaps this is alluded to by *Chazal* when they state:

"כל הכועס, כל מיני גיהנם שולטים בו" (נדרים כה.)

"Whoever is angry is prone to all manner of ills"

"Thirty-five million glands producing juices?" If you say it quickly it sounds routine; but take a closer look under a microscope and you will see that every tiny gland is a beautifully designed little machine — complicated beyond belief — faithfully producing the gastric juice and squirting it into the stomach. Where does it obtain the raw materials to manufacture hydrochloric acid, where did it receive the recipe — who taught the little gland all the tricks of the trade — the Designer knows.

The acid serves to activate another substance — the enzyme called PEPSIN, which starts protein digestion. Without pepsin it would be very difficult to digest your *Shabbos* meal. This enzyme is also produced in the stomach wall. Another enzyme clots milk, converting it into easily digestible curds and whey. Think of the inner-tube of a football, which is made of tough rubber and is inflatable. That is all. You blow it up, cover it with leather and kick it. The stomach is also a form of rubber bag covered with leather. The difference is that the wall of the stomach is a teeming site, with millions of chemical factories, busy producing vital substances twenty-four hours a day. The total number of trading estates, business parks and industrial areas in the whole country do not contain as many individual factories as one stomach!

Besides chemical factories, the stomach also contains powerful muscles. Muscular contractions sweep down the stomach, in a wave-like motion, churning over the food and mixing it thoroughly with the digestive juices until it resembles a thick gruel. And you thought your Food Blender was a modern innovation! Gradually, the muscular action drives the semi-digested food towards the far end of the stomach, where it opens into the small intestine. Here is a danger area! If too much food was released into the small intestine (called the DUODENUM) too quickly, there would be an over-abundance of acidic gastric juices suddenly appearing, causing havoc. Fortunately, there is a valve strategically positioned at that precise location which restricts the rate at which the food passes through. It allows it past in little squirts, no more than can be instantly neutralised by the normally alkaline duodenum.

How on earth does the duodenum (the little intestine) come to be alkaline? It is all very simple. The duodenum produces a substance called SECRETIN which empties into the blood stream. This prods the PANCREAS into instant secretion of its alkaline digestive juices, and all this juice pours into the duodenum, neutralising the invading acids.

It all sounds so wonderfully simple! Wonderful it is, simple it definitely is not. The pancreas is approximately six inches long, grey-pink in colour, weighs about three ounces and lives behind the stomach, and plays a key role in digestion. It produces about two pints of digestive juices a day. That means thirty-two ounces of fluid from a three ounce gland! (Think of any machine producing ten times its own weight of complex chemicals per day, and you get an idea of the efficiency, planning and design of this and every bodily organ). As soon as you sit down to the table, tens of thousands of tiny glands in the pancreas receive a message through the nervous system to produce alkaline juices. When the food reaches the duodenum, the pancreas moves into top gear to perform its life-saving feat.

If you think that neutralising acids is impressive, then take a look at some of the other tasks that the pancreas performs to aid the digestive process. Most of the food that we eat must never enter the bloodstream in the form in which they are consumed — they would be deadly if they did. Fortunately, they don't, and the pancreas plays the major role in rendering them harmless. For this task it produces three enzymes. One of them, TRYPSIN, initiates the breakdown of protein into amino acids which the bloodstream can pass around the body for tissue building. Another enzyme, AMYLASE, converts starch into sugar. A third, LYPASE, attacks fat globules, breaking them into fatty acids and glycerine. All these enzymes arrive, right on cue, through a special duct into the small intestine.

The unity, harmony and co-operation that operates in the body is remarkable. The liver produces bile salts, which break big fat glob-

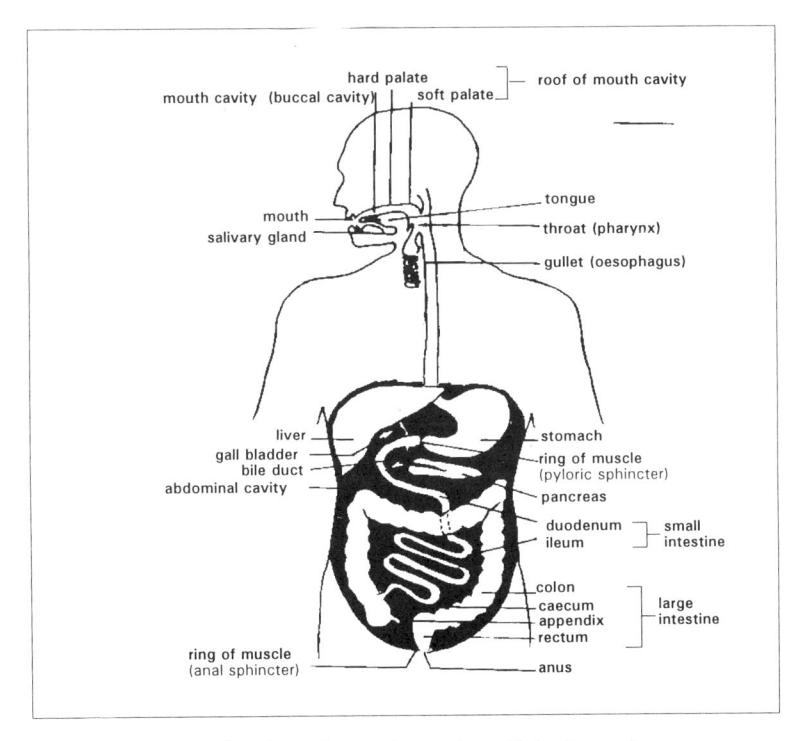

Diagram showing the main region of the intestines

ules into minute ones that the pancreatic enzyme (the above-mentioned lypase) can process.

Further juices are secreted by the intestine wall itself, through which the digestive process advances yet further. Altogether, two gallons of digestive juices are produced by the body each day! It is in the small intestine that the soluble products of digestion are absorbed. How this is done, is incredible beyond belief. The walls of the intestine contain millions of microscopic finger-like projections, called VILLI, each of which is a perfectly constructed tower containing a lymph vessel to absorb fat, and capillaries to absorb the amino acids and glucose into its blood vessels. Millions of marvellous machines specifically designed to extract all the goodness from the food, and circulate them around the body, giving strength, energy, and life itself.

Impressed by a car-wash? In comparison to the strategic split-second fully-integrated system of enormously complicated chemical factories working in absolute harmony which we find in the human digestive system, the car wash is about as complex as a plastic duck.

Thank you liver for doing the hard work. Thank you pancreas for completing the job. Thank you both for disposing of the potential threat that everyday eating poses. Thank you Creator...

ברוך אתה ה'... אשר יצר את האדם בחכמה...

וברא בו נקבים נקבים...

ברוך אתה ה' רופא כל בשר ומפליא לעשות.

7

ಏ DEFENCE FORCES ಲ

Y ou have to stick up for your own country. Americans go crazy over baseball, the Spanish enjoy nothing more than to sport with a rampaging bull, and the greatest excitement imaginable for the Englishman is to watch a cricket match which lasts for five days and ends in a draw. Each to their own! The same nationalistic fervour is evoked when describing weapons. Each country is fiercely proud of the weapons and systems that it produces, and claims, naturally, that their product is the finest in the field. Americans fight in their Shermans, French fervour is aroused by the elegant might of the Mirage, and John Bull's heart pounds proudly as he watches his squadron of Chieftain tanks roll past, Union Jacks fluttering proudly from the rear aerial.

Even to the unbiased mind, a Chieftain tank is a fearsome sight. Fifty-one tons of mechanised might, capable of fighting day and night — blasting anything in sight with a 120 mm gun at a range of up to five miles — shaking the earth as it surges forward, flattening everything in its path at a speed of thirty m.p.h. It is equipped with every sophisticated device — from VHF radio to smoke dischargers, from its own generator to a capability to lay a seventy-five feet bridge

A Centurian tank. 51 tons of mechanised might.

over a raging river in just three minutes! This gigantic Goliath is no mindless monster, but the result of years of development and research, at a cost of millions of dollars.

The great worry amongst professional military men is that with the seeming elimination of the threat from Eastern Europe, all the huge armaments industries might become a thing of the past. Countries are trimming down their armed forces, and new expressions such as 'peace dividend' are entering the dictionaries. However, until the advent of *Moshiach*, the beasts of war will not be quietened. As long as Nations have expansive ambitions, so long as aggressors stalk the earth, countries will require armies; armies will require tanks; and the powerful Chieftain will still have a role to play. Keep the flags flying — the Chieftain is alive and well.

We see what we want to see, and we see nothing. People will rush to the window to watch a low-flying Concord, but no-one will pay attention to a low-flying pigeon. And yet, the Concord cannot fly in fog, land on a window-sill, or produce little Concord*lech*, all of which the pigeons have been doing most successfully ever since Creation. Crowds will line the Avenues and cheer with a thrill in their hearts as the armoured columns trundle along, accompanied by pomp and circumstance and a big brass band, proud of the impregnable defence forces of their country. And yet, a humble hedgehog, capable of resisting attack simply by rolling into a tight ball surrounded by an impenetrable bundle of spikes, attracts no crowds and excites little interest.

Practically every animal, and humans also, possess defence mechanisms to ward off an attacker — or better still — to deter him from attacking in the first place. All the defence-mechanisms share the common features of well-planned, intricate and intelligent design.

There is a little beetle, be careful don't go near. It shoots out boiling poison, its name is Bombadier. This interesting creature is a supreme expert in chemical warfare and weaponry. When provoked, the bombadier swivels the end of its abdomen and shoots a lethal mixture of hydroquinine and hydrogen peroxide into the face of its enemy. These two chemicals, when mixed, literally explode. How on earth does the beetle store explosives in its body! An ingenious mechanism keeps the two compounds separate until ignition is required. The slightest alteration in this delicate balance would immediately result in a race of exploded beetles. The fact that we still have them with us today means that the system has worked successfully since its inception.

The whole mechanism is anything but simple. Mr Bombadier Beetle heats these substances to absolute boiling point — 100° c. And this in a cold-blooded insect! Inside its body is a double-chamber, rather like a rocket engine. The inner reservoir holds the raw material of the noxious spray, and the second chamber contains the activating agent. The beetle squeezes fluid from the reservoir into the reaction chamber, and, as with a rocket, an explosive series of reactions takes place, creating heat in the process. The chemical reactions are so violent that you can actually hear the explosions. As a vital part of its armoury, the beetle has a nozzle, that, precisely like the turret of a tank, can swing in any direction, under its legs or over its back.

The spray of foul-tasting burning vapour shoots out at boiling point at the rate of five hundred to one thousand pulses per second! (If you want to know just how fast that is, try placing some frozen peas in your mouth, pick up a pea-shooter and begin firing. See how many peas you can shoot in one second. If you are fast, you might manage one. Our little hero manages five hundred if he is slow, double that amount if he is angry!) The reason why the burning liquid is emitted in pulses rather than in one continuous spray is to allow split-second cooling between each pulse in the combustion chamber (much like the heart's brief rest between each beat.) Without a cooling process, the bombadier beetle manufacturing boiling spray under attack could easily cook itself! The almost unbelievable co-ordination, complexity and efficiency of this mute little creature that has never learned chemistry, never studied military strategy — but simply and faithfully follows its instincts — is eloquent testimony to a Master Chemist and Designer. The Chieftain tank is as advanced as a bow and arrow and as swift as a rhinoceros with lumbago in comparison with this wonder beetle.

In equipping all creatures with the ability to defend themselves, humans have not been forgotten. Besides possessing a voice to shout, legs to run, and fingers that can curl into a hard fist, we have been equipped with two tiny wonder-machines that are of enormous benefit at all times, but most especially in times of danger. They perch on top of each kidney, they are the size of a finger-tip and weigh practically nothing. They are called ADRENAL GLANDS. For all their modest appearance, they are immensely talented and produce some fifty different hormones, or hormone-like substances. It would take acres of chemical plant to try to synthetically produce all these chemicals. The weight of hormones produced daily is minute — something like one thousandth of an ounce — yet they are vital to life.

The core of the adrenal gland has a direct 'hot-line' to the brain. If you have any sudden strong emotion — a sudden rage or an overwhelming fear — the gland receives the information instantly. What the adrenal gland does not know, is the precise nature of the emergency, so it prepares the body for either flight or fight. Immediately, two hormones — ADRENALINE and NORADRENALIN are poured into the bloodstream. The body's response is extraordinary. The liver immediately releases stored sugar — instant energy — into the bloodstream. The hormones shut down skin blood vessels to protect against injury, with the resulting pale complexion. This extra blood is diverted to the muscles, giving extra strength, and to the internal organs. The heart speeds up and arteries tighten to hoist blood pressure. The body is racing into top gear! Digestion comes to a halt — now is not the time to worry about processing food — and the clotting time for blood is quickened, in case of injury.

All this is accomplished in seconds. Suddenly you are a virtual superman. If your survival necessitates running faster, jumping further, hitting harder or lifting more than ever before, you are now capable of it. If you have heard stories of people lifting overturned cars to release trapped passengers, it is the master chemist adrenal glands which provide the capability.

If these tiny little but vital machines — acres of chemical wizardry compressed into a finger-nail — are so essential to life, it is logical to assume that they were always with us. Imagine telling an implacable foe:

"Don't hit me just yet — wait around a couple of million years, by then Superman will have found his cape."

The fiendish enemy just might not wait!

In today's world, defence systems have never been more sophisticated. Electronics, radar-controlled, computerised and automatic machines have replaced the ponderous primitive weapons of the past.

In *Hashem Yisborach*'s world, defence systems in every creature have always been super-sophisticated, more advanced than we can really comprehend, and the clearest possible evidence of a Designer and Creator who created His world with infinite wisdom.

8

ಏ MY GOOD FRIEND ಌ

Some people say that the dog is man's best friend. It is everything that a friend should be — loyal, faithful, uncomplaining — and best of all, he is there whenever you need him. Phone up a friend when you are in trouble, and hear him say, "Sorry, I'm busy right now, — can I get back to you.." and you will realise that people have their limitations.

Not everyone likes dogs. There is a certain *Possuk* in *Parshas Bo* which hundreds of children know by heart and repeat many times whenever a member of the canine species appears within fifty yards. So there are other best friends. Someone was recently persuaded to invest in a word processor. At first highly sceptical, he quickly became enamoured by this electronic wonder, and at the drop of a floppy disk will go into raptures about how his life has undergone a metamorphosis.

"My word processor is my best friend. In the morning I cannot wait to see it, whenever I am away from home I miss it terribly, and at night I cannot bear to leave it."

How useful his friend would be in a power failure is debatable — even best friends have their limitations.

Cold weather does not have to be described, especially to those living in the northern hemispheres. Those old enough to have experienced childhood before central heating became the norm will remember ice-cold bedrooms, frost glistening on the inside of the windows, long chilly corridors with only an isolated paraffin heater to cast a small oasis of tepid warmth on the frozen expanse of lino. The memory of frigid mornings, and the daily drudge of making a fire in the hearth are surely more vivid than the warm recollection of the glowing coal fire, casting its fingers of warmth into the living room, the area of real heat.

All that is a thing of the past. Central heating is now our best friend. A boiler, fuelled by oil electricity or gas, heats up water which it then circulates throughout the house, generating warmth in areas and rooms that no other heater ever reached. The luxury of a warm bathroom, a heated corridor, and even the ultimate in cosseted living — a centrally heated *Succah*! A turn of a dial, the touch of a

56 / Designer World

thermostat, will guarantee that your home is heated day or night, whether you're in or whether you're out. But even your best friend has limitations. Without a pump it will not work. The pump, electrically operated, sends the heated water against gravity to every furthest recess of the system. If the hot water circulates, surging through the pipes, then it is thanks to the tireless efforts of the pump, operating unseen and unthanked under the floorboards, or behind the boiler. Pump, — you are a true friend, loyal and reliable — just let there be no power failure!

All the best friends in the world are only of value, if one particular pump continues to work ceaselessly and tirelessly. That pump lies within us, weighs about twelve ounces, less than the weight of half a bag of sugar, and is suspended by ligaments in the middle of the chest — the heart of our body. A person requires a continuous

It looks unsightly, but you could not manage without the central-heating pump

supply of blood in order to function. For the blood to carry out its many tasks, it has to circulate around the body. This is powered by the tireless and indefatigable heart, which receives oxygenated blood from the lungs and pumps it to all parts of the body.

The amount of work carried out by the heart is astonishing. The heart contracts approximately seventy times a minute throughout our lives — that is over one hundred thousand times a day, making four thousands three hundred and twenty million beats in a lifetime. The workload is equivalent to a man lifting a fourteen pound weight to a height of five feet once each minute. After lifting the weight a few dozen times, a man would probably be exhausted. But the heart goes on pumping, day after day, year after year עד מאה ועשרים שנה. Heart muscles differ from other kinds of muscle in that they do not become tired. Try a little experiment. Clench your fist and open it at the rate of seventy times a minute — and see if you can even reach seventy without suffering excruciating pain. It will certainly not take too long for your hand muscles to give up. Heart muscle, however, has no difficulty in working at that rate. How did that develop — and how did we survive whilst it was developing?!

In fact the heart does rest — between beats. It takes about three tenths of a second for the left ventricle — the part of the heart that pushes oxygenated blood around the body — to contract. Then it has a rest for half a second. Imagine being given a holiday for half a second! Also, whilst you sleep, a large percentage of the capillaries are inactive, so the heart beat slows down.

Certain statistics stagger the imagination. The blood flows round the body in tube-like blood vessels, which eventually lead back to the heart. The blood vessels which carry blood away from the heart are called arteries, and those that bring blood back to it are called veins. The arteries and veins are connected by narrow thin-walled capillaries. As blood flows through the capillaries, oxygen and other useful substances pass out of them to the surrounding cells, and unwanted substances pass in the reverse direction. In this way, capillaries bring life to the cells, and maintain them in a state of health and repair. The capillaries are numerous, and every organ contains thousands of them. No cell is more than a twentieth of a millimetre from the nearest one. If a person's capillaries would be laid end to end, they would stretch around the world two and a half times! (That is one reason why being overweight is no laughing matter. Every pound of excess fat contains some two hundred miles of capillaries which the heart has to push blood through — in addition to the work of carrying around each extra pound.)

What is incredible is that every single minute, the heart has pumped nearly nine pints of blood — the total volume of blood in a man's body — and a complete circulation has been made to every distant capillary. The vast network of capillaries are supplied with fresh, life-giving oxygenated blood once every minute, without rest. And we are impressed by the hard work and dedication that results in two pints of fresh milk being delivered to our doors each morning! No central heating pump has to work so hard, or works so efficiently.

Not only that, it is capable of greatly increasing its pump rate at almost a second's notice. If someone takes extremely vigorous exercise, its output can increase almost instantaneously from nine, to forty pints a minute. In order to maintain such an output, the heart must pump at 180 beats a minute. When maximum effort is made, as in a sprint race, the muscles use energy faster than the heart can supply them with oxygen. Extra carbon dioxide is produced in the

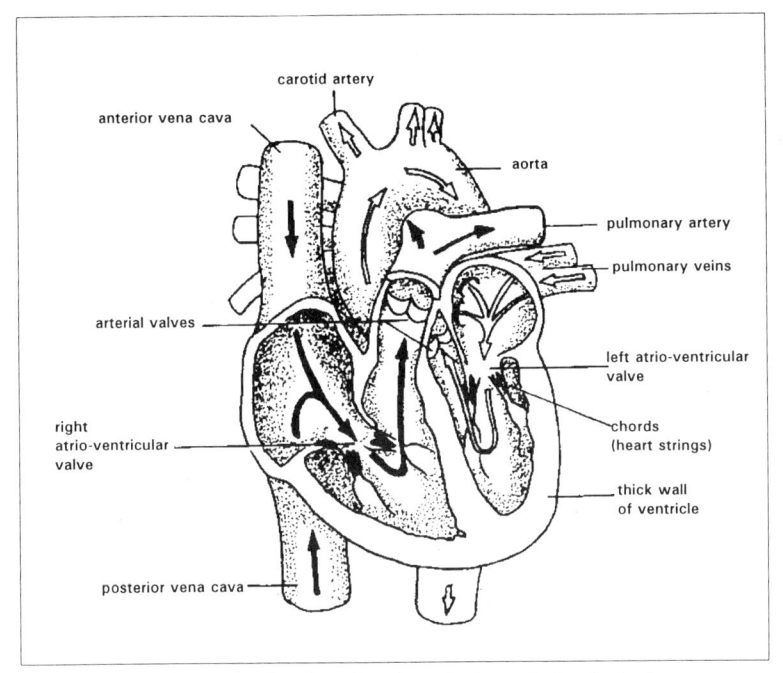

```
                    carotid artery
    anterior vena cava
                                        aorta
                                          pulmonary artery
                                          pulmonary veins
    arterial valves
                                          left atrio-ventricular
                                          valve
    right
    atrio-ventricular                     chords
    valve                                 (heart strings)
                                          thick wall
                                          of ventricle

    posterior vena cava
```

The heart in detail – the most vital mucle in the body.
Oxygenated blood – black arrows
Deoxygenated blood – hollow arrows

muscles, and waste products such as lactic acid begin to accumulate in them, and they begin to ache. The brain senses this is happening, and sends a message to the heart telling it to beat faster. This is an automatic reflex which takes place without you having to think about it. The result of the heart beating faster is that more blood can be sent to the muscles. The arteries serving the muscles widen, whereas those serving less needful organs contract. The result is that extra blood is diverted to the structures that require it most.

The heart — the second most powerful muscle in the body — stronger than the biceps of a heavyweight boxing champion, or the leg muscles of a sprinter, needs nourishment. This nourishment, vital to its existence, is obtained, naturally, from blood. Although the heart represents only a two-hundredth of the body weight, it requires a twentieth of the blood supply. That means that it consumes about ten times the nourishment required by the body's other organs and tissues. However, the heart does not extract nourishment from the blood passing through its chambers, but is fed by its own blood supply through two coronary arteries, little branching trees with trunks not much larger than lemonade straws.

Modern watches are often powered by a tiny quartz which sends out regular electrical pulses. The heart has a similar mechanism. Without any stimulation, the heart muscle would beat at about forty beats a minute. This would be insufficient to meet the extensive range of the body's demands. Fortunately (!) the heart has been 'provided' with a pacemaker which raises the pulse rate as the situation demands. This little pacemaker, which is housed on the top right of the heart, is made of nerve tissue, connected to the brain, and sends out electrical impulses which keep the heart pumping regularly. What a *Chesed*!

The whole system is so complex, yet so brilliantly designed, that it makes the Central Heating system look as advanced as a water-pistol. The valves in the heart are specially constructed to guarantee that blood flows only in one direction. As the blood flows back to the heart along the veins, it must travel upwards, against the force of gravity for most of its journey — so the large veins in the legs have valves that only open towards the heart, preventing the blood from falling back.

Reliable and loyal, brilliantly constructed and dependable — it is the best friend of all.

מה רבו מעשיך ה' כלם בחכמה עשית

9

ഌ A BREATH OF FRESH AIR ଔ

Down in the Underground, you hear the train before you see it. Passengers waiting impatiently for the next train to arrive sense when the train is approaching. Some feel a cold draught emerging from the tunnel, others hear the hum of the vibrating rails. Soon enough the evidence is transformed into fact as the multi-carriaged machine roars out of the blackness. The tens, perhaps hundreds of waiting passengers involuntarily retreat a step or two as the hundred-ton train hurtles past, races along the platform and screeches to a stop. The doors open, numerous passengers step onto the platform, whilst those who were waiting push into the train. The doors clang shut, the train departs and in seconds all is again silent. The exchange has been made. Those who were on are now off, and those who were off are now on.

What resembles a chaotic jangle of noise and movement, people swarming, trains rushing, is in reality a study in planning and purpose. Each train is directed by central control, its timing is synchronized to fit in with all other trains, and much time and energy is expended to ensure that every piece of rolling stock is correctly located. The people who make up the swarms of passengers are also not haphazardly placed. Each one is an individual, quite unique, embodying a myriad of details and characteristics. They are embarking on the train for a specific reason, and to arrive at a definite destination. Everyone is there for a reason, nothing is accidental.

The co-ordinated activity and purposeful movement of a busy station is an apt allegory of that which takes place whenever we engage in that most vital of tasks — breathing. Approximately sixteen times each minute, or twenty three thousand times per day, we breath in a pint of a most precious commodity — fresh air. Air may be colourless, odourless and tax-free, but it is far from free of content! It contains 78% nitrogen, 21% oxygen, and a minute amount of carbon dioxide. Apart from those gasses you will also find water-vapour, dust pollen and germs.

All living cells need a constant supply of energy, and in the human body the source of this energy is food. Digestion breaks down the food that we eat into sugars, simple fats and amino acids. By a chemical reaction with oxygen, these products of digestion are converted into energy, carbon dioxide and water. This process, which is similar to burning fuel in a boiler to supply heat and power, calls for a constant supply of fresh oxygen, and a method of removing waste carbon dioxide.

"May I have a standing order from Central Bank for a fresh supply of oxygen?"

"How often Sir?"

"Sixteen times a minute if you please!"

"Certainly Sir, without fail!"

Our Supplier has given the blood circulation the responsibility to deliver the oxygen around the body, and at the same time cart off the unwanted carbon dioxide. How exactly does it work?

If you place your finger beneath your Adam's Apple (LARYNX), you can feel you windpipe, or TRACHEA. It is a straight tube, about twelve cms. long and it descends into the chest. It then splits into two short tubes, called BRONCHI, one to each lung. The bronchi are similar to the windpipe, only narrower. Within each lung, the bronchi split into numerous branches, like an upside-down tree. They divide and subdivide into tiny air passages. Each narrow air pipe leads to a bunch of tiny sacs — gathered grape-like around its stem. These tiny air sacs give the lungs their spongy texture and appearance — they are the railway stations in which the oxygen passengers embark, and the carbon dioxide passengers disembark. Each person possesses some three hundred million of them! Each little air sac (called ALVEOLUS) is surrounded by a network of blood capillaries, rather like a net bag. The capillaries are separated from the air sac by a thin membrane covered in fluid. This is where the exchange takes place.

The blood cells go past the alveolus in single file. The breathed-in oxygen is dissolved into the fluid and then into the blood. At the same time, the red blood cells give up their carbon dioxide waste in the opposite direction, and this is breathed out. It is the most brilliant railway station. The air arrives on time, like a train, sixteen times each minute. Each time, the platform is crowded. Silently, millions of carbon dioxide passengers jump on the train for their journey to the atmosphere, and millions of oxygen passengers hop onto the platform — an ever-moving red-coloured escalator which will take them around the body. Not even the Moscow Metro could compete with a system which has three hundred million stations, with each station entertaining a train every 4 seconds!

If you learn in a *Beis Hamedrash*, you will know that there exist two kinds of human beings. There are those who just have to open every window, no matter how frigid the outside temperature. At the sight of a closed window, they throw a nervous fit, pretend to gasp for breath, dramatically mop their brows and clutch their throats. The other half of humanity loves warmth, and the snug conditions that closed windows produce, and the sight of an open window makes them shiver and reach for their pure-wool cardigans. That's people! The lungs, however, are most particular. They only like air which is as moist and warm as that in a tropical swamp. Producing this very special air in the space of a few inches is no small task.

When air is drawn in through the nostrils, there at the rear of the nose there is a large space called the nasal cavity. Inside the cavity it is moist and warm. Moist, because its lining produces mucus; and warm because there are numerous blood vessels close to the surface. If you have ever had a nose-bleed you will know what a lot of blood there is in the nose. The nasal cavity is divided up into several bony shelves called TURBINATES, which give it a large surface area, rather like the radiator of a car. The air is warmed and moistened as it passes over these surfaces, and it is cleaned at the same time. And we thought a car was a modern invention!

Hair in the nose traps large dust particles. Sticky mucus in the nose, throat and bronchial passages act as fly-paper to trap finer particles. But the real cleaning job falls to CILIA. These are microscopic hairs — tens of millions of them — which sit along the air passages. They wave back and forth, like wheat in the wind, about twelve times per second. Their upward thrust sweeps mucus from the lower passages to the throat, where it can be swallowed. If you smoke — here is a health warning! Reading the following could make you stop!

If you could watch your cilia under a microscope when cigarette smoke passes over them, you would see that the waving action stops. A paralysis sets in. If this irritation continues, the cilia simply wither away, never to be replaced. Mucus just drops into the air sacs, interfering with breathing as effectively as a lungful of water. The quiet efficiency of the cilia is replaced with the noisy inefficient smoker's cough, the only cleaning method left to the poor smoker!

In the length of time it takes to read this phrase, the superb air-conditioning system has warmed, cleaned, moistened and tested the air we breath, delivering it in prime condition to the lungs. Imagine the machinery necessary to provide that kind of service to each train prior to its entry into the station — at four second intervals! But it is all there, inside us, working away, for the most part unknown and unnoticed.

One of the main blessings of breathing is that you do not have to think about it. It is under automatic control, like the pre-set control box which governs the central heating. If every breath depended on conscious effort — how could one ever go to sleep? The automatic breathing control is housed at the rear of the brain; and it is an amazingly sensitive chemical detector. Hard working muscles burn oxygen rapidly and pour out carbon dioxide. As it accumulates, the blood becomes slightly acidic. The respiratory control centre detects this instantly, and orders the lungs to work harder. If the acid level rises really high, as it does when you do heavy exercise, then it commands deeper breathing as well — your 'second wind'.

The extra demand poses little problem. Normally one breathes in one pint of air — but the total capacity is much more. Just try taking a deep breath! A man at rest breathes about ten pints a minute — with maximum muscular effort this can rise to two hundred and fifty pints each minute! When a person is tired, his breathing tends to be shallow. When the body requires more oxygen — automatic control tells you to yawn — take a long deep breath, and the extra oxygen has been taken on board. It is interesting, and planned, that the air we inhale contains 21% oxygen, yet the air we breath out still contains 16% oxygen content — more than enough to perform successful artificial respiration.

Everything co-operates to enable us to breath, yet it is anything but simple. It is a muscular-chemical-electrical wonder, working with brilliant precision and harmony to enable us to enjoy that most beautiful breath of life.

על כל נשימה ונשימה שאדם נושם צריך
לקלס להקב"ה (בראשית רבה יד. יא)

10

℅ AYIN TOVAH ☙

Part I

The new cleaning lady was keen. That was the problem. She was too keen. It wasn't that you could blame her; she had been employed to clean the office floor, and she was only doing her job. But she did it constantly. How many times a day does an office floor need cleaning? It was hard-wearing lino, and once in a while it would need a good sweep, a wash and a polish. This cleaning lady just did not know when to stop. She was forever washing that office floor, around the cupboards and under the door, mopping and slopping just more and more. If it would have been confined to night hours only, when the place was deserted, no-one would have complained. But during the day! When everyone was at work, amidst the hustle and bustle of a busy area, there she would be with her ubiquitous mop, getting in the way, tripping people up — mind your feet, move your chair — it was just so impractical. If only they could devise a system where the floor could be cleaned, efficiently, silently and regularly without anyone being inconvenienced. "If only" — we are not yet in Utopia, and such things do not seem possible.

Wait! A system has been devised! It is claimed that this one-stop washing system will automatically remove all dust and dirt, whilst at the same time spread antiseptic cleaning fluid over the total surface area, using a unique spreading device. The whole area is guaranteed to be spotlessly clean, germ free, and — most amazing of all — the whole area will be thoroughly cleaned once every five seconds. Before you complain that such frequent cleaning (twelve times every minute!) will be completely disruptive, there is a built-in guarantee that no-one will even notice that the cleaning is taking place. It will all happen, at all times of the day, without anyone being aware of it.

Could you believe that such a system exists? Strange though it may seem, it is happening right now, even as you read this sentence. The surface of the eye must be kept constantly moist and clean. Above each eye is a small factory, called a tear gland, producing a wonder fluid containing a germ-killer. Each blink spreads the fluid over the surface of the eyeball by means of the eyelids, which act like windscreen-wipers. Silently, efficiently, and with no conscious effort, the surface area is kept germ-free, moist and clean. It is all done so swiftly that the work of the eye is in no way interfered with. We blink and we blink, without so much as a think — the most efficient cleansing system ever devised.

The fact that we possess two factories producing a highly specialised chemical cleanser constantly is amazing enough; but do not overlook the co-ordination. Tears, without eyelids to apply them to the eye's surface would be useless. Similarly, for eyelids to open and close over the eye's supersensitive surface area would be an excruciatingly painful experience without the lubrication of tears. Water without a mop will clean nothing, and a mop without water has no value. Like so many organs and systems in the body, this is an example of the inter-dependence of two completely separate functions, where each is totally dependant on the other, and one without the other has no function — a clear indication of the total co-ordination of the whole.

No method of cleaning would be sufficient without provision to remove excess liquid. Fortunately, there are two little drainage ducts in the inner corner of the eye, down which surplus fluid trickles. This duct leads directly to the nasal cavity. When a person cries, he has to blow his nose, but sometimes so much fluid is produced that it cannot all be drained away, and so it rolls down the cheeks as tears. Look your good friend in the eye. Would you believe that in the top outer corner, tucked away under the skin lies a chemical factory producing specialised antiseptic, twenty-four hours a day, and in the lower inner corners, skilfully hidden, but operating beautifully, is an intricate drainage system linking the eyes with the nose!

It is the mark of a good Designer that He is able to combine pragmatic practicality with pleasing looks. No car has its engine resting on its roof. Dust and rain, knocks and bumps would soon ruin it. Instead, it is tucked away, safe and sound, snug and secure under a hard metallic bonnet. Similarly, the delicate mechanism of a camera is shielded by the hard durable casing, whilst the ultra-sensitive lens is protected by lens caps and leather cases. The Designer of our eyes well understood that it is the precision instrument par excellence, and that any camera by comparison is as sophisticated as a *matzah* box with a pinhole — and as such has been provided with adequate protection.

The outer parts of the eyes are protected by eyebrows, eyelids and eyelashes. Each eyebrow is a bony ridge covered with thickened folds of skin. It shields the eye from sunlight, helps to protect it from blows, and disperses sweat and rain so that they run off the face at the sides of the eyes. A man was once walking along a road lined with shops. As he walked, he was looking sideways at the shops when suddenly he felt a crash on his face, and he saw stars even though it was midday. When he recovered his senses, he looked around and saw that he had walked straight into some scaffolding standing on the pavement. Gingerly, he felt his nose and was gratified to find it still there. Had the eyebrows not taken the force of the blow, or had his eyes protruded beyond his eyebrows, it could have been much different... Besides the eyebrows, protruding cheekbones and forehead complete the ring of shock absorbers which essentially shield the eye from damaging force.

The eyelids are a protective cover for the eyes, much like metal shutters that guard a shop window. Except, that the eyelids glide open and shut in a split second without the clanking noise of their metal cousins. The opening and closing of our very own shutters does not happen merely by chance. They are powered by muscles which in turn are operated by direct messages from the brain. It is an interesting example of a mechanism which is both voluntary and involuntary. That means that you can blink quickly if you wish, or

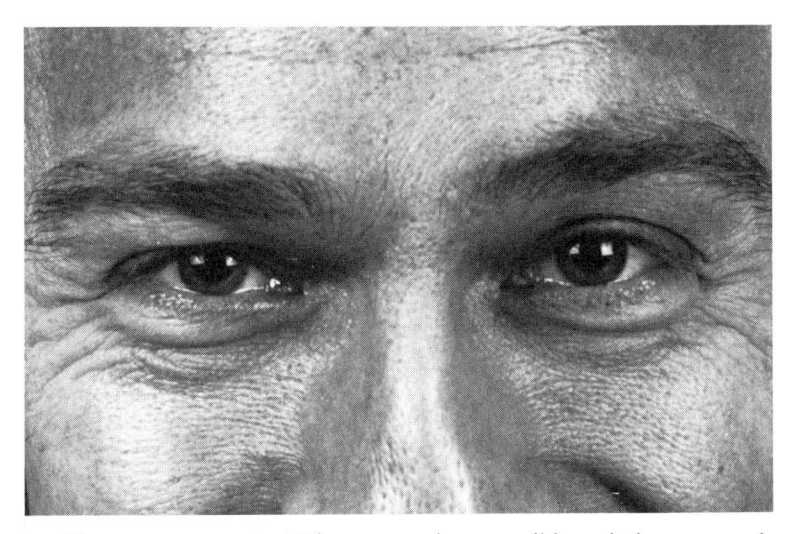

Smiling eyes – no wonder! The tears, eyebrows, eyelids, eyelashes, nose and forehead provide a remarkable protective barrier for those two priceless cameras

try not to blink at all. Normally however, it is a reflex action, which increases under stress or in times of danger, and decreases during times of concentration.

What is perhaps most amazing to see is the construction of the eyelid, which is much more than a flap of skin. On the outside are housed the muscles which move it, in the middle is a plate of cartilage, to give it rigidity, and on the inside of the eyelids are housed tiny TARSAL glands which secrete an oil, which together with the tears, provide lubrication. (These glands by themselves would not be sufficient to allow the eyelid to glide smoothly across the eye. Tears are essential.) The eyelashes only grow on the outer edge ensuring that they do not come too close to the eye's surface! This whole complex of muscles, cartilage and oil factories conveniently folds away out of sight when not required.

The eyelashes form a fringe of stiff hairs protruding from the eyelids, which catch and brush away particles that might become lodged in the eye. Observed an eyelash. See how stiff it is, unlike any other hair, how it never grows beyond a certain length and never needs trimming, how they are perfectly shaped, the top set curving upwards, the lower set downwards, in order not to obscure vision. How do you curve a hair! Nothing happens by chance, especially the fact that each single hair has a most intricate construction, and is the product of its own individual factory.

The eye has been blessed with super-sensitive nerves which sound the alarm should they sense an intruder, such as a particle of grit or a single hair. How do you react if a hair touches you heel, or a grain of sand comes into contact with your hand. Would you even feel it? Yet if either touches the surface of your eye, the result is a frenzy of distress. Why the difference? Everyone has nerve endings near the surface of his body — as many as are required to protect that particular limb. If you prick your finger with a two-pronged fork, you will feel two pricks. If you do the same to your back, you will feel only one prick, because the back has far fewer nerves than the hand. It does not need so many. The eye needs much protection, and so has many more nerve endings. If a piece of dirt, however tiny, enters the eye, a message is flashed to the brain which in turn instructs the tear glands to flood the area to wash away the intruder. The approach of an onion, with its potentially damaging pungent aroma, produces the same effect.

Iyov said: "*From my own flesh I perceive G-d*" (19:26). The way our window to the world is cleaned and protected, with wisdom and design, is an excellent illustration. The way the eye actually works is more amazing still...

11

ॐ AYIN TOVAH ॐ

Part II

Any child will tell you. It is easier to take thing apart than to put them together. A jigsaw, painstakingly completed over a long period can be dismantled by careless hands in a second. In a nearby neighbourhood, old terraced houses were being demolished to make way for new improved dwellings. A row of the old houses were knocked down in a cloud of dust, timber and bricks, and the site cleared in less than a week, whereas their replacements took months to rise slowly — Phoenix like — out of the rubble. To discover something that can be taken apart and then reconstituted perfectly in split seconds, is a rare achievement, and would appear worthy of further investigation.

Imagine the following invention. You have a tube filled with a substance composed of two chemicals. When a light shines on that machine it causes the substance to break into its two constituent chemicals. That in turn causes a little bell to ring — a light detector. Having done their job, the two chemicals join together again in perfect combination. They are happy to repeat the performance incessantly for as long as you like. The only condition is that you feed them carrots! The purpose of this little invention is to provide a signalling device to inform you when a light is shining, together with a

The mechanical eye – the best of modern technology

complete analysis of the nature, source and meaning of the light. Its advantage is that it costs nothing to operate, apart from a few pence for carrots, and its brilliance is that its constituent chemicals break apart and join together again as quick as a flash.

Are you interested in such a machine? How many can we offer you? We have good news for you — you already have some. Not only some, but many. To be precise, one hundred and twenty five million. You don't remember receiving them? Well, you wouldn't; they came with you at birth, one hundred and twenty five million in each eye!

When light passes through the aperture at the front of the eye (the PUPIL) and through the lens, it is focused on the back of the eye, the RETINA. In this area, covering less than a square inch, lie minute machines (approximately 150,000 to each square millimetre) shaped like rods. Each rod is a distinct machine, connected by a nerve fibre to the brain. Each tiny rod contains a chemical substance called RHODOPSIN, or 'visual purple'. When the minutest amount of light strikes the rod it causes some molecules of visual purple to break down, or be bleached. This in turn generates a tiny wisp of electricity — a few millionths of a volt — far too little to tickle a mosquito. This electricity feeds into the straw-sized optic nerve, and is transmitted to the brain at about three hundred miles an hour. The brain interprets the signals flooding in, and hands down its verdict. (The sight that you saw is then stored away in your personal photograph album, called a memory, able to be recalled at any time). The visual purple is then resynthesized, and is ready for action once again. All of this electro-chemical activity has been competed in about two thousandths of a second! Here is your machine that falls apart and re-joins quicker than a blink.

The rods work best in dim light, or at night, and can only detect black and white. When people tell you that eating carrots helps you to see in the dark, believe them! Visual purple is made from Vitamin A, which is particularly abundant in carrots. Anyone who is not obtaining sufficient Vitamin A in their diet may indeed experience difficulty in night vision. Have you noticed that when you enter a gloomy room from bright sunlight, you cannot see anything at first, but gradually things become visible? This is known as dark-adaptation, and is caused by the fact that all the visual purple has been broken down by the sunlight, and it takes a few seconds for the millions of rods to re-constitute it and start working!

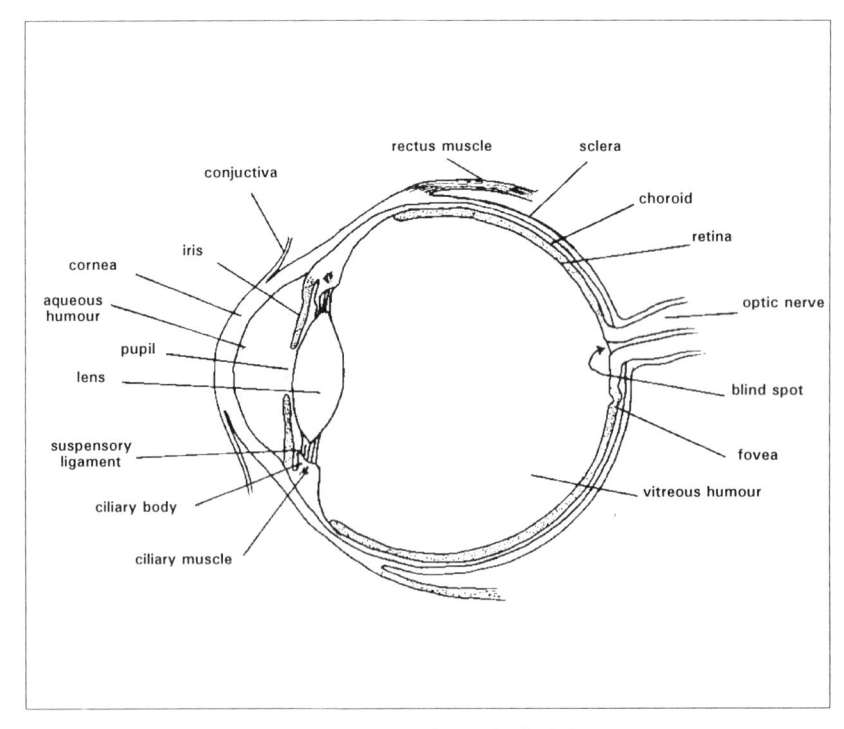

Horizontal section through the left eye.

How do we manage to see in broad daylight, and detect colours? For that, our Creator has kindly provided us with a different machine, this time, cone-shaped. Each eye is equipped with approximately seven million cones, and they are concentrated on one small area of the retina, and they become active as illumination rises. It is thought that the cones, too, have bleachable pigments, which react to the light waves of different colours. Like an artist mixing paints on a palette, our brain blends the electrical signals that different colours trigger, to make scores of different hues. In dim light, the activity of the cones diminishes, colour sense vanishes, and everything becomes grey as the rods take over. ("From when may you recite *Shema* in the morning, Rabbi Eliezer says, from the time that you can differentiate between blue and green" — light enough for the cones to have taken over from the rods. הפלא ופלא!)

Imagine what would happen if one hundred and thirty million separate machines sent in their electrical reports to the brain simultaneously — it would not be able to cope with so much data. In order to resolve this problem, an ingenious arrangement has been built into the system whereby many nerve fibres combine and connect, thus greatly reducing the number of signals. In so doing, there is a great advantage in that the image is enhanced, and blurring is eliminated. This system is so sophisticated that it has been adapted to process the images that are received from spaceships. The difference is that the little retina performs the function of a complex image processor in an area the size of a pin head, whereas the pictures from space are processed by a computer that fills a large room!

It is chastening for us to realise that every time we look our good friends in the eye, we are observing two ultra-sophisticated tiny cameras, complete with lens, shutter, automatic iris (aperture) control, with automatic focusing, not forgetting the self-cleansing mechanism, where every image is processed instantly, stored away in the memory bank, whose complexity is so great that our ability to comprehend, let alone duplicate it is as limited as an apprentice mechanic taking his first awed glimpse into the opened bonnet of a Rolls-Royce car.

Although the eye itself is an extremely sensitive instrument, it is extremely well protected. As it lies in its bony cavity, it is cushioned by fatty tissue. The outside layer of the eye is made of a tough protective (as you read this paragraph, think, Design, Design, Designer...) tissue, which holds the eye in shape due to its non-elasticity. It counteracts the outward force of the eye fluids, and maintains the shape of the eyeball, essential for good vision. This tough outer layer also provides points of attachment for the muscles that move the eye.

The eye muscles are amazing! You can move your eyes up and down, sideways or rotate them all about. Six muscles, anchored to the skull at the rear of the eye socket, are attached to various points of this outer cover. The muscles are co-ordinated by the brain so that both eyes move in the same direction. One of the refinements of the muscular action is that you can look at a moving object, and a reflex action will ensure that you follow the path of that object without any conscious effort. Nothing is accidental! The muscle that enables you to rotate your eye actually runs through a pulley made of fascia to be able to bend backwards and be attached to the eyeball at the correct angle. There really is a real pulley above your eye through which the superior oblique muscle runs smoothly and freely!

Another remarkable refinement is that each eye sees a slightly different view of the same object. The brain receives these differing views and blends them together to give a three-dimensional complete picture. Hold your right finger in front of your face. Look at it with each eye in turn, with the other eye closed, and you will see slightly different views. With both eyes open, all is remarkably fused into one all-round picture.

Our eyes, the size of table tennis balls, are not filled with air. There is a clear liquid in front of the lens (AQEOUS HUMOUR) which contains dissolved salts and glucose. It also contains dissolved oxygen, and it supplies the lens and cornea, which contain no blood vessels, with nutrients and oxygen. This wonder liquid is manufactured in a specially designed factory inside the eye. An intricate, specially constructed drainage system ensures that the pressure of this liquid remains constant. The large space behind the lens is filled with a jelly-like VITREOUS HUMOUR, which is a protein-jel which helps maintain the spherical shape of the eye. It is no accident that the *Loshon Hakodesh* for an eye is עין, which also means a well of water. (The word עין is also contained in מעין, a spring). The connection is phenomenal. The only organ in the body entirely filled with liquid is a beautifully constructed little well; our window to the world, our עין טובה.

12

ଌ FLIGHT ଊ

On any long journey, the view from the passenger seat is often tedious. Cows follow fields, sheep follow moorland, and boredom soon sets in. Pass by an airport, though, and everyone wakes up. Eyes are strained in the hope that a plane is taking off or landing. If an aircraft is indeed in the process of taking off, it is extremely difficult for the driver to concentrate on the road ahead — instinctively he feels the urge to watch

A British Airways B757 taking off. Think of the technology necessary to make this huge machine defy the forces of gravity. It's almost as impressive as....

the colossal metal structure surge upwards in a gravity-cheating exhibition of technological wonder.

There is no doubt that aircraft are fascinating. A low flying Concorde passing your house will bring all the inhabitants racing to the window. A helicopter hovering overhead will turn all heads upwards, mesmerised by the sight of an enormous machine cutting through the air in a clatter of noise. A bomber screaming, scraping the tree tops, is a frightening sight, yet strangely leaves the cows munching as before, undisturbed and unperturbed. Aeroplanes fascinate. A photograph from 1927 shows Charles Lindbergh in his 'Spirit of St. Louis' approaching Hendon aerodrome watched by tens of thousands of spectators. So many people enraptured by one aeroplane!

Yet the greatest aerobatic display of all takes place all around us, and for the most part remains unnoticed. Lift your eyes on high, and see the wonders in the sky. If you are fortunate enough to live near the sea, see the seagulls with their wide wings, wheeling, soaring, gliding gracefully, sliding through the air with just the barest flick of their feathers, sometimes hovering almost at a standstill in perfect aerodynamic control.

If five small jet planes flying in close formation leave you speechless with amazement, observe a flock of starlings at dusk as they come in to land on a tree. Thousands of birds, twisting turning and changing direction almost as one. There are never any mid-air collisions, and no-one knows how such perfect harmony is achieved. On a hot day, stop and ponder at a cloud of midges, not with irritation or repugnance, but with awe, as they weave around each other at breakneck speed in a dizzying blur, never ever hitting each other. How do they do it? As far as we know, there is no midge control-tower with little midges staring at computer-screens, guiding the airborne midges in their intricate and co-ordinated waltz! If you can, watch the tiniest of all birds, the humming bird, which weighs just 1.5 gms, perform feats that would make the most sophisticated helicopter green with envy. They are not only quick and agile in forward flight, but they can also fly up, down, sideways, backwards and upside down. In addition, they can hover perfectly, keeping their beaks quite till as they suck nectar from the flowers. As it hovers, the humming bird's wings twist into the shape of a propeller, and the wing tips move in a figure of eight to give perfect control. Their narrow wings beat up to ninety times — each second! Most remarkable of all, the tiny bird, as with all members of the bird family, lay eggs to produce the next generation of flying wonders. No Concorde, to the best of our knowledge, has ever produced diminutive Concorde*lech* which one day will grow to be long and graceful, giving much *nachas* to their parents.

The larger the aeroplane, the longer the runway it needs to land or take off. Hours of training are required to develop the expertise necessary for the pilot to bring the plane down safely and approach the ground at the correct angle and appropriate speed. Any too sudden contact with terra-firma would give the passengers a nasty jolt. Bearing this in mind, give a thought to how a bird flies through the air and manages to land, first time, with perfect safety, on a telegraph line. What technique does a fly use to land upside down on a ceiling? It is interesting to notice that before landing, most insects extend their six legs out as soon as the landing surface comes within a few body-lengths of them. The legs are constructed to function as efficient shock-absorbers, since, unlike aircraft, insects and most birds never run forward after touch-down. They arrive at their landing spot from almost any angle without slowing down at all, alighting with a sharp jolt. Some idea of the efficiency of the landing gear is given by the estimates that some beetles are subjected to a force about forty times that of gravity when they strike an unyielding surface — a force which would cause the complete disintegration of any aircraft!

Anyone who has ever flown in an aeroplane will have heard that dreaded word — overweight! Food blenders and mixers, *peckelach* for the cousins, together with all the vital food supplies for friends' children, must all be contained within twenty kg. or else pay for the consequences. The reason for this cruel imposition is obvious. The heavier the aircraft, the greater the power it needs to get it off the ground, and fuel costs money. For that reason, special metals are chosen which combine minimal weight with maximum strength, and all the interior fittings of the plane must be of the lightest materials. The consideration of minimising the weight is an obvious precondition of aeroplane design. Just look at the design of birds! To reduce weight, the skeleton is remarkably light. Normally, the skeleton is the heaviest part of the body, but many of the bones of birds are honeycombed with air spaces. Should you think that this would weaken the bones — fear not, for additional strength is given by a criss-cross of internal bracing struts. Aeroplanes, naturally, have adopted the same system.

Pause for a moment and think. However strong your desire to lose weight, how can you reduce the weight of your bones? Who taught the thousand of species of birds to design bones with air spaces?! How do you develop an air space in a bone?! There is a bird called a gannet which plunge-dives into the sea from heights of up to one hundred feet to catch fish. To help them survive the impact of this tremendous crash, they have spongy bone around the head and beak, and air sacs under the skin around the throat.

Although the designers of aeroplanes try to copy as many features of birds as possible, their streamlined shape, the retractable under-carriage — one characteristic of birds has not yet been adopted, and perhaps can never be. That is the special covering with which birds have been created — feathers. Feathers are fantastic! Without them, the bird would remain grounded, cold, waterlogged and unrecognised. With them, they give the wing a large surface area which helps keep the bird in the air. They keep the bird warm by trapping a layer of air against the skin. Air is a poor conductor of heat, so this layer of air holds heat inside the body. Are you feeling cold? Go on, try to grow some feathers! Feathers keep the water out, because they are oily. Where on earth does a bird find oil? No problem — the oil is produced by a gland on the bird's back, close to the tail. The bird rubs its beak in this oil before it preens itself! Because the feathers are oily, water runs off the oily surface without wetting it. For that reason, a duck can swim in its pond for hours on end without getting cold or even wet! Besides everything else, feathers enable birds to recognise each other and camouflage themselves. Terns, for example, and many other fish-eating sea-birds have white underparts. Unsuspecting fish cannot see them against the bright sky, as they swoop down for their supper. Other feathers help birds follow their leader. Brent Geese migrate in flocks from Siberia to Europe. To make sure they keep together and do not lose sight of one another, the birds have a white rump that is easily seen from behind in flight.

The beauty and complexity of the feather can only be fully appreciated when viewed under a microscope. The vaned feather is made up of a central shaft which is hollow up to two-thirds of its length. Beyond this point it becomes solid to increase its strength. Design! Growing out from the central shaft are hundreds of barbs. Each barb in turn carries hundreds of tiny filaments (called BARBULES)

... a duck coming in to land on a railing – a ½ inch runway. There isn't a plane in the world that can achieve that!

and these are equipped with minute hooks which interlock with the next row. The whole structure works much like a zip fastener. Or rather, the zip fastener works very much like a feather! If the web splits, the bird simply draws the feather through its beak a few times, and perfection is restored. Amazing, amazing design.

The next time a jet plane roars overhead, and you instinctively look skywards, do yourself a favour and look for the immensely superior flying marvels all around you.

"שאו מרום עיניכם וראו מי ברא אלה" (ישעי' מ')

"Lift your eyes Heavenwards and see who created all these"

13

෩ COMPUTER SPEAK ෪

Part I

Great-great-grandfather is coming again! What a *simcha*! The last time he came he was simply amazed at the dazzling array of unbelievable machines that you had in your house. To think that you were always of the opinion that you had an unostentatious, unassuming home, without any unnecessary luxuries or lavish furnishings! What, you wonder, will he discover on this occasion?

Soon enough the great day came, a cold and wintry day, with the outside temperature well below zero. As the revered gentleman came through the door, his greeting was warm, but you could see that he was shivering from the cold. Stepping into the hall, he immediately remarked on the cosy warmth of your home, and asked to be taken in front of the fire so that he could warm himself through. Somewhat taken aback, you remarked that you did not possess a fire, but that your house was heated by radiators in each room. Now it was the elderly gentleman's turn to look baffled, never having heard of or seen this mysterious 'radiator'. You patiently pointed to the white thin metallic structures standing demurely by the wall, with little lace doyleys and dried-flower arrangements gracing their otherwise featureless shelves, and explained that what he was looking at was indeed the source of your heat. You continued your discourse by explaining that inside the radiator lived piping hot water, and that was that!

"But where does the hot water come from," asked the amazed gentleman. "Where is it heated?"

It is strange how the simplest question can sometimes stop you in your tracks. Where did it come from? Of course, how silly of you to forget, in the boiler!

"Can you show me where the boiler is?" asked your inquisitive sage.

Again you were flummoxed. Where on earth was it — I haven't seen it for a long time! Inspiration suddenly struck.

"Why, how could I forget — it's in the bathroom, but the control panel is in the kitchen."

Barely able to control his emotion, your respected guest asked if you were seriously expecting him to believe that in your bathroom, you kept a fire which heated all the water in your house, and that you controlled that fire by a little dial and switch in your kitchen? At that stage, you did not feel like reminding him that hidden beneath his waistcoat was his very own beautifully designed personal central-heating boiler (the Liver) and that the reason that he had been shivering in the cold was that his automatically controlled thermostat was working so efficiently. That would do for another time. Instead, you swallowed hard — it promised to be an interesting afternoon.

You led him into the kitchen to make him a hot drink, passing the chugg-chugg of the meaty dish-washer and the orbiting gyrations of the washing-machine which was in midst of its long spin. The poor man looked shell-shocked as he gaped at these gurgling enigmas. As you plugged in the electric kettle and switched on, you patiently explained the wonders of cleaning a dinner-load of dirty dishes and a mini-mountain of soiled clothes at the flick of just two switches. He would barely believe his ears as he visualised what these major activities involved in terms of hard laborious labour in his day. He decided not to ask you how the hot water now residing in his cup came to be boiled, since there definitely was no flame visible underneath the kettle, and instead retired to the front room to regain his composure.

Now prepared for anything, you joined him in the front room, and saw him staring fixedly at a square screen, which stood on a rectangular box, with another small box by its side. He was also now prepared for anything, and if you would have told him that he was looking at a miniature moon-rocket which was fuelled by orange peel, he would have accepted it with equanimity. But, you told him the truth.

"That, my dear *elter elter Zeide*, is a computer-word-processor, with a small printer attached."

As he appeared somewhat uncomprehending, you continued to explain, as best you could.

"*That, my dear elter elter Zeide, is a computer – word-processor, with a small printer attached!*"

"It really is quite simple," you began, not really convincing yourself, "All you do is type your message onto the screen by means of the keyboard, add, remove, or change the text as much as you like, and when all is finished, you can either just store the text in the computer's memory for future use, or else press this little button and print it out on paper — like this!" With little more ado, you wrote an appropriate message on the screen, and with a whir and a whizz, out came the message in beautiful bold black typeprint. Amazement is much too mild-a-term to describe his reaction at this display of almost futuristic technological wonder. In a voice quivering with emotion he declared that never in his wildest dreams would he ever have thought such a phenomenal fantasy possible.

The strange thing is that not only was this fantasy a reality, but — perhaps without realising it — he was actually using the very same machine that he could not comprehend to describe his incomprehension! His brain was the computer, his thought were the keyboard, and his vocal cords the printer that articulated those thoughts.

Modern man stands in awe of his own achievements, and can hardly believe that he can accomplish so much. At the very pinnacle of human prowess stands the ubiquitous all-powerful world of computer technology. It is a humbling thought, but an essential one, that the brain with which we have been endowed, which works so faithfully and fantastically, is far, far in advance of any computer yet designed. When a person purchases the wonder machine, it is as useless as a lump of scrap iron without the thick, *lomdishe* Manual of Instructions, condensed into five volumes. As you wend your wearisome way through the intricacies of the 'easy-to-follow' instructions, you come to the conclusion that life is anything but simple. For every one operation you do correctly, there is a good chance that you will do five wrong. Eventually, you do master it, but even then, you have to do everything precisely and correctly for the machine to operate and be of any benefit.

Just think of the things that you require. Assuming that you have already purchased the computer, and that is no small sum, you need an electricity supply, with the correct outlet, plug fuse and wire. To connect the computer to the printer requires yet another specialised wire and plug.

"Sorry sir, that will have to be purchased separately, plus V.A.T. naturally..."

And then you are ready to print. That's what you think! You haven't got any paper! Back to the shop.

"What quality of paper would you prefer, Sir? We have 80 grain superior, or if you prefer we can supply 100 grain de-luxe. I should mention that our better customers do prefer the 100 grain, and the slightly higher price, plus V.A.T. naturally..."

And we have not mentioned the most important word DISCS. Hard, floppy, big byte, little byte, manuals, electricity, fuses and flexes, paper and warranty, bubble-jets and laser beams — give me back my pen!

Move over, proud technology, let us introduce the brain and its print-out partner, the vocal cords. You are supplied with them at birth, and they cost nothing. You can take them anywhere, and they work everywhere. They are compatible with millions of brains throughout the world, and the fuel they require to keep them working is anything that you fancy. Potato crisps, corn flakes, *heimishe* cucumbers, or cream cake will all keep your machine working at peak efficiency. What memory capacity does your brain-computer have? Just try and see if you can fill it! Many of our greatest leaders were busy for decades for twenty hours per day filling their memories, and never once did the "Full up" sign appear. There is never a danger that by pressing the wrong button you will erroneously erase all that you have ever learnt. It requires no servicing, cannot overheat, and there is no possibility of the model ever becoming obsolete!

"אתה חונן לאדם דעת". You *Hashem Yisborach*, have graced mankind with intellect and understanding. That means that we have the unique capacity to ponder, reflect, deduce and analyse. Of what use would this wonderful capacity be if we were not at the same time given the machinery to express those thoughts, or to communicate those reflections. It is therefore perfectly logical that the One who bestowed upon man the capability to utilise his intelligence, should at the same time supply him with the necessary tools to record his thoughts and ideas for posterity. Thus, the brain and the vocal-outlet go together as naturally as pollen and bees.

Just a superficial look at the computer with its attendant printer will show volumes of design. The keyboard is neatly laid-out, with the keys in the same position no matter which model you buy. It has no sharp edges, and the colour is pleasing to the eye. The printer, with its daisy wheels, bubble jets of laser beams is mind-boggling in its ingenuity, and it does produce beautiful work. The computer itself is nothing less than amazing in its complexity and capability. Would you for one minute believe that having left out your old tin cans in the back yard one windy night, you came out the next morning to find that somehow they had all been transposed into a gleaming, shiny perfectly operating computer with all its accessories!

Just a superficial listen to the voice will provide you with a host of features of design. Being a wind-instrument, it is housed just where it should be — in the wind-pipe. Everything that it requires in order to operate is located nearby — tongue, palate, lips and teeth, not to mention the lungs themselves. If your computer and printer demonstrate intelligence, then your brain and its voice shout out for all to hear "Design!" "How great are Your deeds *Hashem*!"

But how exactly the voice operates, is a story on its own...

14

ಲ "COMPUTER — SPEAK!" ಇ

Part II

The story is told of a young by who was attempting to do his Biology homework, whilst his father was immersed in his *Sefer*.

"Daddy," asked the son, "where are the appendix?"

The father heard the question and absent-mindedly answered:

"Ask Mummy, she puts everything away!"

This little tale teaches us two important lessons. First of all, it is important to listen carefully when someone speaks to you, and secondly, order is a wonderful thing! The father could rely on the fact that the house was indeed orderly, thanks to his good wife.

The importance of orderliness cannot be over-emphasised. Every one knows that there are two types of people in the world. There are those who career through life like a runaway hurricane, completely disorganised, never knowing where anything is, always in a state of panic because they cannot find the vital piece of equipment that they desperately need. Such people are often highly intelligent, and can solve the world's greatest mysteries with the greatest of ease, but have the profoundest problem in remembering where they placed their left shoe. Other people, on the other hand are totally organised. If you ask them for a piece of lemon, they will lead you to a little container in the fridge marked 'Partially consumed Lemons', and inside there will be lemons. If you ask if they have such a thing as a paper clip, they will unswervingly go to a desk, open a drawer, and without a moment's hesitation, pull out three paper clips, of varying designs. Such people always know where the appendix are!

It is true that extremes of any nature can present difficulties — (a polite way of saying get on your nerves) — but the advantages of being systemised are obvious. There is no point in having to go to the fridge when you need a pair of pincers, or to the tool-box when you require a pickled cucumber. The scatter-brained genius might be a lovely fellow to have around, but you would never ask him to pack your suitcase before going on holiday, or to dissemble a car engine to repair a fault, and then re-assemble it. When you need to rely on something working efficiently, there is no alternative to orderliness. This idea, expressed in a slightly different way, would tell you that any object in which everything is precisely positioned in its correct place indicates clearly that intelligence and design have been at work.

A cow has no profound thoughts that it needs to articulate. A frog has no philosophical questions that it needs to ask. A chicken has no heritage that it needs to transmit to other chickens. That being the case, although these animals can produce sound, they cannot manufacture speech. They have no need to. Man, on the other hand, has thoughts, questions and a heritage all of which must be transformed into meaningful sound capable of being received and comprehended by others of the same species. The machine that produces this meaningful sound requires a passage of air to activate it. It is therefore not coincidental that the machine — the vocal cords — is housed in the wind-pipe, the only place in the body where they would actually work. The voice box could have been placed on the right knee, or the left toe — and would have proved totally useless. Conversely, therefore, the fact that they are precisely where they should be, entirely compatible with their surroundings and able to work beautifully indicates the greatest degree of advance planning and design.

At the top of the windpipe there is a little box. This little box, called the larynx, is made of cartilage, a firm but flexible material identical to that found in the ear. It sticks out slightly at the front of the neck, especially in men, to form the Adam's apple. Who exactly coined this phrase is not known, but what is known is that the reason why a man's Adam's apple is more prominent is because his larynx is large in order to hold his larger vocal cords. Inside the larynx, stretching from the front to the back, are two ligaments (bands of tough tissue). These are the vocal cords. When you breath gently, the air moves past the two vocal cords in the voice box without producing any sound.

Have you ever thought what the difference is between a whisper and actual speech? What do you do when you speak that you do not do when you produce a whisper? It cannot be the volume of air that you exhale, because you can produce a loud whisper which demands a lot of air, whereas soft speech requires very little, yet it is definitely speech. Whisper — speak; speak — whisper; what is the difference? Try it out, and see if you can solve the problem! If you have ever driven a car, then you will know the answer. You can switch on the engine, press your foot on the accelerator, yet not move an inch. What could be the problem? Before calling out the garage, just check that the car is in gear. If the gear lever is in the neutral position, then you may rev the engine to your heart's desire, but it will remain stationary. The voice is precisely the same. When you whisper, you pass air through your vocal cords without activating them in any way. They remain in the neutral position, and sound is not produced. When you wish to speak, the cords receive a message from head office to position themselves, which they jump to do, restricting the passage of air. The air is then forced between the cords, making them vibrate. The vibration of the cords produces sound, in much the same way as the plucking of an elastic creates its distinctive noise. The faster the air is forced past the vocal cords, the louder the sound that is produced. The pitch of the sound, (a high note or a low one, and the many in between) depend on the tension in the cords, which are pulled by muscles, which are in turn controlled by the brain. The cords open wide to produce deep sounds, and narrow to slits for high-pitched sounds.

Place your finger on your Adam's apple, swallow, and you should have noticed that its position rose. That signals the closing of the flap-valve called the epiglottis that sits perfectly over the windpipe. Besides that, the vocal cords also close tightly when you swallow something, explaining why you cannot talk whilst you swallow. These days, cars are designed with many safety features. If the engine overheats, a little red light glows; if you are running low on fuel, another little light flashes — we take these things for granted and happily acknowledge the thought that went into its planning. Two safety features on the windpipe to prevent food slipping down and causing much distress demonstrate similar forethought which no little baby could have had, yet he is born with them! Every time we negotiate a meal with safety, we should use the vocal cords to thank our Designer!

There are many interesting features in the production of speech which deserve our attention. If you have heard one piano, then you have heard them all. It is true that some people are more adept than others in their ability to use the instrument, and some pianos are 'baby' whilst others are truly grand. But all instruments of mass production sound identical. If you think about it, the species called man is one which has been produced quite prolifically. Although the precise number is a little vague, there are certainly more people in the world than there are pianos, even allowing for pianos of all description. Then think how many people there have ever been in the world since its creation. The number is quite large — definitely more than all the musical instruments ever manufactured. The amazing fact is, as *Chazal* tell us, (*Sanhedrin* 38), that there have never been two people with identical faces, fingerprints — or voices. Everyone's voice is different. When the telephone rings and you hear the voice at the other end, you can recognise the caller even before he identifies himself. Many wonders are manifested there. Firstly, that every human being is unique and individual. There is no-one else in the whole wide world, past present or future who is the same as you in every way. Secondly, your home computer (brain) has a prodigious memory that can instantly identify any voice of the million that it has heard, and stored. As soon as you hear the voice, out pops his file with a mental picture attached, and all the information relevant to that person.

Often, you greet the caller by his first name, only to hear an embarrassed voice at the other end tell you that he is the said person's son. Your comment is "Why, you sound just like your Dad!" It is true, children do inherit their parents' voice identity to a large degree, as much as they inherit all the features of their parents. It is quite amazing that given the fact that every one of the billions of voices ever created have all been different, the father is still recognisable in the son's vocal cords.

The fact that mens' voices are deeper in pitch is also no accident. If men are designed to assume the role of leadership, then they require the tools for the job. Whatever your views on a previous British Prime Minister, it must be admitted that the male voice carries a greater degree of authority than its female counterpart, which is obviously designed for softer, quieter roles.

What the vocal cords produce is raw sound, only partially refined into speech. Lips, tongue, nasal tract, teeth and palate modify this raw sound into comprehensible speech. Everything is where it should be. All the cavities of the chest, throat and head give speech resonance and quality, much like the resonating chamber of the guitar or violin.

Many questions have not been answered. Why are some people musical, and others (usually unknown to themselves) tone-deaf? What is a sore throat, and how can you lose your voice? How can your voice travel through solid matter to be heard by your neighbours? Not every question needs an answer, but to question and observe is the unique quality of man and the special tradition of children of *Avrohom Ovinu*. We stand amazed at the technology of the computer print-out. People pay thousands for a Stradivarus, the Rolls-Royce of violins. Listen to someone speaking fast. Ideas formulating, rushing onto his computer screen and pouring out of his vocal print-out at breakneck speed in an absolutely spectacular demonstration of electronic/muscular/ technological wonder. At the same time, it pours into your computer (mind), is immediately absorbed, comprehended and filed into your memory bank. All at the speed of sound. Impressed? It all comes free, never needs re-inking, replenishing or servicing, and will serve you well, *b'ezras Hashem*, for one hundred and twenty years. Use it. Open your mouth, put your vocal cords into gear, and, using the fabulous machine for its best possible purpose, say...

"מודה אני לפניך מלך חי וקים..."

Just open your mouth, put your vocal cords into gear, and say "Modeh Ani Lefonechoh"

15

ೞ TAKE A LOOK AT A LEAF ಌ

It had started out as a harmless *Chol Hamoed* outing. A visit to a stately home, with extensive grounds to explore and enjoy. The novel feature of this particular location was that some of the walks were a little off the beaten track, adding some spice to what might otherwise be a rather dull experience. And that was the problem. After consuming their packed *Chol Hamoed* lunch, the two intrepid explorers, father and little son, (little son in a buggy) strode forth into the untamed wasteland of rural England. Every-

Just a simple leaf, until you see...

thing went well for the first mile; the air was fresh, the vegetation lush and verdant, timid squirrels and even fat toads were spotted with the excitement usually reserved for duck-billed platypuses. Then the trouble began. The path had disappeared. Ahead, behind and on both sides, everything looked identical. The going was rough, rocks appeared, and the buggy with its diminutive wheels did not take kindly to the rugged and rocky terrain, nor did the buggy's young occupant, who was vociferously voicing his eager desire to rejoin civilisation. The father reassured his young charge that they would soon be home, convincing no-one, least of all himself. He was now worried. Where on earth were they? Would they ever see human beings again? Panic welled up as the afternoon advanced and still they pushed on — but then, hope and optimism drove out the despair. They were safe. Everything would be fine — there in front of them as clear as a summer's day, was a trodden path. It was just flattened earth, true enough, but it was clearly marked with wooden borders, and that demonstrated intelligence. Where there was intelligence there were people, and that meant civilisation. Soon they found their bearings, and the panic in a teacup ended happily.

If a muddy path with a few wooden markers is such a clear indication of intelligence, what would you say about a motorway? They are designed for high-speed motoring, so that traffic going in opposite directions is clearly separated. They have gentle curves and easy gradients so that traffic does not have to slow down. There are no traffic lights or junctions, and other roads pass over or underneath them by means of flyovers. Their construction involves surveying, bridge building and tunnelling. The machinery used includes all the members of the heavy brigade — bulldozers, scrapers and excavators, giant cranes, Herculean lorries and massive steam-rollers. What looks to the uninitiated like a simple road, is in reality a many-layered marvel, from the sub-soil base, through the sandstone, compressed pebbles, gravel and up to the tarmac (named after Mr McAdam who invented it) which covers the road like the icing which graces the patisseur's masterpiece. Even that is not the finished article. A slightly cambered surface ensures the flow of rainwater towards the side of the road, and naturally, guttering and drainage form an integral part of the system. Travellers in the night rely on the reflections of the cats' eyes — inserted equidistantly into the road's surface like cherries on a cake — to tell them where the road is going. The next time you zip along the motorway, spare a thought for the vast amount of planning and intelligence which enables you to zoom from A to B in comfort and safety.

So you think that a motorway is complicated? Welcome to the wonderful world of the leaf. I suppose the more we see things around us, the more we take them for granted. On any given day we probably see thousands of leaves, and if you live in a wooded area, the number runs into the millions. Yet a leaf, a blade of grass — does it have anything special to tell me?

If you think of a leaf in terms of a food-producing factory, then you have the general idea. Any plant, or tree, is a living organism, and its leaves are the mechanisms which provide the plants with the nutrition that enable it to survive and grow. First of all, take a look at its structure. You will notice that the leaves have a network of veins which stiffen them and help to prevent them from drooping. If they would hang limp, they would not be able to catch the sunlight, and not perform their vital task. Imagine an aeroplane's wing made out of a single sheet of metal, somehow attached to the side of the plane, without any strengthening struts or network of supports. The wings would droop like a daffodil that has been three weeks in a vase without water, and it would not fly too far! Well, naturally the aeroplane's wing has been constructed with design — and the leaf not?

In some plants, the leaves and stems are hairy or have spikes which help protect them from attack by insects and other animals. The famous English rose has prickly thorns all along the stem, and the good English ladies who spend Sunday afternoon pruning their roses all wear special protective gloves — and all the thorns point downwards. The rose obviously knows that its predators crawl along the stem from ground level upwards, that they have nervous systems which react adversely to pain, and that a sharp point can cause pain.

Who told them all this classified information — how did they then manufacture all the weaponry, and how did they all manage to survive before they were told! It would seem that all was known, and designed, right from the beginning.

Take a look at a road — it just looks so very ordinary, with nothing to arouse any interest. A closer look reveals marvels of intelligence and layers of creative talent. Take a look at a leaf — are you serious? It looks so very, very ordinary, humdrum and unexciting. Now take a closer look under a microscope. There you will find layers of cells with a level of complexity indicating the profoundest intelligence imaginable. The top layer of the leaf is covered with a waxed protective layer, which makes it impervious to water, but still allows sunlight to penetrate. Along the centre of the leaf runs a stem — an irrigation channel that carries water from the soil. That stem is linked to the National Water Board, whose network of roots, channels and pipes ensure a continuous supply of the life-giving liquid. Other channels within the leaf carry away the food that has been manufactured in the factory. Take a look at the leaf — it doesn't look as if there are any holes in it. It has — thousands of them (called pores) — and they allow the vital gas carbon dioxide to enter, to help in the production of food. Where exactly in the leaf is the food manufactured, and how does it all work?

Grass is green, most leaves are green, England is referred to as 'This Green and Pleasant Land' and someone who enjoys gardening is thought to have green fingers. Why the emphasis on green? Prepare to be amazed.

Inside the leaf are layers upon layers of cells. Around the edge of each cell are tiny bodies — tiny green bodies. These tiny things (they are so small that ten thousand would happily fit onto the full stop at the end of this sentence) are green because they are filled with a substance called CHLOROPHYLL. Each tiny body (called CHLOROPLASTS) contains millions of molecules of chlorophyll, and chlorophyll molecules are laid on the chloroplast membranes like library books are stacked on shelves. In this way, a great many chlorophyll molecules manage to pack together in a small space. In view of the important job that the chlorophyll has to do, this, like everything else in the created world, is no accident.

When sunlight strikes a chlorophyll molecule, some of the energy from light is absorbed by the chlorophyll. The energy trapped in the chlorophyll molecules combines with the carbon dioxide and water in the leaf cells to produce glucose and oxygen. Plants breath in carbon dioxide, they breath out oxygen, the catalyst is green chlorophyll, the process is called PHOTOSYNTHESIS, and what has been described is really an over-simplification of the many complex chemical steps that actually take place! Imagine feeling decidedly peckish. It has been a long time since breakfast, and your stomach is sending signals that the fuel-level is low. Don't go to the fridge, leave the cupboard alone, and forget about the shop. Just go out into the sun and soak in some sunshine. As you do that, energy flows back into your system, and you have that contented feeling that a full stomach engenders. A dream? For human beings who were cursed to work hard for their living, perhaps, but not for a leaf. This miracle of converting sunlight into food takes place all around us, and each one of the millions of leaves that we see so regularly is nothing less than a fully fledged food factory bearing silent, yet eloquent, testimony to the brilliant design of the Creator.

Even secular textbooks describe chlorophyll as 'the miracle molecule'. Its colour is green. It is a fascinating fact that the *Loshon Hakodesh* for green is ירק — *yud, resh, koof*. Those same letters can

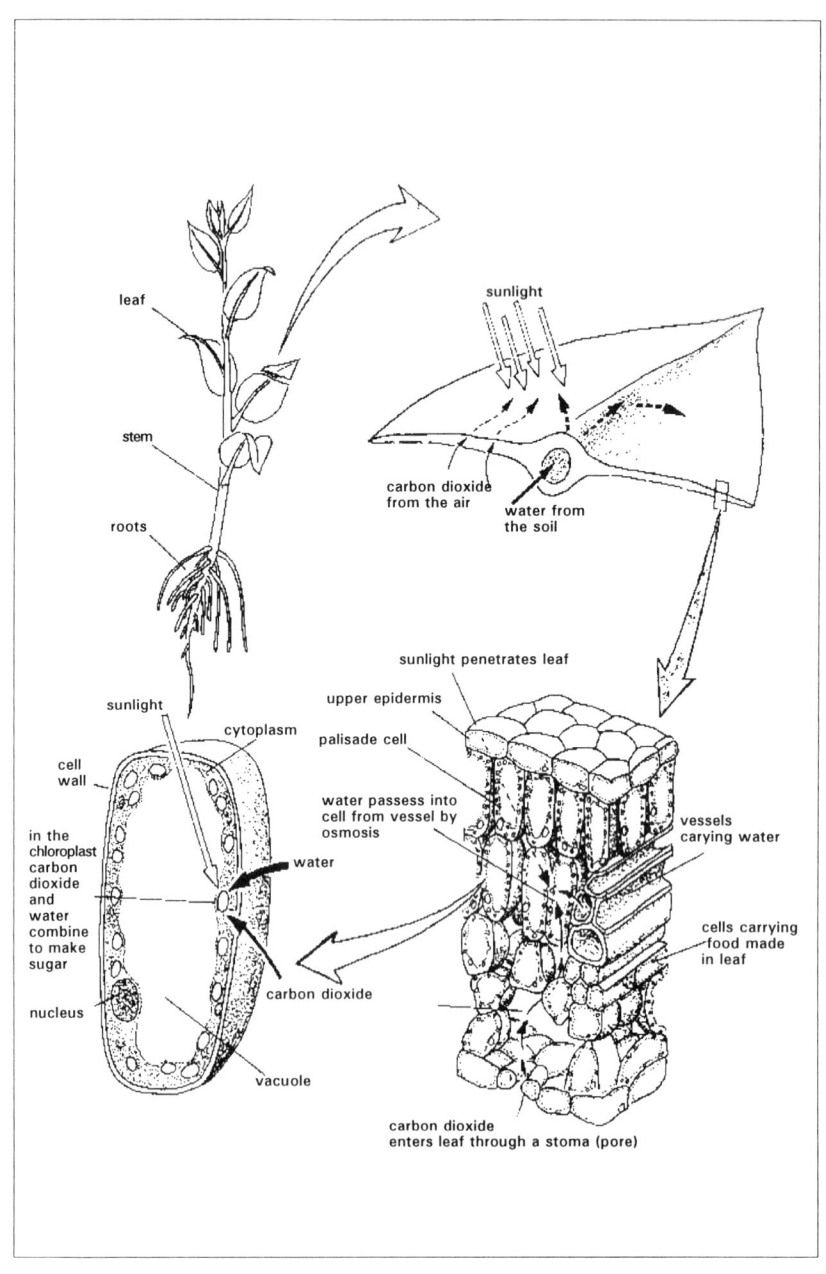

...the vastly complicated miracle of photosynthesis

form the word קרי, meaning coincidence or pure accident; alternatively they can form the letters *resh, koof, yud* — רק ה׳, only *Hashem*. Look at a road and admire its construction. Take a look at a leaf, which is immensely more complex than any motorway — do you see accident or design? The choice is yours.

"ובחרת בחיים".

16

ॐ THE CRANE ☙

You see them in City Centres. You see them trundling along the road, slowly and ponderously with as many wheels as shoes on a centipede. Some are mighty, some are slender — and some are both. Of one thing you can be sure, wherever they are situated, they will always attract attention. For some reason, the crane is a machine that fascinates. On building sites, the contractors thoughtfully provide gaps in the wooden hoardings which surround the construction area so that mesmerised members of the public can satisfy their curiosity in a dignified manner. There is something magnetic about a crane performing its acrobatic skills that compels onlookers to stand and stare in boggle-eyed wonder. Perhaps it is the very size of these machines, massive monstrosities that flex their iron muscles accompanied by billowing blue clouds of diesel smoke, lifting enormous loads aloft with a clanging and a banging and a whir of cables and hiss of hydraulics. It seems impossible that something so large and cumbersome should be capable of performing such skilful feats of dexterity. People stand transfixed as mighty bulldozers burrow and dig, then hoist vast quantities of rubble aloft in their oversized shovels, and with a seemingly effortless flick, disgorge their contents accurately into the waiting truck. De-

"For some reason, the crane is a machine that fascinates."

spite their size, these blue whales of the construction industry cavort and pirouette in the smallest of areas, to the avid fascination of the open-mouthed spectators, who would happily watch the gripping display, just standing and gaping, the length of the day.

There is something remarkable about human beings that enables them to be much impressed by wonders outside of themselves, but fail entirely to notice the very same wonders in their own bodies. Why that should be, is an interesting question, but the fact remains that in every way possible, that piece of anatomy which is presently holding the book (your arm), is far, far superior in every way to any crane, however large, nimble or powerful it might be. A crane is usually made of metal, which needs to be painted regularly to prevent it rusting, for rust will corrode and eventually damage the machine. Stand in the rain for prolonged periods, and you will become damp depressed and disconsolate, but you will not rust. A mechanical shovel can do several jobs, including digging, drilling, spreading, shovelling and demolishing. Like many hand-drills, the different jobs require specialised heads, which are attached and removed as needed.

Just consider how varied are the skills and tasks that your very own specialised wonder-tool — your five-fingered hand — can perform. Just with your bare hands, you can lift, dig, drill, write, type, cook, grip, pound, wrench, throw, compress, pluck, twist, squeeze, press, smear and smooth, pull and shake. All these actions, and hundreds more, involve skill and dexterity, yet all can be performed by the very same hand. The hand can descend with crashing force, and the same hand can stroke a baby's face with feathery gentleness. No-one has yet stroked a baby's face with the mechanical shovel of a bulldozer. A crane is severely restricted where it can travel, how far it can reach, and where it may stand. You own personal crane can go anywhere, and is totally flexible and versatile. Hold your hand out in front of you and turn in as far as you can to the right. Now turn it to its fullest extent in the opposite direction. You will see that it has turned a full 360 degrees. Forwards backwards sideways up down in any direction — find a crane that can emulate your arm!

And look at the speed. Your Herculean crane is slow, ponderous and deliberate. In comparison, watch two hands making *Challos*, pouring, mixing, kneading, rolling, stretching, pulling, plaiting, patting, sprinkling, all with speed and all in a twinkling. Each action is a skill involving memory and intelligence, yet each and every one is done with accuracy and precision, never a finger out of place, and each *Challoh* a masterpiece. If a crane were human, it should be labouring under a severe inferiority complex by now! Put it a different way. Imagine placing two mechanical excavators on either side of a tennis court, each holding a racket in their unwieldy hands, and asking them to play a fast game of tennis! Not only is your own personal shovel and crane accurate swift and nimble, it is also a highly sensitive sensor that simply at a touch will inform you of the texture, moisture and temperature of every single object that it touches. And we think that the brilliant new digital thermometers that have just been invented are the last word in advanced design!

And that is not all. All cranes require fuel, special diesel oil. If you poured orange juice in their tanks, your kind gesture would not be appreciated. Your arms and hands also require fuel — but their fuel is obtainable anywhere. You can fill your fuel tanks with the greatest variety of foodstuffs imaginable, from potato crisps to *Yerushalmi Kugel*, and your arms and hands will work uncomplainingly. The mechanical crane and all its bulldozing cousins require regular maintenance, oiling and overhauling. Without it they will seize up and refuse to work. If you are a typist, your two hands are capable of putting 120 or more words on paper each minute. Even if you are not a typist, you will flex and extend your finger joints more than twenty five million times during a long lifetime, yet whereas legs and shoulders tire with sustained activity, how often do you hear people complain of tired hands? People would be amazed if a car or any machine could be invented that never requires servicing, plugs changed or oil replacing. Be amazed — you have one, and the machine is you! Not only do you have a stupendous machine, it has been carefully coded with your own personal identity, guaranteeing that you are unique in the world. No-one, past present or future has your personalised fingerprints, which cannot be lost, stolen or borrowed.

You do not need to be a genius to know how cranes actually work. A pillar with a long inclined arm is the main ingredient of the common jib crane; the lifting machinery consists of pulleys and a winch, which in turn is powered by a motor, to wind the wire, from which hangs the lifting hook. Derrick cranes, cantilever cranes, giant cranes that build skyscrapers and mechanical excavators are all developments of the same principle. The idea of a hydraulic press was invented by an Englishman (naturally) by the name of Joseph Bramah, nearly two hundred years ago. He discovered that a piston pushing water downwards in one arm of a close-fitting 'U' shaped cylinder will force a piston upwards in the other arm. This simple principle is really a kind of hydraulic lever, and the landing wheels and flaps of an aeroplane are worked by hydraulic machinery, as is the machinery of our friend, the bulldozer. In actual practice, thin oil is preferred to water, as it will not freeze or cause rusting, and

The Crane / 115

keeps the moving parts well oiled. Because of Mr Bramah's ingenuity, flying by plane is so much easier, whilst bulldozers can perform their powerful feats of strength effortlessly. As complex as a real crane is in comparison to its Meccano model, so the human hand and arm are when compared to their huge mechanical counterpart.

Structurally, the hand is the most intricate part of our body. In no other piece of body machinery is so much packed into so small a space. You have eight wrist bones, five in your palm and fourteen in your digits — a total of twenty seven bones. The two hands together contain more than a quarter of all the bones you possess! The supply of nerves to detect heat, touch and pain is extraordinarily elaborate. Thousands of nerve endings per square inch, most heavily concentrated in the fingertips, provide the greatest degree of sensitivity imaginable. Every time that you rotate your thumb, you are witnessing an amazing event. Thousands of messages from the brain are required for the simple act, ordering this muscle to contact, that one to relax; causing this tendon to pull, that one to rest.

If you think that the thin oil in hydraulic pistons demonstrates design, then listen to this. Wherever two bones meet, a joint is formed. The elbow, at which the forearm meets the upper arm, is a case in point. The joint at the elbow moves like a hinge, as do the two bones that meet at the knee. How can two bones move about each other without painful friction? The answer is amazing. First of all the two ends of the bones are covered with a special layer of cartilage which is very smooth and shiny. Then, the whole area of the joint is surrounded by a special capsule. The inside of this capsule is lined with a remarkable membrane that actually produces a specially designed lubricant. This lubricant, called SYNOVIAL FLUID fills the whole area of the capsule, acts as a cushion between the two bones, and ensures that all movement is smooth and friction-free. The more physical activity that is done, the more your little factory will produce the vital fluid. Besides this wonder fluid, movement of the joint is made possible by the fact that the relevant bones are held together by strong ligaments which prevent dislocation during normal movement.

It's as simple as that. Fluid in a joint — it's like the oil between the moving parts of a machine. The label on the oil-can for the car or crane will proclaim, 'New Advanced Design' — 'Special Improved Formula'. What label will you put on your elbow or on your hand? Move over, mighty bulldozer; stand aside, colossal crane — and give due recognition to the greatest machine of all — the one created by the *Yad Hashem*.

17

෨ THE EIGHT-LEGGED ☙

෨WONDER☙

Of all the outdoors activities that attract thousands of participants, and hold many more in a web of fascination, rock climbing is near the top of the list. It looks relatively easy to the onlooker, safe and happy with his two feet firmly on the ground. To the participant, it is anything but. Just imagine that you are about to descend from an overhang. It does not have to be too high, say one hundred feet. Your lifeline to this world is a thin rope, which the manufacturers claim can take the weight of an elephant, large variety. You just hope that they were not exaggerating. You attach one end of this slim nylon cord to a rock, and pull for all that you are worth hoping that it is secure, and will remain so for the foreseeable future. You then thread the rope through a metal pulley which is bolted to a harness around your waist. This pulley is designed with a special feature that, in the event of a sudden release of the rope, will lock the rope, ensuring that the climber cannot suddenly plummet out of control. Everything is ready.

This is the moment of truth. The climber feels anything but brave, his mouth turns dry and his head palpitates with fear. He cannot understand why he ever agreed to such a foolhardy and scatter-brained activity. But there is no way out. People are watching and waiting, and they have already performed this feat of bravery. Sick with fear, he places one leg beyond the overhang and turns round. There is no turning back. He leans out, gripping the rope for all he is worth, which at that moment is not very much. He is already defying gravity, and the rope is taut, mirroring his own terrified tension. Slowly, hand over hand, he jerks downwards, his boots kicking against the rock face, feeling the exhilaration of controlled downward motion, coupled with the joy of having conquered his own fear. Jubilantly he reaches the end of his descent, his surging adrenaline making him feel on top of the world.

If the way down fills you, the petrified onlooker, with dread, the way up is much worse, for now you are trailing the rope, instead of hanging from it. You are all ready; sensible shoes, bag of chalk hanging behind you to give your fingers extra grip, muscles flexed. The first three feet are easy, because you can jump down, give a

"Sick with fear, he places one leg beyond the overhang... there is no turning back!"

nervous little laugh and try again. Beyond that, you can't. Slowly you go higher, reaching from hand-hold to hand-hold, your feet instinctively feeling for those cracks and little ledges on which your life depends. There comes a point where you cannot go back, and the way forward is unsure, you are stuck like a fly on the side of this great rock, the wind is picking up and you have never felt more alone in your life. At that moment, when one wrong move could... you are experiencing the incomparable joy of climbing, that great outdoor feeling, at one with nature... HELP!! At that point, we take our leave from our intrepid friend, wishing him much success in all his endeavours.

If mountain climbing is such a hazardous occupation even with a rope, imagine what it would be like with no rope at all. In any case, ropes are such costly items. You have to go to a specialist climbing shop which supply the lightweight yet strong nylon rope which is guaranteed unbreakable, the special footwear, again, strong yet light, the weatherproof clothing, the sunglasses which protect against glare — the list is endless. If we want to be practical, what is really needed is a specially designed body for climbers which will allow them to climb any surface in any direction, and enable them to produce nylon rope from a special aperture in the body. Climb as high as you want, whenever you wish, wherever you want, swing from overhang to underpass, sail from peak to peak, your rope smoothly and silently paying out from its place of manufacture, somewhere within you, keeping you safe and secure as you perform your Tarzan act.

"Come on," you say, "wake up from your daydreams, you know jolly well that these things are impossible!"

Are they? Have you ever heard of the spider?

Everyone has their likes and dislikes, and lots of people dislike spiders. In reality, spiders should be welcome in homes and gardens, because they feed on flies and other insects. Of the many species, some are so small you can hardly see them, and others, the ones which form the chief ingredient of horror stories, are as big as your fist. There is indeed one delightful species (you might meet it next time you go for a stroll in a tropical rain forest) that preys on lizards and even small birds. Although there is such a variety, all spiders big and small have two things in common. They all have eight legs, (as opposed to insects which have just six) and they all produce silk from their bodies. If you can, look at a spider very closely. You will see that at the end of its body are six tiny tubes. These tubes are called SPIN-

NERETS, and the silk thread comes out of them. Naturally, it does not just come out — the spider uses two of its eight legs to pull out the thread. The thread is so thin that very often you cannot see all of it, unless it is covered in early-morning dew, but it is very strong. It has to carry the weight of its owner, which is sometimes substantial, especially after a sizeable lunch, and it must be able to withstand the impact of a flying insect without shattering into fragments, allowing the potential victim easy escape. This silk is at first a liquid, and is manufactured in specially constructed glands inside the body.

No other animal uses silk in so many different ways as our spiders. They make it into houses, diving bells, cocoons, traps, parachutes and lifelines to save themselves if they fall. Just imagine what specialist machinery is required to produce the precisely specified silk, — too thick and it could never leave the spinnerets, too thin and it would be useless for its multitude of purposes — which has to be converted from a liquid to a powerful thread the instant it meets the air. How would you care to manufacture that mind-boggling set of machinery to a size that could comfortably fit into a body so tiny that you can barely see it!

Whenever you see one of the world's great suspension bridges — the Golden Gate, or the Humber Estuary — you gaze at the graceful arch spanning the river, suspended by seemingly delicate cables, and you admire the wisdom, design and technology that made such feats of civil engineering possible. Clever men— they learnt it from the spider!

The familiar garden spider spins its thread, and attaches one end to a twig. It allows the other end to flutter in the wind, knowing that it will soon blow onto a leaf. Once a horizontal line has been secured (nothing is simple — how do you secure a rope to a leaf!)

the spider constructs a frame, resembling a pentagon, within which the web will be spun. Lines are strategically laid from corner to corner, resembling spokes of a wheel. Starting from the centre of the web, the spider constructs a spiral, moving ever further from the centre. Then, an amazing thing happens. The spider leaves its work, and runs to the outer section of the frame, and begins to build a spiral from the outside working inwards. The difference is that this thread is different to that which has been used thus far — it is now special adhesive thread — all the better to catch you with. Please bear in mind when planning your machinery, that you require two distinctive grades of thread, one smooth and one sticky. It is interesting to note that these garden spiders have specially designed oily legs so that they do not become trapped by the sticky strands of their own webs!

Such amazing creatures need specialist equipment. That which enables a spider to run up a wall and along ceilings (much to some people's displeasure) are their tiny claws and pads at the end of the eight legs. Some spiders can climb tall buildings, but like a trapeze artist, it always attaches a line of silk behind it, so it will not fall too far if it misses its footing. One particular Australian species, called the Bolas spider, has a unique method of going shopping. It sits on a leaf, and spins a long thread with a wad of shiny, sticky material on the end. It then gives off a smell like that of a female moth. When a male moth flies towards the smell, it is attracted by the twirling shiny material flickering in the moonlight, and is then caught in the sticky trap.

Little spider — cunning hunter, master rope maker, mountain climber, and civil engineer; from where did it obtain its training, skills and highly specialised equipment? If all of its skills and tools of its trade are vital for its survival, how did it manage during the thousands of generations that were trying so hard to develop these skills, but not quite succeeding! Which clever spider*'le* first thought of producing silk (after conducting market research into the tensile strengths of other materials) from spinnerets that did not exist! The answer to all these questions is so very clear:

"מה רבו מעשיך ה' כלם בחכמה עשית..."

"Little spider – who taught you your incredible skills?"

18

℘ A MASTER OF GOOD ℘

℘ TASTE ℘

Just like with everything, there are extremes in shop-assistants. The first extreme is typified by a surly, rude individual, who is most definitely not there to please the customer. It could be a female, who is engaged in a heated and earnest conversation with a like-minded individual, and when you, the customer, approach the counter and cough politely for service, you are completely ignored. Well, she obviously did not hear you. You cough again, a little louder, still maintaining your good humour. The assistant gives a glance in your direction, not pausing for a second in her dissertation, and with an attitude which reflects both contempt and disdain, ignores you again. Now you feel annoyed. With rising indignation and undisguised sarcasm, you courageously say, "Excuse me, do you have a moment to spare?" With the speed of a tortoise with lumbago, the Assistant-of-the-Year graciously turns her head in your direction, and deigns to ask you what you want. You place your request. Almost with a cry of triumph, the less-than-charming crea-

The perfect shop assistant – this one certainly knows his plaice!

ture announces, "We've none left!" and with lightning speed, turns her head away and carries on her conversation with animated enthusiasm.

The other extreme is equally oppressive. You no sooner have set a foot in the shop, and the ever-so-eager person is by your side. Dripping with pseudo-charm and obsequiousness he remarks how young you are looking and isn't it a simply splendid day. You also thought so until you walked into the shop, and are not too responsive. You are asked, with a sugary smile, what you would like. At this point, you know that you cannot win. If you tell the want-to-help-you-so-much assistant that you are happy just to look around, you can be sure that breathing down your neck as you do your grand walkabout will be you-know-who, cooing words of advice and encouragement whilst offering to wrap everything up for you and deliver it free of charge.

There is a happy medium, everyone's dream. Someone who is helpful and efficient, friendly without being overbearing, ever-present yet unobtrusive. There is good news. You have a little friend, it weighs just two ounces. It is an expert in many vital jobs, making life pleasant and happy, yet is humble and knows its place. It knows when to make a noise, but can sit quietly and unnoticed if required. It serves you faithfully, asks for no reward, and is the master of good taste. May we introduce you to your very good friend, your very own tongue.

In as much as a car can be described as a tin box with four rubber wheels at each corner, the tongue can be described as a muscle covered with mucous membrane which lies on the floor of the mouth. The muscles within the tongue consist of bundles of fibres which run along its length, height and width, and they can change its shape. (Some very fortunate people are extremely skilled and are able to roll their tongues long ways into a U-shape. Others, who do not possess that particular gene, cannot roll their tongues, however much they try, yet manage to live happy lives nevertheless!) Carefully positioned muscles attached to the tongue externally enable it to be protruded, depressed or pulled into the mouth. (However far you and I are able to poke out our tongues, we are no match for some creatures. There is an interesting animal called a chameleon, which during the day moves slowly along the branches of trees in the forest hunting for insects and spiders to eat. When near enough to its prey, it wraps its tail firmly round a twig, watching its target. Suddenly it shoots out its tongue, which stretches up to the length of its own body, with amazing accuracy. At the end of its tongue there is a suction pad, that sticks to its prey. The tongue then springs back into its mouth, bringing in the meal. The whole action takes less than a second! Similarly, however fast we can flick our tongues in and out, we are no match for snakes and lizards. However, here we see something amazing. The much-feared forked tongues of snakes and lizards are not poisonous, as is often believed. They are harmless, and are used to 'taste' the air. The flicking tongues pick up smell particles from the air and ground, and deliver them to a special sense organ housed in the roof of their mouth — called, believe it or not, the Jacobson's organ — which detects and identifies the smell of a meal or mate.)

The human tongue might not be as gripping as the nightmare scenarios mentioned above, but for versatility it has no match. Extend your tongue from your mouth, and clamp it lightly between your teeth, and then try and speak. What comes out is hardly recognisable. In the course of one sentence, your tongue is deftly darting from place to place, now clinging to the roof of the mouth (say

'Lamed'), now rolled behind the front teeth (say 'Tes'), now completely inactive (say 'Vov'). Just consider the subtle difference of tongue position that can differentiate between a 'ssss' — as in 'Samech'— and 'zzzz' — as in 'Zayin'. Listen to an accomplished *Baal Koreh* at speed, where every vowel and consonant is carefully articulated, and picture to yourself the electrical messages racing from the eyes to the brain through the nervous system into the muscles controlling the movement of the tongue, where every instruction has to be faithfully carried out without error in a flash of a second before the next message races in. Besides the tongue, remember to send messages to the lips (two of those), the teeth and the whole breathing mechanism in order to produce intelligent and lucid speech. Remember too that all the messages regarding the vocalisation and singing of the words have to be taken from the memory bank, since all the *leining* is prepared in advanced and 'somehow' memorised. Be honest — isn't that an efficient machine? And do you think it happened by accident?

 Living in the world of dishwashers, the next stage in labour-saving devices would be an apparatus that cleans the table and sweeps the floor after each meal. Wouldn't life be wonderful? Dream no longer, you have one already. After each intake of food, your tongue cannot keep still. Darting here and there, it keeps its domain clear of debris, acting as an efficient toothpick and broom-cum-hoover. Throughout the eating process, the tongue is busy distributing the food inside the mouth so that it is evenly chewed and made acceptable to the stomach. One of its most complex tasks is to assist in the swallowing process, without which no food could be digested. What appears at first sight to be quite simple, is actually a masterfully co-ordinated feat, a reflex so vital that it is programmed into us before birth.

For those of you with an inventive streak, here is a little project. Using your skill and initiative, construct a machine which, simply by touching food, will be able to identify the type of food, its sweetness, sourness, freshness, and gauge its temperature and texture. The machine would have to be kept inside the mouth for immediate readiness, and obviously not hinder any of the other functions of the mouth. You have guessed right. You already have one of these amazing machines, conveniently housed in the tongue-complex. (It should not be taken for granted that the sense-of-taste apparatus is situated exactly where it is needed. In an accidental haphazard world, the sense of taste could have just as easily 'developed' on your right knee. In a world of design, everything makes sense.) How does this remarkable machine actually work?

The organs of taste are microscopic nerve-endings known as taste buds. Have a close-up look at a tongue, and you will see the familiar small bumps. These bumps are called PAPILLAE, and they are surrounded by tiny trenches. In the lining of some of these trenches are the openings of the taste buds. (Each person has approximately nine thousand of them, and although most are to be found on the tongue, there are others to be found in the throat, on the palate and on the tonsils.) A single taste bud looks like a rosebud, and in this little bud are housed the sensory cells that reacts with food to produce 'taste'. Only liquids can be tasted, and for that reason a dry piece of food placed in a dry mouth produces no sensation of taste whatsoever. When dissolved, however, the fluid containing the particles of food washes over the taste buds to produce a chemical reaction. How precisely the sensory cells are activated by the chemicals in the food is not known. Amazing! We know how to put man on the moon, but we are not sure precisely how a taste bud works. But work it does, and the chemical reaction triggers off an electric impulse which travels to the brain, and there the interpretation is given.

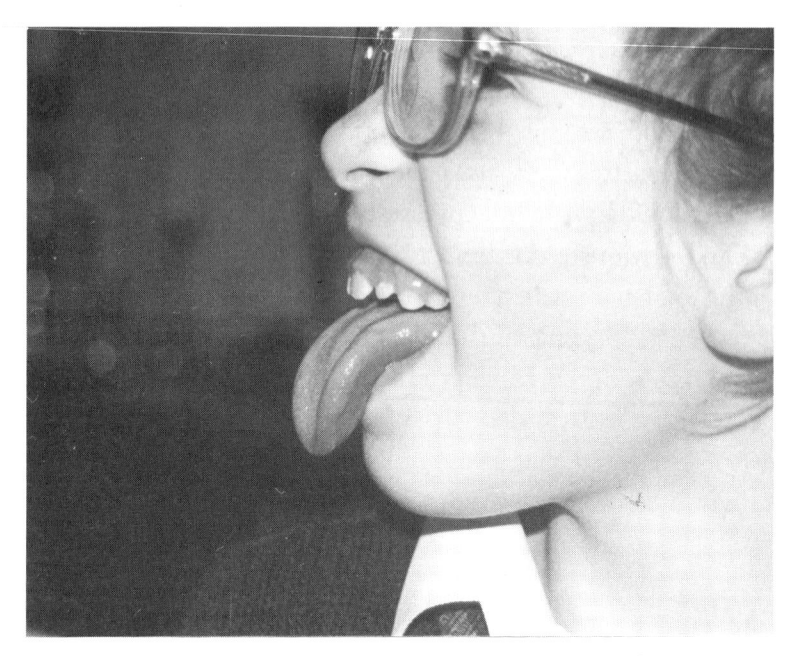

Sticking out your tongue might not be so rude when you realise that it is a wonder machine which enables you to talk, swallow and taste!

This information is then stored away in the memory bank, so that the next time you taste French cheese, it will be a familiar taste.

Different parts of the tongue detect different tastes. The taste buds at the front are sensitive to sweet and salt, those at the side to sourness, and the ones at the back are particularly sensitive to bitterness. An indication of just how magnificently the machine works is the fact that the tongue can detect bitterness in a dilution of one part in two million!

A machine that incorporates so much, enabling us to talk, swallow, clean the mouth, taste and enjoy our food is a machine to be treasured and appreciated. Thank you *Hashem Yisborach*, for such a faithful efficient pleasing servant. Thank you *Hashem* for our tongue!

19

ᛞ THE PHENOMENAL ᛜ

ᛞ FILTER ᛜ

Water, water everywhere, and not a drop to drink, is a well-known maxim that should make us stop and think. You hear stories, and it should never happen to anyone, of seafarers, even holidaymakers, who found themselves adrift in an endless expanse of ocean, parched and tortured by raging thirst. They are surrounded by water — wherever they look — water. Why not drink some? Anyone who has ever taken a gulpful of sea-water whilst swimming at the beach will know the answer. It is unpalatable, containing such a high concentration of salt that the immediate reflex is to vomit, and the after-effect is a profound desire to drink. How do you feel after eating a *heimishe* quantity of *heimishe* salt-herring? Very very thirsty. That is the effect of salt, and the reason why all the water in the seven seas will not quench the thirst of the marooned mariner.

Many places in the world with low rainfall face a growing water-shortage. Times have changed since Queen Elizabeth I of England claimed with some pride that she took a bath once a month, whether she needed it or not! We all use a vast quantity of the precious liquid, besides the gargantuan appetites of industry, (a family of two adults and two children uses approximately eight hundred and fifty pints of water per day — the equivalent of fifty buckets — and that is not counting *Nagel Wasser* and *Netilas Yodaim*; it takes eight pints of water to produce one pint of beer, and an unbelievable six thousand and six hundred gallons of water to manufacture a single motor car.) Not surprisingly, the natural water supply is often inadequate. What is the solution? Around the time of the destruction of the first *Beis Hamikdosh*, there lived a Greek philosopher called Aristotle. (Details of conversations which he had with the *Novi Yirmiyohu* are recorded by *Chazal*.) Aristotle noted that when salty water is boiled, the steam that rises leaves the salt behind. Condensed into water again, it is pure. That process is called desalination, and you can do it yourself. A simple solar still can be made with a glass dome over a pool of salt water. The water is heated by the sun, vaporises, and then condenses on the glass, and runs down it to gather in channels around the edge. A still which is one yard square in area should produce a gallon (four and half litres) of fresh water per day.

In order to produce really useful amounts of distilled water, a very effective method uses membranes made of plastic which have tiny holes in them, sufficiently large for water molecules to pass through, but too small for salt molecules. The plastic membranes are formed into a tube and salt water is pumped into them under pressure. Pure water then drips from the outside of the tube. In far off Bahrain, one of the world's largest desalination plants produces over twelve million gallons of fresh water every day using this method.

Isn't that a clever system? What made them think of such an ingenious idea that could so effectively and efficiently filter contaminated liquid? The answer is simple — they looked at the kidneys. However complex the machinery needed to operate a large desalination plant, however complicated and synchronised all the component parts must be for the plant to work efficiently, either of the two kidneys is more complicated, better synchronised and more efficient.

A single kidney is reddish-brown, shaped like a bean and is about the size of your fist. This humble-looking organ is nothing less than the master chemist of the body. A chemical factory of breathtaking magnitude which weighs just six ounces! Not surprisingly, these precious little machines are well protected, firstly by being surrounded by a capsule of tough fibrous tissue, and then held in place at the back of the abdomen alongside the spine by a bed of fat, which also cushions them from knocks. They are given extra protection by nestling safely inside the lower ribs. The kidneys have two main functions — to remove waste products from the blood, and to regulate the salt and liquid content of the body. In addition, they help production of red blood cells, watch over potassium, sodium chloride and other substances in the blood — where even the smallest quantity too much or too little could be extremely hazardous. The kidneys ensure that the blood is neither too acidic nor alkaline, and so many other jobs that a complete catalogue of all its activities is simply not known!

The little that we do know is sufficient to create quite an impression. Each kidney contains more than one million little filtering units (called NEPHRONS). If you would untangle and stretch out all the tiny tubes that connect all the units, there would be seventy miles of them. Please bear in mind that each single little unit is an independent machine of dazzling complexity, yet is part of a co-ordinated structure, the total of which is able to achieve wonders. Every minute, about two pints of blood are pumped along the artery to the kidneys, but the kidneys do not filter it all at once. It takes about fifty minutes for the entire bloodstream to be purified, all in a six ounce little machine. Would you like to know how it's done?

Let us have a closer look at one of the million microscopic nephrons. Blood is pumped under pressure into the kidneys through the main tube, called the renal artery. It then flows through very fine tubes, called capillaries, still under pressure, until it reaches a filtration plant — the nephron. Because the path of the tubes in the nephron is so tortuous, the pressure causes fluid to filter out through the capillary walls to collect in a special receptacle. The capillary walls act like a very fine sieve, allowing smaller molecules to pass through, but blocking the way to others. The molecules of water and salt, for instance, are small enough to pass through the holes in the membranes, whereas molecules of proteins and blood cells are too large to go through and so stay in the bloodstream. The fluid which filters out of the blood contains glucose, amino acids, salts and waste dis-

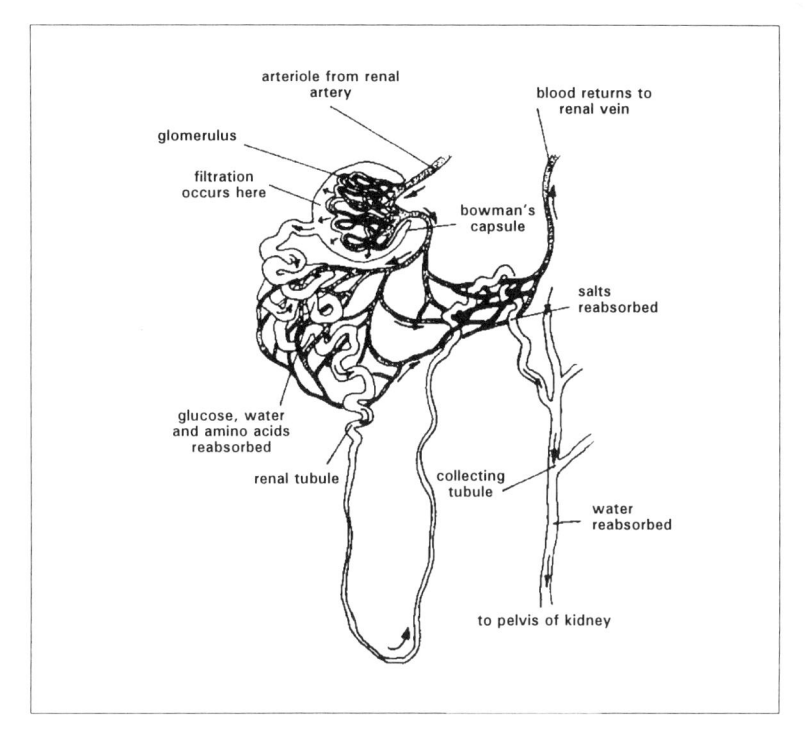

Diagram of the nephron, one of the million marvellous machines which make up your kidney.

solved in water. Effectively, what has happened is that many vital substances have filtered out of the blood together with the waste! What happens next is simply incredible. From the special receptacle (called the Bowman's capsule) the filtered fluid passes into a maze of tubes which are surrounded by a network of capillaries. There, 99% of the fluid (the amino acids, the glucose and much of the water) is re-absorbed into the blood through the capillary! What is NOT re-absorbed are the waste products such as urea, uric acid, excess salts and water, and these microscopic droplets of waste-laden fluid gather in collecting tubes eventually passing down to the bladder. The purified blood is then carried back into the body's circulation by the renal vein. The method by which the kidneys are able to selectively re-absorb substances from the filtered fluid is not fully understood!

Apart from removing waste products from the blood, the kidneys also monitor the amount of fluid in the body. If you have not drunk sufficiently, and also lost fluid through perspiration, your blood will contain less fluid than normal. When this blood passes through a certain part of the brain, special receptors detect the drop in level of water, and the pituitary gland (housed in the brain) is stimulated to release a special hormone into the circulation. When this hormone reaches the kidney, it causes the wonder organ to increase the amount of water it re-absorbs from the filtered solution. Thus, more water is retained and less water is evacuated through waste. Apart from this, there is a mechanism that produces the sensation of thirst, which is complex to the extent that it is not well understood, which serves to regulate the intake of water and so maintain the concentration of the blood.

Similarly, if you have absorbed a large amount of water, this extra fluid will find its way into the blood stream, tell the brain receptors of the increased level, which will in turn inform the pituitary gland to release less of the special hormone, consequently the kidneys will receive the message, and re-absorb less fluid back into the system, and more water will be evacuated. Interestingly enough, there are certain drugs that can effect the production of the hormone produced by the pituitary gland. Alcohol retards the gland's ability to produce less of the hormone, which in turn allows the kidneys to produce more waste liquid. As a result, people who consume a lot of alcohol become mildly dehydrated, and crave water the next morning. Caffeine in coffee has a similar action, which is why a large mug of coffee might not be the ideal thing to drink just before bedtime.

Nicotine in cigarettes has the opposite effect, and steps up production of the hormone. People who smoke heavily need to visit the bathroom far less frequently than those who are free from the influence of the drug.

It is safe to assume that in the construction of a desalination plant, every component, from the largest piece of metal to the smallest screw, is carefully designed, and its function understood. Each little kidney, weighing just six ounces, contains a factory which does everything a desalination plant can do, plus a mighty lot more. It is so advanced and complex that all of its functions are not understood. What would you say about its design?

ברוך אתה ה'... אשר יצר את האדם בחכמה
וברא בו נקבים נקבים...

20

ഓ THE MOST MODERN ‌ൠ

ഓ BUILDING ‌ൠ

Times change. When trains were first invented, whole new worlds opened up for towns and cities. Whereas previously a town might have been remote and largely inaccessible, the railway unlocked the doors and let in the world. All of a sudden, towns that found themselves at the junction of several lines, gained importance and earned prosperity overnight. And their railway stations mirrored their newly-found prestige. Large edifices with Gothic facades and ornate brickwork, resembling resplendent Town Halls, were built in the town centres; emphasising the railway's pivotal function in the town's development. Turn the clock forward, and go to a station now, and you might be excused for imagining that you have by mistake entered a shopping-mall. Surrounding you is a structure made primarily of glass and tastefully decorated steel girders. In our open society, modern design does not seek to hide the steel structures that perforce hold up the building, it paints them pretty colours, moulds them into interesting shapes, and rather like Toytown come to life, exposes them to the full gaze of the public who view with fascination, or perhaps do not notice at all, the intricate array of metallic bones clothed in a skin of perspex and glass. The indoor trees, the automatic doors that glide open at the hint of a tread in their direction, and the electric trains that silently slide in and out just complete the picture of a super-efficient dreamland that we expect our modern world to be.

Do you think that is modern? Just wait until you hear what we have planned for the future. You see, all those steel girders are so expensive to erect, and extremely difficult to lift. The fact that they are painted in pastel shades does not make them lighter! What we have in mind is a new type of steel that you place in the ground, which then grows to precisely the length and shape that you require. Effectively, it means that if correctly placed, the whole structure will take shape entirely by itself. And that is not all. The new steel girders will be much lighter and stronger than the old-fashioned version. But the best is still to come! Who needs a building that is rigid and cannot move — stuck to the ground like an immovable... building! What we propose is a structure composed of the new steel that can pick itself up and move around with complete freedom to wherever it is required. Whenever the population changes location, just tell the station to move along with it, and it will gladly and efficiently do so. Now that is what we call progress — your glass and steel travel-centres of which you are so proud are positively archaic and primitive by comparison. Excuse me. Is this a dream, an excerpt from a land of fantasy and futuristic wishful thinking?

Or is it simply a description of the steel girder structure that we already possess — our very own bones. Looked at superficially, more than two hundred and sixty bones support the body and provide protection for vital organs such as the brain, the heart and the lungs. They also store minerals necessary for the body, and are the place where blood cells are manufactured. We owe our shape and support to the scaffolding consisting of hundreds of jointed bones, and contraction of the muscles anchored to the bones allows for all bodily movement, such as grasping, carrying, bending, walking and running. Such facts are common knowledge, but when looked at in greater detail, prepare to stand (thanks to your bones) and be amazed.

When it comes to strength, there is little to beat the bone. Bone is hard and tough, but at the same time has properties of elasticity. Its strength under stretching is several times greater than steel, and yet, volume for volume, it weighs only about a quarter as much. This tremendous strength (the thighbone for instance, can bear thirty times a man's weight) is due to its strength in composition. It is two-thirds calcium, phosphorus and other minerals, giving hardness and strength, and one-third a protein fibre called COLLAGEN. The thighbone (or femur) has to be strong in order to bear the weight of the body, and this is achieved by its remarkable structure and composition. The outer part consists of dense compact bone, but beneath this, at the end of the bone there is a criss-cross network of bony

The Most Modern Buidling / 141

fibres called spongy bone. The fibres form a frame very much like the metal lattice in a crane (or rather, the lattice work in the crane is very much like the spongy part of the femur) and is thus able to bear a tremendous load.

The bones are a store-house of virtually all the body's mineral supply. 99% of our calcium, and 88% of phosphorus plus smaller amounts of copper, cobalt and other essential trace elements, are stored in the bones. The warehouse is open twenty four hours a day, and goods are being moved in and out constantly. If you wish to know just how important this information is, listen to the following. The role of the bones in storing and releasing calcium is crucial. The bones conduct their business via the blood, and in the bones there is a rich supply of blood vessels. The bone exposes its mineral crystals to the current of blood, taking excess calcium from the blood, or supplying it if there is a shortage. The surface of mineral crystals that the bones expose to the blood is so vast that if it would be flattened out it would cover one hundred acres of land! Altogether, the bones contain a large amount of calcium, about one kilogram of it, whereas there is only one fortieth of an ounce of calcium circulating in the blood, yet, this very quantity plays a vital role in a person's health. Without calcium, no impulses would travel along nerves, and blood would not clot. Muscle contraction would cease — together with the heartbeat! On the other hand, too much calcium would be equally serious, contributing to the formation of kidney stones and various serious conditions. This demonstrates the necessity of the bones having a supply of calcium always ready, and that the EXACT amounts are fed into the blood. Who tells the bones what the situation is?

The answer is two little pairs of glands (called PARATHYROID GLANDS) which are embedded in, or near the thyroid glands in the neck. If the level of calcium in the blood drops, the little glands — silent and unknown guardians of health — register the information and secrete a hormone — a chemical messenger — to instruct the bones to release calcium. Too much calcium in the blood will register with the gland which will then send out a hormone to instruct the bones to absorb calcium from the blood. This finest of balances, on which our good health depends, is hardly accidental.

No steel girder has ever produced fuel or food in its unfeeling steely interior, yet the humble bone is busy producing life-giving liquid at prolific rates. The body needs a constant supply of new red-blood cells to replace those which die off naturally everyday (about one hundred and eighty million red blood cells die of old age each MINUTE), and bone marrow is the source of most of the blood cells. This soft, jelly-like substance fills the pores and cavities of certain bones such as the ribs, skull, spine and the short bones of the hands and feet. A little more than half a pound of marrow provides five billion red cells a day! If the oxygen content of the blood falls too low, the production of red cells in the marrow speeds up. This makes it possible for the body to adjust to unusual conditions, such as high altitudes, where the air is thin and low in oxygen. In the spongy interiors of the marrow chambers, white-blood cells are also produced, which protect the body against infection. The shafts of the long bones (arms and legs) are filled with yellow marrow, and this specifically acts as a reserve of marrow for any sudden demand for blood cells in case of heavy bleeding. And you thought your bones were simple?

To the best of our knowledge, no steel girder has the capability to repair itself if it breaks. It really is a shame that no-one has yet invented this capability, it surely would be most useful, yet bones have always had the capability to mend themselves. A bone mends in three main stages. If the bone is fractured, blood vessels are broken, and bleeding occurs. The blood congeals around the fracture, forming a clot. Bone cells then multiply and move into the blood clot, where they lay down new bone tissue, squirting out collagen to be calcified into bone. In this way the two separated parts of the bone become joined together again. In the mending process, a ring of new bone tissue is formed round the fracture, so the mended bone is slightly thicker in the region of the fracture. The new bone is now modelled, and unwanted bits are broken down and re-absorbed. This phenomenal service is performed by special cells which destroy bone, trimming off rough edges and helping to sculpture the bone back to its original shape so perfectly that the final mend of a well-healed fracture is invisible even under X-ray examination!

Take a close look at the scaffolding or the steel-work supporting a building. Isn't it a well-planned and intricately designed building? Yet it is lifeless and immovable, inert and primitive when compared to the living organs, masters of movement and regeneration, wizards of chemical technology that are our bones, the work of the Greatest Designer of all.

21

ઠ A BALANCED VIEW ଓ

It's funny how some places have gained fame throughout the world because of some triviality. I imagine that the good citizens of Timbuktu have credibility problems, with people out of their locale not believing that such a place actually exists amidst the sand-dunes of North Africa. Perhaps people from Chelm had the same problem. There is one city, happily situated in Italy, where a single mention of its name will immediately conjure up a word inexorably associated with the town. Whether the town has any other claim to fame is of little interest to the tens of thousands of tourists to whom a visit to this notable place is high on their agenda of fascinating places that they just have to see. The city? Pisa. Pisa used to be a flourishing port; it had its own fleet; Galileo lived there for a while and discovered the effects of a pendulum; and it would have remained an obscure backwater had it not been for some second-rate architect who left his spirit level at home when he began to build his tower. Built originally as a bell tower, it probably began tilting during building, but they continued building it anyhow, all one hundred and seventy nine feet of it. Built from beautiful white marble, it stands seven stories high, and the top is currently leaning about seventeen feet out of the vertical. Intrepid tourists are allowed to climb to the top (as long as they don't stamp their feet too hard) and each year the leaning tower tilts over a little more. Opinion is

How long can the famous leaning tower continue its balancing act?

divided as to how long the tower can continue its balancing act — the souvenir manufacturers of Pisa and the tourists currently taking photographs at the top hope it will be a long time in the future.

Whilst gazing in mesmerised fascination at the leaning tower, several questions become apparent. The first is to understand why it does not actually topple over. If you would be told that it is because its centre of gravity (the point through which the weight of the building acts) just about falls within the boundaries of the actual building, you would certainly want to know why it is that a man is capable of leaning much further than the leaning tower, with the centre of gravity falling well out of the area of his body, and yet not topple over. When you look at the leaning tower, how do you know that it is actually leaning and the nearby buildings are perpendicular. Maybe it is the other way round? When fathers play with their childrens' toy building blocks and excitedly attempt to build the tallest tower ever, whilst the little toddlers look on in resigned boredom, the daddys know that as soon as the miniature World Trade Centre begins to sway, it's time to run for cover. Instability in building blocks is bad news. Why is it therefore, that although many of the things that we do make us unstable, (even in a simple action like walking, the body constantly becomes unstable for a moment) we are still able to retain our balance? Why, when sitting on a bench which has no back, do we not fall backwards? What enables an ice-skater to glide across a frozen rink, executing the most hair-raising contortions and flourishes, supported by nothing more than two knife-thin blades? How on earth does he keep his balance?

Take a look at a spirit level. You will see a carefully constructed tube, sealed at both ends containing coloured liquid and a bubble. If the bubble is sitting happily between two calibrated marks, then you know that the surface on which the spirit level is resting is absolutely horizontal. It is a very useful machine, quite simple in its construction, indispensable to anyone wishing to build a straight wall. As far as we know, no-one has ever claimed that the little instrument, humble though it may be, came about as a result of an explosion in a glass factory. That being the case, would you like to have a look at three tiny spirit levels in you own body?

The clue where to look for the apparatus that controls balance is given in its very name. A balance in *Loshon Hakodesh* is מאזנים. Take away the מ and you have אזנים. Have a look inside the ear, and there you will find the organs of balance. When exactly the scientific world discovered that balance is maintained in the ears is not known to me, but the Creator of *Loshon Hakodesh* revealed this information to us 5754 years ago. The ear can be divided into three sections. The outer ear, which is the interestingly shaped instrument you notice on the side of people's heads. The middle ear, which contains the ear drum and the three little bones which amplify the vibrations of sound, and the inner ear, set deeply inside the bone of the skull, which contains the coiled cochlea, the organ concerned with the perception and transmission of sound to the brain. Just above the fluid-filled cochlea, and connected to it, lie three tiny semi-circular canals. Each one is about 15 mm long, is U-shaped, and is set at right angles to its two other partners. These three angles, each one at a different plane, can be visualised by looking into the corner of a room, where the two walls and the ceiling join together.

Each tiny tube, resembling a complicated spirit-level, is filled with fluid, and each one has a little swelling at one end. Into this swelling reaches a sense organ (called the CUPULA), which extends most of the way across. The cupula is perched on top of tiny hairs, and as you move, the canals inside your head move too. However, the fluid inside them tends to lag behind the movement of its enclosing canals, and the tiny difference of pressure on the cupula in turn make it tug on the little hairs holding it up, sending nerve signals to the brain, not very far away. The brain analyses these signals, and interprets them as movement. The three canals have been set at right angles to each other specifically to enable them to detect movement in a particular direction. One will detect up-and-down movement, such as jumping over a fence, the second will detect side-to-side movement, as a cyclist bends sideways to turn a corner, and the third detects back-and-forth movement as will occur on a swing, or in *shockling*. Any movement of the head will produce a current in at least one of the canals, informing the master computer of a change of direction, so that the appropriate instructions can be issued to regulate the situation. There your have it — three electronic spirit levels on each side of your head.

If you spin round and round (on a round-about, or just turn and turn), and suddenly stop, the fluid in the canals continues moving for a while, telling the brain that you are still spinning. However, the rest of your body is setting up impulses that give the brain the impression that the body is stationary, so for a while you interpret the conflicting impulses in a manner that informs you that the room is spinning! Sometimes, when our bodies are in moving vehicles, particularly one that is moving in all planes, like a ship in a rough sea, contradictory and confusing impulses can be set up causing changes in the pulse, and in the direction the food travels in the digestion department (you will notice the strong brown bag directly in front of you...!).

Even when your eyes are closed, you know the position of your head. When you wake up in the morning, it is not possible to imagine that you are standing on your feet. What informs you of the exact position of your head, even when it is not moving? For this we have two interconnected little chambers just below the three canals, which are filled with fluid, and contain a tiny ball of chalk which is attached to a group of sensory cells. If your head is upright, the ball sits neatly on top of the sensory cells, however, when you bend your head forward, the minute little ball pulls on the sensory cells, causing them to send messages to the brain informing it of the head's new position. What can you say about such fantastic machines! You can now understand why, if you have too much alcohol, you cannot walk in a straight line, and the familiar drunken stagger is observed. Alcohol befuddles the brain, so that the messages being transmitted by the organs of balance are not properly dealt with, and balance goes on holiday until sobriety returns.

Stability is also maintained by our eyes, which, by looking at fixed objects such as the skyline and the sides of buildings, keep us aware of the true horizontal and vertical planes (enabling us to know that the leaning tower is really leaning!), and explains why it is difficult to keep our balance in the dark. Another amazing facility is evidenced by the fact that when you stand to attention and lean forward, you can feel the extra pressure on the front of your feet. This makes you lean back again, so that you don't fall forward. This feeling in your feet comes from receptors in the skin (table legs do not possess it) which are sensitive to pressure and pass the message to the brain. Similarly, when you lean forward, you can feel tension in the muscles at the back of your leg. All our muscles have special receptors inside them which are stimulated by being stretched, sending messages to head office enabling us to take remedial action to prevent falling.

So many machines, each more complicated than the next — stretch receptors, pressure receptors, eyes, canals at special angles, tiny balls of chalk, all wired up, flashing electronic messages by the thousand each second — all specially constructed to enable us to keep our balance. Let us take nothing for granted, and give fulsome thanks to the Designer and Creator —

"ברוך אתה ה' — המכין מצעדי גבר".

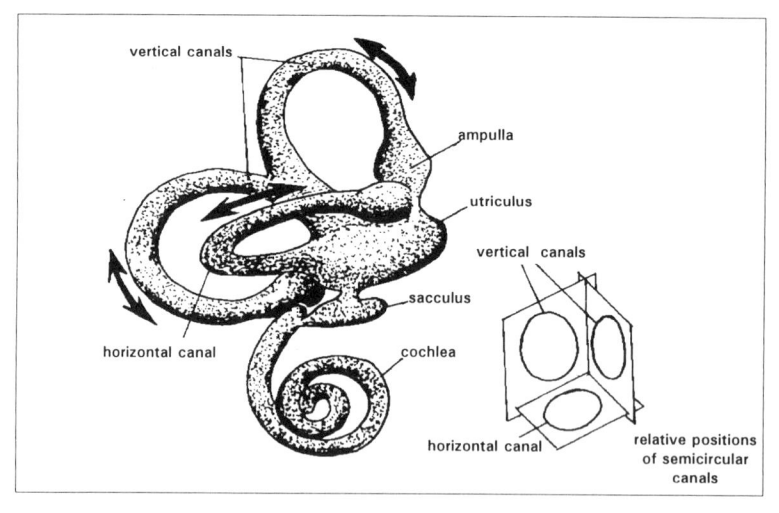

Diagram of the 3 semi-circular canals that enable you to stand straight.

22

ℬ RADAR PATROL ℛ

Fog. Swirling clammy fog descends without warning, shrouding all landmarks in a hazy indistinct thickening mist. Where before stood clear and well-focused objects, a lamppost, a tree, a building; now in their place loom fuzzy and threatening shapes, emerging menacingly out of the darkening gloom.

Imagine that you are the captain of a 100,000 ton oil-tanker, sailing up the English Channel, a crowded sea-route just twenty miles wide. You are standing on the ship's bridge, the steering wheel in your hand. The massive machine under your command is surging through the water at a steady fifteen knots, when, suddenly and ominously, the dreaded fog descends. You can see nothing but the yellow clouds which obliterate all else. For all that you can see, you might as well have your eyes closed. The ship which relies on your instructions for its safety takes about one mile to stop. Panic rises! You don't know where you are going or what is ahead of you. All you know is that all around you are other ships, in exactly the same predicament. At any moment you expect the calamitous noise of grinding metal... Quick, what can you do?!

The year was 1939. England was at war. Technology had advanced since World War I. No longer would the battles be fought across trenches with sct-piece strategy, but, indicative of times to come, the country with the most efficient air-force would gain the initiative. But England was an island. It had a severe disadvantage. How would they know from which direction the enemy aeroplanes would come? How would they know when the bomb-bearing deadly machines would fill the skies — by the time the planes would be within hearing, or sighted, it would be too late. Should the Royal Air Force maintain a 24-hour vigil around the shores, such a proposition was not practical. The sky is a big place, there were not sufficient planes, and how would you spot the enemy fliers at night — with Ever-Ready torches tied to the tips of the wings?

Come in Sir Robert Watson-Watt. This gentleman discovered in 1935 that radio waves could be used to detect a distant object. The principal he used was that of an echo. If you stand about three hundred metres from the foot of a cliff and shout, the sound of your voice returns as an echo after an interval. What happens is that the sound waves travel through the air until they hit the cliff and are

Radar scanners send out radio signals – effective and efficient.

reflected back to your ears. It is a harmless method of talking to yourself! The further away the cliff, the longer the interval. Sound has its limitations, not least of which is the time it takes to travel, which is 340.5 metres per second, and sound waves dissipate quite rapidly. Sir Robert discovered that radio waves, which travel slightly faster at 300,000 kilometres per second (the speed of light), are the ideal form of detecting objects even at great distance. The waves are sent out by a transmitter, and the reflected waves are received by the antenna, and the distance and shape of the object calculated. Radar had been born. By 1939 Britain had a radar network on its south and south-east coasts to detect aircraft, and this system proved invaluable to the country's defences during the Battle of Britain in 1940.

Breath again captain of the oil tanker. On your bridge there is an anti-collision radar screen which, thanks to the radar pulses which are being sent (and bounce back before the next one is emitted), shows other ships as dots, and their direction of travel as short lines. Radar allows ships to travel in the thickest of fogs in the greatest of safety, allows planes to fly and land in darkness, and even enables a pilot to have a map of the weather ahead so that he can avoid storms.

What a tremendous invention radar is! How intelligent we are for having invented it! It may be slightly humbling to know that what mankind has managed to perfect during the latter part of the century, animals have been doing since they were created.

Have you ever heard of echo-location? The little bat probably hasn't either, but it uses this unique means of orientation in order to survive and flourish in the darkest of caves. Very few bats rely on their eyesight for detecting obstacles, which is understandable in view of the fact that they love to live in caves which are pitch black. Instead they have a system of emitting sound waves, and picking up the echoes reflected from objects in their path, in precisely the same way as radar sends out signals and detects the reflections from solid objects. If we go to the airport, and watch how atop the control tower the radar scanner turns around and around, silently and efficiently sending out and picking up its signals, so allowing the operators to guide the flying machines in safety, we feel proud of the scientific achievements of modern man in devising such a system. By all means get excited — but take a closer look at the diminutive bat, see his level of sophistication — and there you will have something to really become excited about.

The bats send out bursts of ultrasonic sound pulses. These have a short duration, and a very high frequency, which are beyond the hearing of you and I. Consequently, if you saw bats flying around, you would hear nothing. The brief pulses enable the bats to time the echoes accurately, and so determine the distance of the object producing the echo. The reason that the bats use high frequency sound rather than low frequency is simple. In natural environments, the sounds produced, for instance, by the wind blowing through trees, or by other animals, are of a relatively low frequency — you can hear them. If the bat also sent out low frequency sounds, the returning echoes could be a confused mixture of sighing trees, mooing cows and its own signals. Instead, by using a high frequency sound for echo-location, the bats are unlikely to be bothered with interference from other sounds in the environment. Isn't it clever of the bats to think of that!!!

Go into a quiet corner, and try and produce an ultrasonic squeak. You might find it rather difficult. How then does the humble little bat manage? It has been designed with a highly specialised larynx (voice box) and the sounds are emitted through special horn-shaped nostrils.

If you would like to know more about specialised equipment, listen to this. Since the sound of the loud pulse must be compared with its relatively faint echo, many bats have relatively large ears, specially shaped to enhance directional sensitivity. The sensitivity of the ear is reduced by special muscles in the inner ear when each loud outgoing pulse is produced. In other words, the bat has special muscles to ensure that it doesn't deafen itself every time it emits its outgoing squeak. The sophistication of the system is even more staggering. In order to enhance the efficiency of its echo-location, one species of bat, the greater horseshoe bat, adjusts its call so that the frequency of the echo falls within the most sensitive part of the hearing range, whilst the call itself is emitted at a frequency to which the bat is least sensitive. The technology that the bat requires to be able to achieve this is beyond description.

Just how efficient the radar system of the bat is, can be demonstrated by the fact that many bats feed upon flying insects at night, and are able to capture them whilst flying, detecting them and tracking them by means of their brilliant echo-location. The little creature knows how to differentiate between a caterpillar, for example, and the leaf on which it rests, so that it will eat only the caterpillar and leave the leaf (obviously preferring a good meaty meal to plain salad!). Their unique radar capability enables them to fly without risk or hesitation, even in total darkness. A certain brave individual once met with a striking example of this ability when he disturbed a colony of several hundred bats in a small dark cave in the West Indies. They all immediately took to the wing, swirling around in every direction, yet at no time were there any collisions. The orderliness of the seething, seemingly disorganised mass was incredible. It would appear that each bat produces its own special sound, which it recognises, so that it does not confuse them with those of its neighbour.

Experiments have shown that a little brown bat can fly through a fence of vertical wires spaced twenty four centimetres apart in complete darkness without touching any of the wires. Presumably, the wing span of the bat is not much less that twenty four centimetres.

Have you ever driven through a foggy night where you can see precisely nothing, when even though you wipe the windscreen and screw up your eyes, you just see a yellow glare? Would you care to do that at seventy m.p.h.? With obstacles all around? How would you avoid them? The answer is develop a radar system — but quickly!

The bat's superior radar-system enables it to fly in total darkness in absolute safety.

Just how do you 'develop' an ultra-sophisticated complicated radar system, on which your life depends! The humble and unpretentious little bat has a system, special larynx, special ears, special muscles, all brilliantly co-ordinated, which rival the most advanced system which modern technology can produce, and was happily using it whilst the ancestors of the scientists were discovering that the round wheel is more efficient than the square one.

מה גדלו מעשיך ה'

23

ॐ THE THERMOSTAT ॐ

Getting up was hard to do in winter. Sometimes it was so cold that the *Negel Wasser* froze and your socks stood up by themselves next to your shoes. Think of it — lying in bed in an isolated island of warmth, staring glumly at the fascinating patterns which the heavy frost has drawn on the window, watching the vapour from your breath float away in the still coldness of your room. You know that as soon as your feet touch the icy surface of the bare linoleum, they will recoil with shock, and you shiver at the prospect. You can delay it no longer — you have to get up.

The first job of the morning in those days was the most unpleasant and the most difficult. Making the fire. Clean the grate, and remove the cinders. Take out the cinders into the freezing outdoors, bracing yourself for the shock of exposure. Run back with coal from the coal shed and sticks from the wood pile. Crunch up some paper and lay it on the grate. Strategically place the small sticks around the paper, and little pieces of coal on the sticks. When all was ready, your hands stiff and blue with cold, dusty and soiled with coal dust and ashes, you struck a match and held it to the paper — and hoped for the best. The fire then had to be carefully tended, sometimes provoked and other times mended, shifting the coalies here and there, poking it gently to give it some air, until, until those flames red and gold, over the cold black adversary had taken a hold. Then sweep up, and allow the warmth of the fire to slowly seep through the room, providing heat and comfort, a focus for the whole family.

If it was hard during the week, then *Shabbos* in winter required all the ingenuity and planning of a field-marshal. The coal fire had to be stoked up on *Erev Shabbos* in such a way — with brick-like coals arranged as a jigsaw — that it would burn slowly and steadily throughout the long *Shabbos* evening.

If you want to know the real truth, the kitchen was the focal point for the whole family, because it was the only warm room. The rest of the house, from the bathroom, bedrooms to the passages were all reliably freezing. The little paraffin heater in the downstairs hall did more to fumigate the house than provide any real heat.

How things have changed. Bliss and comfort! Convenience and warmth! Just reach for the switch and set the timer. An hour before

160 / Designer World

your delicate feet have to make contact with the fitted carpet, a gentle *whoof* from the bathroom tells you that the boiler has ignited, and soon the house will be basking from attic to front door in the regulated glow of central heat. The greatest calamity that can happen is if some thoughtless person fixed the thermostat too low, so that when you return from your shopping expedition the heating is off. With a little shriek of dismay at not being greeted by the familiar warm air wafting on your cheeks, you run to the little box on the wall and turn up the dial, confident that in minutes the temperature will rise, together with your serenity and comfort. Three cheers for oil, gas and electricity, three cheers for thermostats, and above all one hundred and three cheers for the modern times which have made coal

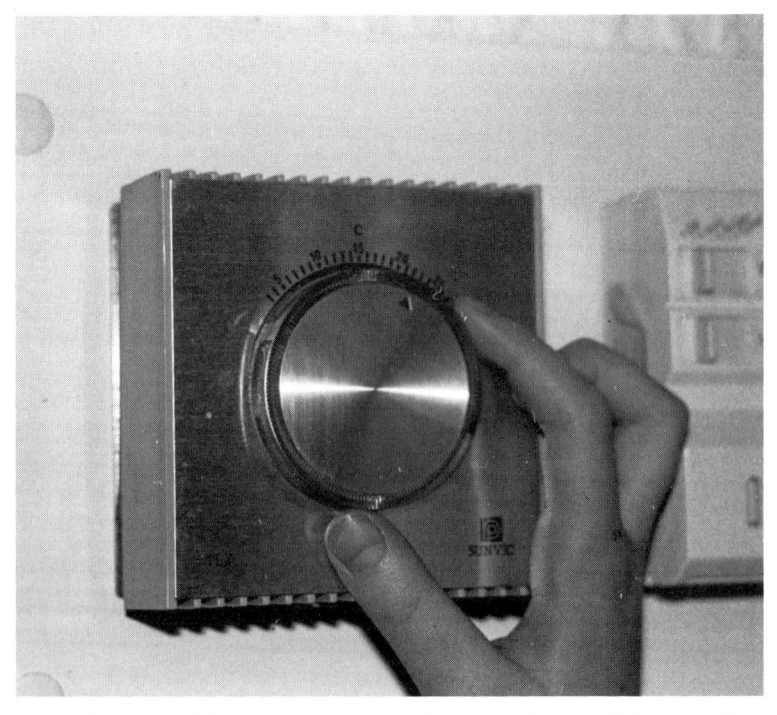

A Wall-mounted thermostat. What a clever machine – a flick of the dial keeps the house in constant comfort.

fires a thing of the museum, and have allowed us the luxury of guaranteed warmth at all times.

That's what you think! Would you like to hear about a system of thermostatically controlled central-heating which provides a constant level of heating both day and night, summer and winter, and is as old as the world? Are you serious? Where is it? Right inside little old you!

If anyone ever asks you if you have temperature, please say yes. Every human being needs a temperature of approximately 98.4 degrees F. or 36.9 degrees C. That temperature needs to be constant if we are to be able to settle anywhere in the world. Whether you live in Siberia, where the temperature drops as low as "minus 90 degrees F", or in Libya where it climbs to 136 degrees, you will survive, with a steady 98.4. Reptiles and fish, on the other hand, have a body temperature which is only a few degrees above that of their surroundings, and varies accordingly, with the result that in cold conditions, their body temperature slows down most chemical changes, and reduces their whole organism to a state of inactivity. Insects can be completely immobilised by a sudden fall in temperature. A fly in the fridge won't fly for too long!

We take it for granted that our body temperature remains constant no matter where we live, and no matter what the season. But how does it work — where is the thermostat? It is very modest, no larger than a small prune, and lives on the underside of the brain. Its name — the HYPOTHALAMUS. It is just one three hundredth of the mass of the brain, but has a richer blood supply than any other part of the body. For good reason, for the little hypothalamus is the thermostat that monitors our body temperature and maintains its constancy in a number of most remarkable ways. It is so sensitive that if your blood temperature would rise (or fall) by as little as one tenth of a degree, it would immediately detect it and set to work. Let us say that your blood has heated up slightly due to vigorous exercise. This fact is monitored as the blood passes through the hypothalamus. Messages are sent out through the nervous system to the sweat glands which are situated beneath the skin, and tells them to start working. Fluid from the blood is filtered into the glands, and passes through their little ducts to the surface of the skin, so that a layer of moisture is produced on the skin's surface. Does that cool you down — why should it! The answer is an amazing law of physics (created by the Creator). When any liquid turns into vapour, it removes the heat from its immediate surroundings. Therefore, as the sweat evaporates, it takes its latent heat from the body, and so reduces the body temperature. (This remarkable fact has been utilised in fridges. A gas is condensed to a liquid, and then it vaporises. As it does so, it takes the heat from the surrounding area, in this case the inside of the fridge, and Hey Presto — a freezing cold fridge!) Thus the sweat of your brow is your body trying to cool down. (In very humid conditions, the air might contain so much water vapour that the sweat cannot evaporate rapidly enough to produce an adequate cooling effect, and may lead to extreme discomfort and serious overheating.)

Another set of instructions go to the blood vessels near the skin's surface. Expand! This allows more blood to flow near the surface (giving you a flushed look) enabling you to lose heat through the skin. Yet more instructions are flashed to other brain areas to speed up breathing, carrying away yet more heat.

If it is a very cold day, and your blood temperature drops by as little as one tenth of a degree, your built-in thermostat registers the change. (Just think how complicated that little statement must be in reality — a tiny piece of — what? — noticing a drop in temperature and sending out a barrage of electrical messages... messages that mean something!) Immediately the messages are transmitted. Decrease sweat production, minimising the heat lost through evaporation. An emergency message to all blood vessels that are near the skin's surface — constrict yourselves! This will reduce the volume of blood flowing near the surface (and explains why people who are cold look pale or even blue) and reduces heat loss. Other glands are told to instruct the liver (the main central heating boiler of the body) to increase its rate of chemical reactions, and thus release more heat to the body. If your temperature drops significantly, a reflex action will be activated which makes your muscles contract in spasms. This strange activity produces heat and is called shivering!

You and I are not the only ones to have been created with specialised heat-sensors. There is one little creature that you would not like to meet, called a pit viper. This snake has been endowed with a special extra sense that 'sees' heat. On its head are two sensory pits (a little hollow next to each eye) that are so sensitive that they can detect a change in the air temperature of less than one degree. It uses this sense to track down warm-blooded prey, particularly at night when it cannot see them. For example, it can detect the presence of a rat at a distance, follow it down its burrow just by detecting its heat, and then introduces itself when it is ready for a late-night snack (and you thought that the heat-seeking missile was a modern invention?!).

Take a look at a modern fridge and marvel at its ingenuity and advanced technology. What it is to be modern! Just one hundred years ago or less people were buying blocks of ice from the fish-monger to keep their food cool. Take an admiring look at your neat little thermostat on the wall, the very latest in 'state-of-the-art' technology, quietly and efficiently regulating the temperature in your modest home and be grateful that the age of coal fires is receding. What it is to be modern! Take a closer look at yourself, discover the technology that is so brilliantly designed, sophisticated and advanced that it makes your fridge and central-heating system look as clumsy as a Penny-Farthing, and be very grateful.

מודה אני לפניך מלך חי וקים

24

ஐ INVISIBLE MENDING ରେ

Mother was indignant. And quite rightly so. She had lost count of the number of times that she had told him not to run in the street. It was undignified, unsightly, unnecessary, and he could fall. He agreed wholeheartedly, but still ran. His logic was unimpeachable. Running was faster than walking. Why take five minutes when you could take three? They agreed to differ, and life continued happily and runningly, until one bright day the young man was racing at full pelt down a sloping road. The road was covered with concrete and gravel, and the surface was uneven. One second he was happy and carefree, his legs eating up the distance with a hearty appetite, the next, his foot struck a projection on the rough surface. What happened then could be described as the vain attempt by a human without wings to become airborne. He took off in a graceful arc, but very quickly the forces of gravity overpowered the upward movement, and in a non-too-graceful crash he plummeted to the ground, sliding down the loose gravel in an undignified position of complete prostration.

His first sentiment upon rising from the ground was to hope that no-one had seen his humiliating downfall. He then surveyed the damage. It was extensive. Where his knees had careered along the concrete were now the tattered remnants of once smart trousers, with badly grazed knees prominently visible and red. The brunt of the damage had been taken by his hands. In seeking to cushion his fall, the palms of his two hands were ripped and bleeding, with small pieces of dirty gravel liberally embedded in the torn skin. Slowly and painfully, he retraced his steps back to his home, where the daunting prospect of facing maternal wrath was more than offset by the instinctive desire to be cleaned and nursed.

He need not have worried too much. The medical attention he received was second to none. His hands and knees were washed with warm water and antiseptic, and carefully bandaged. His trousers, however did not merit such sympathetic treatment. They were unceremoniously dumped into the wardrobe, and there they lay, ignominious and forlorn. Within two months, two miracles had occurred. Both his hands and knees had completely healed, to the extent that there was not the slightest sign of any damage on either — even the fingerprints had re-joined. Life returned to normal, the runner still ran, albeit with a little more care. Sadly, no similar miracle happened to the trousers. They still lay, torn, crumpled , muddy and forgotten

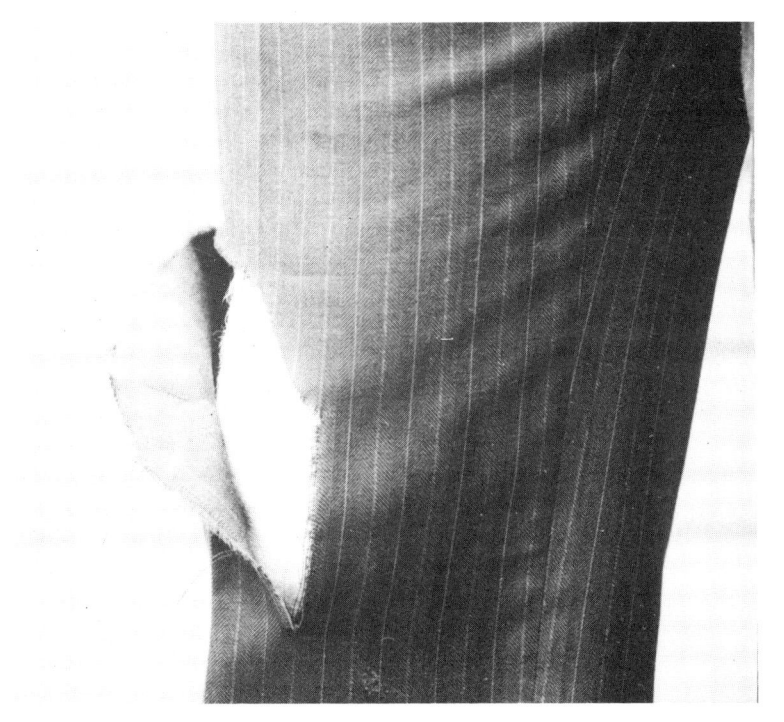

Ripped Trousers. Six months after the accident – and still ripped!

on the wardrobe floor, with absolutely no sign that they (the trousers) were going to do anything about it. Why did his skin regrow, but not the trouser fabric? Why did the bleeding gradually stop and the wound close, but the hole on the trousers remain as gaping as ever? Why is there no invisible mending as invisible as that of a wound healing? How is the brand new skin on your fingers able to reproduce the pattern of your very own personalised fingerprints? How precisely do wounds heal?

Imagine that someone cut his finger accidentally. The skin barrier is broken, and blood vessels have been cut open. Result — bleeding. There is an immediate reaction from the body's emergency services. Tiny platelets (these are pieces of special blood cells produced by the bone marrow, and there are between 250,000-500,000 of them in each cubic millimetre of blood) rush to the breach. Within seconds they make a temporary patch. What happens next requires a vivid imagination. You have to imagine a reservoir with a gaping hole in its side, and water pouring out of the yawning gap. Some superman then flies in and attaches a hose pipe to a valve that just happens to be at that spot. Superman then sprays the hole in the reservoir wall with a special liquid, which coagulates on contact with the wall, and holds back the cascading water. This super liquid then forms enormously strong metal cables which snake across the cavity, gradually pulling it together. Bricks then appear out of nowhere, and position themselves around the cables complete with quick drying mortar, until the hole disappears, and the reservoir is as good as new. Superman would win world acclaim, and deservedly so. That is exactly what happens to the wound. The platelets form the first line of defence. The heavier defences then move in — in the shape of FIBRIN. Fibrin is a protein, which is released by the blood plasma, and it makes its presence known by creating a meshwork of fibres right across the wound, effectively plugging the hole, stopping any more blood leaking out, and preventing the entry of bacteria and other unwanted materials.

Can you see a problem? If fibrin, the wonder-sealant, is present in the blood, why is it not clogging up the blood with its web of protein inside the body, with unthinkable results? The answer is amazing. Since fibrin is so effective in coagulating the blood, it cannot be kept in the blood in its finished form. Instead, the raw materials are there, ready to be formulated and put into use at seconds' notice. For this to happen, a chemical enzyme called THROMBIN acts on a protein called FIBRINOGEN, and that chemical reaction converts the fibrinogen into the fibrin. (Many different chemical substances are needed for thrombin to form. We are born with some of them; others we get from our food — calcium and vitamin K for example. Vitamin K is found in cabbage and spinach, and is stored in the liver.) The processes of coagulation when a blood vessel is broken, and non-coagulation when the vessel is whole, are both vital, and crucial to the survival of mankind. It is also vital and crucial for us, who seek to discern design in the creation, to know that the biology books admit, 'The details of the coagulation of the blood are very complicated, and not all biologists agree about the different stages...' Putting man on the moon is simple compared with the complexities of our own life-blood!

Now that the blood has clotted, it begins to shrink. As it does so, it hardens and forms a scab which protects the damaged area while new tissue is forming. So there you have it — the repair site has been thoughtfully equipped with overhead protection to enable the construction force to complete their work in safety and comfort! The clot shrinks some more, pulling the tissues closer together, and new cells at the margins of the wound begin to spread over the inner surface of the scab, forming a new layer of skin at the rate of about 0.5mm per day. New capillary branches grow from others in the area, and cut nerves grow out into the tissues. It sounds simple, until you realise what it actually means for new cells to grow to replace the damaged ones. When a cell has been cut, it sends out a distress signal to its neighbours "Help, quickly grow!" This message is sent chemically by means of hormones. The healthy cell receives the message, and immediately begins to reduplicate itself. What ensures that the cell will reproduce another skin cell, and not a liver cell? The answer is that each and every one of the hundred million

million cells in our body is genetically coded with the precise information that it requires in order to be faithful to its calling. Thus, if the skin of your forefinger is removed, the new skin that grows, consisting of millions of single cells, will contain the correct code to ensure that your individual fingerprint (unique in the whole world, past, present and future) will once again be faithfully replicated.

The young man who so badly grazed his hands when he hit the deck could not bear to touch anything, and certainly not to grasp any object until his hands had healed. He imagined that this was because his hands were 'sore'. Nothing of the sort. This was another brilliantly designed defence mechanism which came into action, in which the pain-sensory endings in the wounded area became more sensitive, reducing the movement of and interference with the damaged area, and increasing the chances of successful healing. Nothing is simple in the created world!

People wonder why it is that a healing wound is redder than the surrounding area. Here we discover yet another remarkable feature of design. When the tissue (skin and flesh) is damaged, a special chemical is set free by that damaged tissue, which causes the capillaries in that region to expand. This in turn allows more blood to reach the surface of the skin, and the rate of flow of blood around the wound is increased. This gives rise to the redness and warmth in the vicinity of a wound, and also increases the supply of antibodies and those special cells in the blood that devour any invading micro-organisms. Once again we find something remarkable. If a defending cell (phagocyte) finds any foreign material, it will engulf and consume it. At the same time it will send chemically transmitted messages to its millions of friends — "Come quick and help in the battle". Quickly they come and begin gobbling up the bacteria. The redness around the wound is a sure sign that all the defences are at work, and the good fight is being fought.

Poor trousers, designed by man, useful when they work, but if damaged they will never re-grow. Nor will a girder that cracks, a table leg that bends, or metal suffering from fatigue. Look at those cut hands — ripped and shredded — and look at them now. Wonder of wonders and miracle of miracles — just leave them alone, and as good as new. What design — what a Designer!

25

ஜ THE SPACE CAPSULE ௸

Have you ever thought what it feels like to be a goldfish? Now if you could be a free goldfish, swimming in a large pond or secluded corner of a little river, it would be marvellous. Go where you like, eat what you like — flies, juicy insects or delicious weeds — and whenever you like, that must be the life. But not if you end up in a goldfish bowl. There, in a circular glass jar twelve inches wide, it must be a miserable life. The only choice your have is whether to swim round the bowl to the right or to the left. The same journey every day, no change in the view, it's almost a dog's life. The worst aspect of it must be the total dependence on the human master's generosity and memory for your food supply. No tempting flies, no delectable insects ever come near, just a few flakes of 'Super Concentrated Scientifically Approved Fish Food' — just the thing to make you goldfish sleek and healthy — that's what they say, but believe me, after three months it is utterly and predictably boring. And sometimes master forgets! He goes on holiday and remembers me when the plane is about to take off. Whoever invented goldfish bowls was no friend of goldfish!

So how would you like to be a human goldfish? In the days when countries could afford to send their heroic and patriotic citizens into space, life in the space-capsule was not too different to the life of our little goldfish. Compressed into a circular constricted area the size of an under-stair cupboard, with no method of obtaining food or indeed anything from the hostile outside, with just the emptiness of space to stare at from one end of the dawn-less day to the other, it can't have been much fun. If not for the fact that the President himself would speak to you, if and when you returned, few would have volunteered. The worst part was the total dependence on other agencies for your every need. If you wanted dinner, you had to hope that the ground crew had remembered to pack your 'high calorific super energised' little pill, mushroom flavoured. If you needed to blow your nose, you would have needed special lessons in how to perform that feat where no gravity exists. Oxygen, water, food, radio contact, fuel, tools, and above all the ability to get out of this unusual and confined abode, all had to be supplied by outside forces, on whose efficiency and capability your life depended. Any number of things could go wrong — you could lose radio contact, the oxygen supply might be insufficient, a passing meteorite might like the look of your little craft and collide, or — horror of horrors — there are computer systems controlling the spaceship down on earth, there might be a power failure! Help! Talk about being vulnerable!

And do you think it is any different to being a little chick growing inside an egg? The small goldfish in its bowl; the brave astronaut in his space capsule; and the tiny chicken in its shell — all share a common denominator, the absolute reliance on forces outside of it, and far beyond its control, for their survival. In the case of the spaceman, we understand the complex but well-orchestrated coordination on which his survival depends. Is the same true of an egg?

Have you ever wondered how a chicken manages to sit on her eggs during the incubating period without producing scrambled eggs? Eggs are such delicate things — why does she not crack them? To understand the answer, you must understand an electric light bulb. The glass of a light bulb is not much thicker than the paper of this page, yet it withstands a strong grip when you push it into a light fitting. The explanation for this lies in the shape of the bulb — which is modelled entirely on the shape of the egg. The characteristic egg-shape provides structural strength to withstand all-round pressure, even with a thin shell. (If the shell were too thick, the chick inside would not be able to peck its way out; but more about that later.) Light bulbs and eggs have a rounded profile over the whole surface. When you grip an egg, or a light bulb, the force that you apply is transmitted in all directions away from the point of contact by its curved shape. This results in the force being distributed over a wide area, with no excessive force being set up at any one point. If imitation is the greatest form of flattery, then the millions of light bulbs are the most eloquent testimony to the incredibly efficient design of the shape of the eggs. The phenomenal strength of an egg is attested to by the fact that a chicken's egg survived a 183m. drop from a helicopter, and an ostrich egg will withstand the weight of an 115kg man. It is said that you can balance a table on four eggs, without them breaking, although it is not recommended that you practice the art on your parents' new pale white carpet!

Enormous research is invested into finding the appropriate material for the exterior of the space-module. It has to withstand the great heat of re-entry into the earth's atmosphere, as well as repelling the adverse radiation of space. An egg-shell is no less equipped for its duties. Constructed from chalky calcium carbonate, it protects the egg and is sufficiently impervious to prevent water evaporating from it. If the outside of an egg is impressive, then the inside is a veritable wonderland. The blood spot, although unwelcome in the kitchen, is in fact the beginning of an embryo, the beginning of life, and that tiny blood spot will eventually develop into a chick. The tiny embryo rests on top of a bag of yellow yolk. This yolk is the chick's food supply, and nourishes it whilst it develops, and it develops quickly. At three days the chick's heart already beats, and it has blood vessels. At fifteen days, the chick is already recognisable as a bird, and five short days later, at twenty days, it is fully developed and is ready to hatch the next day!

The embryo and yolk sac are surrounded by a watery fluid (the white of the egg) containing the protein ALBUMEN. The main job of this fluid is to supply the embryo with water during its development. Take a close look at an egg. Do you see any holes in it? Look more closely, and you will see that one end of the egg is blunter than the other. At the blunt end, just under the shell, there is an air space. The shell has tiny holes running through it, which allow oxygen to diffuse into the air space from the outside. The oxygen is then carried via blood vessels to the embryo, and carbon dioxide passes out in the reverse direction — in this way the embryo breathes! A breathing egg! It is obvious that the yolk sac must be kept in place so that the developing chick can obtain the nourishment it requires to survive. What keeps it in place and prevents it slopping from side to side? The albumen twists and densifies like a rope from the two extremes of the egg, holding the yolk firmly and securely in place. Any well-designed capsule in which living creatures develop must take into account the need to produce and store waste. You will not be surprised, therefore, to know that three days after having been laid, the fertile hen's egg with its tiny embryo has an excretory sac attached, in which the developing embryo is able to deposit its nitrogenous waste. Nothing is missing, and everything is in its place.

Every mother bird knows, without ever having been taught, that their eggs require a stable and warm temperature in order to develop. Most birds satisfy this requirement simply by sitting on the eggs, but somehow the mother birds know when the eggs require extra heat. When the air temperature is very low, birds incubate very closely, and shiver to keep both themselves and the eggs warm. In climates where the air temperature rises above that which is beneficial for the eggs, the birds will again incubate very closely to prevent the egg temperature rising above the body temperature of the mother. The egg has no way of regulating its temperature, and relies entirely on its mother, and mother knows exactly what to do! Similarly, the eggs must be turned regularly by the parents to help the chick develop properly. With instinct and devotion, the parents do their job, without ever having been taught.

Soon enough, it is time for the little one to come out into the world. It is interesting that there are no known cases in which parent help the chick by pecking or otherwise breaking the shell open. It has to do it itself. What precisely stimulates hatching is not known

How did this rather large baby manage to squeeze inside a little egg?

to man, what we do know is that the little chick is superbly provided for in order to achieve a successful landfall. Baby birds have an 'egg tooth' to help them break out of the shell. This is a tiny knob at the tip of their beak, precisely designed to allow junior to make a speedy exit. In the case of the chick, it takes approximately one hour from the first crack until the shell cap is broken, **always** in a counter-clockwise direction from the first crack, and the chick, wet and bedraggled, but very much alive and healthy clambers from its shell. Some chicks make peeping calls from inside the egg several days before hatching; the hen replies, so when the chick hatches, it already knows its mother's voice!

When you see a fully grown chick emerge from its shell, you wonder how this rather large baby managed to squeeze inside a little egg! You begin to wonder a little more — if the shell would have been a fraction thinner, it would never have survived being laid, if it would have been thicker, the chick could not have broken through. You wonder what would have happened if the chick would not have had its beak, or its complete supply of food, or bag for waste or if the egg would not have been its perfect shape... you begin to discern design, wisdom, planning... If you think the men at NASA are wise, what would you say about the Designer of the living miracles called eggs?

26

ᛤ MEMORIES ᛥ

You can feel sorry for yourself. Well, why not, it makes you feel better. It isn't that you like to wallow in self-pity, but the problem is that it is so easy these days to feel out of date. Like *Choni Hame'agel* who woke up after a seventy-year sleep and discovered that no-one knew him. Like the man who still drives a little black car which he has to start each morning with a starting-handle, whilst his contemporaries swish around in their automatic fuel-injection 1.8i XJ6 epitomes of luxury. It really is hard, when technology is moving at such a rapid pace, not to feel out of date very quickly. Once upon a time, when people wanted to tell the time, they reached to their waistcoat pocket and opened the lid of their *'goldene Zeiger'*. Time progressed, and the watch was transferred to the wrist, and it was still relatively simple to stretch out one's hand and tell the time. That was in the olden days. Now, if you wish to know the time, at your disposal on your wrist is strapped a mini-computer, with a host of tiny Lilliputian buttons, and a screen. Would you like to know the time in Manila? The temperature in Zululand? The rate of sterling against the yen in Yokohama? Would you like to know the square root of your telephone number? You mean you only want to know the time now where you live — how boring! You are just not with it!

Once upon a time, people carried a little *Luach* in their pockets. Useful little things, they usually came free with the *Rosh Hashonoh* appeal, and they were perfect for noting appointments and finding out which day *Purim* will fall this year. Obsolete. Absolutely obsolete and out of date. Old fashioned is just not the word. What up-to-date people have is a slim little case (looks like a cigarette case, in the days when people smoked) and is called a digital notebook. Open up the flap and there before you is a screen and keyboard. Contained in the memory of this electronic wonder is all the information known to mankind. You wish to know on what day you were born — tap key X. You know a telephone number but you cannot remember whose it is, tap key Y and all will be revealed. Do you wish to be woken up at 5.30am tomorrow morning, and then reminded to wash *Negel Wasser* ten minutes later — no problem, just tap key N. Itineraries, schedules, appointments, notes, information, addresses — the little wonder can store it all. "Just remember to change the battery," comments the cynical bystander, who has not yet received his digital notebook.

An up-to-date version of the old note-book

How sad — does he not know that the marvellous machine lets you know when the battery is running low! Wonder of the modern age! If you are one of those old-fashioned folk of valuable vintage who still has a non-digital notebook, writes shopping lists on bits of paper, and ties knots in his tie for reminders, try to keep it quiet, otherwise you might be looked upon with great sympathy!

The fact is that many machines these days boast memories as part of their built-in features. Computers are based on their ability to store information; calculators would not work without a memory store; word-processors make life a pleasure because of their memory, and even washing machines, once programmed, can memorise their tasks just according to your personal liking. Telephones have memories, so that by pressing just one little button, the tone sings out its plaintive tune, and your are through to Uncle Lou in Texas, saving you that awful time-consuming drudgery of pressing ten buttons. (It really must have been hard in those days. Do you remember when you had to place your index finger in the number hole and turn your hand round? Phew! That was really terrible!) Never has the memory been more in demand. It is true to say that the advent of modern technology is not without its disadvantages. If you go into most shops, the assistants will feel unable to calculate a simple subtraction (giving change) without their ubiquitous calculator, whereas in former times the shopkeeper would write a long list of prices at the back of a brown bag, and with dazzling speed and a blunt pencil snake down the list and tell you an amount that was never (or nearly never) wrong. Children, together with many sections of society have lost their confidence in using their minds to solve mathematical problems. And the digital notebooks have their limits! They can only store a certain amount of information, before the little sign shows 'Full' like a saturated car-park.

Everyone is impressed by the technology of modern labour-saving machines. Although we make gentle fun of them — we take full advantage of them, and we love them. We ask questions about their memories, how so much information can be stored in such a minute space, and we know that the answer involves items such as 'silicon chips, binary digits, electronic switches, conductors, and printed circuits.' We are powerfully impressed to learn that super computers can work at a rate of a billion operations each second, and the working rate is so fast that it generates enough heat to melt the machine, to the extent that it must be continually washed with coolant fluid whilst operating! Instinctively we feel that we do not need to know every detail of how they work in order to be impressed by their design and function. Enough that we know that they have been designed by clever people, that their every component is the result of much research and effort, and all credit to them for their efforts on behalf of mankind. We shall gladly acknowledge their technological skill and knowledge, and happily take full advantage of their hard work.

So how do we feel about our very own memory? It is interesting to note that we all know of great *Gedolim* who spent eighteen hours per day and more filling their minds with *Torah* knowledge, for weeks, months, years and decades. Did you ever hear of the word 'FULL' flashing across their eyes? It would appear that the human memory is capable of storing quite a lot of information! Let us take a little look at some of the features of the human memory, and the results could be interesting.

What is the extent of our memory? Can you bring to mind a familiar face? It seems that we memorise sights. Close your eyes and concentrate. Bring to mind the sound of thunder. Can you? You can remember sounds. Now bring to mind the taste of creamy milk-chocolate, or hot chicken soup. Easy? You remember tastes. Can you evoke in your mind the smell of roasting chicken, the smell of sour milk, the aroma of a summer evening immediately after a shower of rain? You remember smells. Close your eyes again, and try picture in your mind the feel of a peach skin, or a kiwi fruit. The fact that you can indicates that you can remember touch. There is no sense that you have ever experienced, be it sight, sound, taste, smell or touch that is not faithfully recorded in your memory. Think for a minute. Imagine that you had the following project. To take a piece of meat from the butcher, and encode in that piece of meat the memory of

Learning Torah day after day – and the memory is never full.

the aroma of strawberries. How would you do it? What is it that enables us to memorise all our experiences? What system is used? When someone tells you to picture something to yourself, and you do, what have you done? What happens inside your head?

Why do we need a memory? The simple answer is that without a memory you could not read this page. The shapes of the letters would be absolutely meaningless. If someone spoke to you, it would be incomprehensible, like talking to a newly born baby. Put bluntly, without a memory we could not survive. We would not know how to walk, (walking is an acquired skill), how to talk, we would not know who we are or where we live. We could not perform any function, for we would never know what we had been doing a second before. Memory is vital to survival, therefore we have a memory. What we sometimes forget is that the ability to forget is as much a function of design as the ability to remember. Since we have been created with a memory, why should the memory not be infallible? Logically speaking, why should we be able to forget? (In any case, there are many things that you never forget. Once you have learned to swim, you can always swim. Similarly with typing or riding a bicycle.) Have you ever made a fool of yourself, or been hurt, or upset — without the blessing of forgetfulness, how would you be able to carry on living? Forgetfulness is vital to survival, therefore we have forgetfulness.

Why is it that some people have 'photographic memories' and can recall a whole printed page with ease, whereas other people claim to have 'a terrible memory'? Why is it that elderly people can recall events which happened in their childhood nearly a century ago, but cannot remember where they put their front-door key?

The answer to these and many other questions concerning memory is to a great degree a total mystery. 'The exact mechanism of memory is still unknown.' '...The neurophysiologic basis of memory remains for the most part a mystery...' Complicated? Extremely. More complicated than a computer's memory? Much more. 'Instinctively we feel that we do not need to know every detail of how it works to be impressed by their design and function.' Exactly.

27

∽ THE SUIT OF ARMOUR ∾

Every seaside resort likes to create a good impression. Usually, they advertise their particular location as having miles of unspoilt golden sands, guaranteed (or almost guaranteed) azure skies and unbroken sunshine. The travel brochures that they issue might even depict those very scenes. The reality, however, is likely to be very different to that which the brochure would have you believe. What they fail to show you are the flies on the beach, the stomach upsets and the litter in the streets. But, give

188 / Designer World

credit where it is due. Sometimes you are pleasantly surprised. On one occasion, a visitor to a typical resort was very impressed, very impressed indeed. As he was sitting on the beach, there in front of his very eyes was a man hoovering the sand. At first he could not believe his eyes! Hoovering the sand? This was really dedication to cleanliness at its finest; and he was mightily impressed. Then he sat up with a jolt. What sort of machine was capable of sucking in litter without sucking in the sand! Perhaps the man was in fact collecting sand! But surely a spade and bucket would have been more effective,

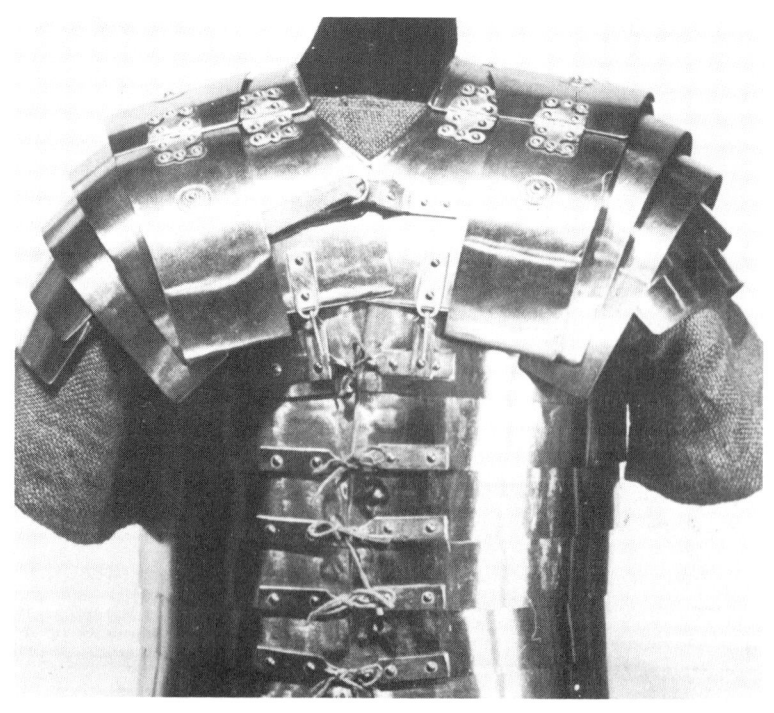

Genuine Roman armour, cumbersome, heavy and insensitive
(Courtesy of Newcastle University)

and in any case, was he not in danger of removing the beach! This definitely required further investigation.

Approaching the man and his machine, the visitor demanded to know what he was doing. As though accustomed to such questions, the man replied, "It's the recession you know. Things are tough in business. So I thought I would try my luck with my metal detector. You never know — perhaps I'll find a buried treasure!" The visitor smiled knowingly, felt an absolute fool, and returned to his deck-chair.

How was he to know? He had never seen a metal detector in his life, and it really did resemble a hoover. Had he been interested in understanding how the detector worked, he would have been told that the machine simply creates a magnetic field, which penetrates the sand and reacts with a signal when metal is detected. Had he ever travelled by plane overseas, and been compelled to walk through a square wooden frame to check that he was not carrying firearms, he would have actually walked through a magnetic field such as the one generated by the beach-comber. The greatest shock, however, to the man who thought that he had never seen a metal-detector would have been the knowledge that he himself possessed something far more sophisticated. And not just one machine, but several million! Just beneath the surface of his skin are housed a whole host of detectors and receptors. These are the touch receptors which tell him about the world through five different kinds of sensations — pain, heat, cold, pressure and contact — just a few of the wonders contained in the remarkable wrapping that we call our skin.

If you want to carry eggs home from the shop, you do not put them in your pocket. The bus might be crowded and your eggs will be scrambled. You place them in a protective wrapper so that they arrive home safe and sound. Sometimes the wrapper is made of cardboard, sometimes of plastic, but it is always cleverly designed to accommodate the shape of the egg. An average man is issued with seventeen square feet of skin, which fits around him perfectly. One of its many functions is to protect the man inside. It is strong and elasticated, and holds everything together, keeping vessels and fat from bulging or falling out. The fatty substance which constitutes the under-layer of the skin acts as a shock absorber to protect internal organs. Apart from cushioning any blows to the body, the skin also protects the body from germs and other harmful substances which are constantly landing on its surface. Inside the skin are millions of cells which produce a pigment called MELANIN. This is the substance that determines the colour of our hair, eyes and skin. Besides that cosmetic function, melanin is a vital protective agent that screens out dangerous ultra-violet rays emitted by the sun. A day or so after you have been in the sun, the tiny granules of pigment start rising from the lower region of the skin to the surface, giving a protective tan. (Excessive exposure to the sun can itself be dangerous, and should be limited.) People who have freckles on their face simply have concentrations of melanin.

Have you ever heard of a shopping bag that produces vitamins? May we introduce you to your skin. The humble protector of your bodily organs (the shopping bag enclosing your precious purchases) supplies much of the body's vitamin D requirement by producing a substance that changes into vitamin D when exposed to the ultraviolet radiation in sunlight. For this reason, vitamin D is sometimes called the sunshine vitamin, and it plays a part in bone formation. Could you imagine purchasing special roof slates which soak up the sunshine, and by means of a magical method convert the sunbeams into strength which they then send to the beams of the house, endowing them with *'koach u'Gevurah'* — you don't have to imagine it, you have it, right there at your fingertips.

Did you know that every day in Great Britain alone 150 million cups of tea are made from tea bags — small paper bags packed with enough tea to flavour one cup when steeped in boiling water. That information might not necessarily excite you (it all depends what you drink) but its implications might. The actual tea bag is made from net-like filter paper that has holes large enough to let boiling water in, but sufficiently small not to let any leaves escape. Just imagine that your skin was constructed from this type of paper — although your insides would not fall out, every time you had a bath you would soak up water like a sponge and become waterlogged. It cannot be an accident, therefore, to learn that our skin is absolutely waterproof, preventing water getting in and equally stopping the body from drying out. The actual skin cells contain a protein called KERATIN, the very same substance that the feathers of birds (and similarly our hair and nails) are made from. This substance is waterproof ('water off a duck's back'). Besides that, every hair that protrudes through the skin is supplied with a tiny gland which produces oil. This oil keeps the hair supple and helps to make the skin waterproof. Oil wells in our own body — riches, in the form of health and design — that we were never aware of!

In much the same way as a ceiling in a large store conceals a maze of cables, air ducts and pipes, so the seemingly smooth skin surface conceals a vast network of tiny pipes carrying blood, glands bringing sweat to the skin's surface, and millions, and millions of tiny nerve endings. These are the touch receptors which tell us about the world through the various forms of sensations. The brain interprets combinations of these sensations to tell us whether an object is

192 / Designer World

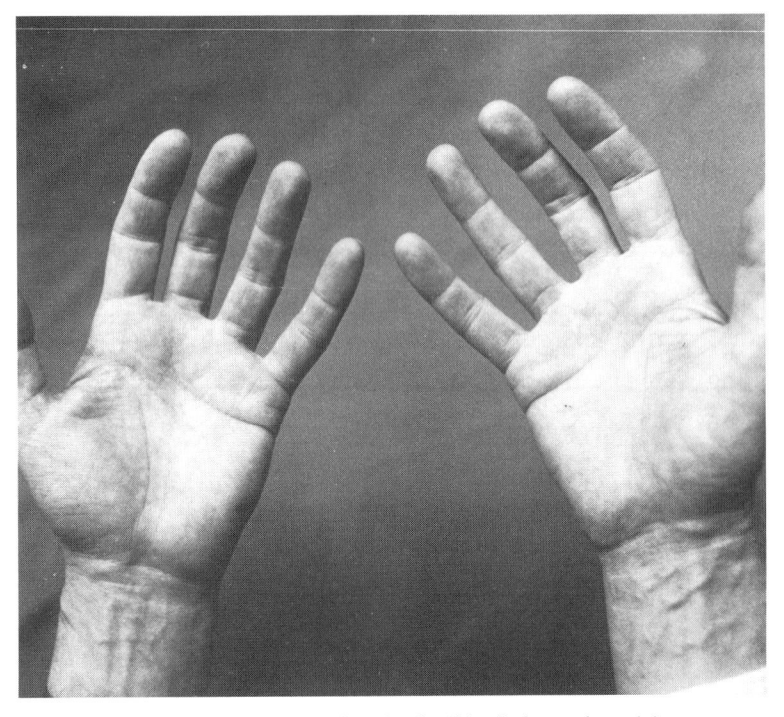

Genuine hard-working hands, flexible, light and sensitive.

hard or soft, dry or wet, hot or cold, or rough or smooth. For example, if a bare-footed man would be unfortunate enough to tread on a drawing pin, the touch receptors in his foot would sent electrical impulses along his sensory nerve in the leg, up his spinal cord to the brain, where they are decoded and interpreted as sharp pain. Ouch! Without the sense of touch, survival would be very difficult. This sense warns the brain when the skin is injured — and gives us information about the objects in the world around us.

Would you care to carry out an experiment? Put on a pair of gloves, and try and thread a needle! Why is it so hard? The answer is that touch receptors are situated near the surface of the skin, but they are not distributed evenly throughout the body. The most sensitive area is the hand, which has up to 1300 touch receptors per square inch (with the fingertips being the most sensitive area of the hand). Covering your hands with gloves simply blankets their sensitivity. Without this degree of sensitivity, even a seemingly simple act, such as holding a glass of water, would be so difficult. Without a highly sensitive degree of touch, how would you know that the grip you were exerting on the glass was not too loose, (the glass crashing on the floor) or too tight, (the glass smashing in your hand)? In a designed body, touch (and pain) receptors are distributed where they are needed most. The eye, a most delicate and complex machine, is very well endowed with nerve-endings, so that just the smallest particle of grit in the eye causes intense discomfort, with floods of tears to wash away the intruder. The sole of the foot, in contrast, is very insensitive, and it is quite possible to walk around with a pebble in one's shoe without too much discomfort. The tip of the tongue can feel the points of two needles when they are only 1/25 of an inch apart, yet skin on one's shoulders can only feel two distinct points when they are more than two inches apart. It's all part of the design. Whilst you might be concerned about buying a new suit for *Pesach*, you don't have to worry about your skin. It is constantly renewing itself, each day millions of skin cells are washed away in the shower or are rubbed away by clothing, whilst others take their place. You will be pleased to know that over a twenty-seven day stretch, you receive a completely new covering of skin, entirely free of charge.

Go on a tour around an ancient castle and see the clumsy heavy suits of armour which were worn for battle (and which, without a tin opener, they could never escape from) and you have an idea of the ultimate in human design. Could they produce vitamins, incorporate a sense of touch, pain and heat receptors — out of the question! Compare that to the enormous sophistication of our skin, and you have some idea, some very small idea, of the extent of the fathomless wisdom of our Designer.

"כולם בחכמה עשית"

28

ଚ CURRENT AFFAIRS ଚ

Just imagine. Excitement gripped the household. Today they would be visited by someone very special. A distant relative was coming — distant, because he was arriving from the fourteenth century. Their very own relative was about to come from the year 1393, and they would have the honour of showing him around their home, humble though it was. Soon enough, a horseman dismounted in front of their door, arousing the curiosity of all who saw his strange and quaint apparel. Never had they seen shoes made from rough leather, which came to a point like the tip of a carrot. His coloured tunic and breeches, not to mention the cloth turban-like hat looked initially like something from another age — until they realised that it was! With courtesy and friendliness they invited him into the house, and with wonder and fear he stood rooted in the hallway. He looked at the floor, not knowing what he was standing on. Where he came from the very richest noblemen had stone floors, and everyone else had earthen floors in their small, one-storey, two-roomed huts. His hosts explained how six hundred years later, we covered the earth with concrete (concrete?) and then floor-

A heavy-duty battery. Designed by man to power his car.

boards, then brown paper, then with rubber (rubber?) underlay and finally with fabric carpets. Their visitor looked at them with amazed wonder, and asked if they were the monarchs of the land! Laughingly they explained how not only were they not rich, but that they were really quite poor, and lived very simply. Well, relatively. It was going to be an interesting evening.

They led their special guest into the kitchen. As it was getting dark, they switched on the fluorescent light, and immediately the visitor clapped his hands to his eyes. Never, apart from the sun, had he seen such brightness. In his own home, those who were very rich had candles, and those who were not, read by the light of the woodfire in the hearth. After overcoming his initial shyness, he began to grow curious, and asked his host to explain the various chests, boxes and containers that he beheld all around him. As if taking a Japanese tourist on a guided tour of a Stately Home, he took him by the hand, and began.

"This square box, with a glass window in the front, is a washing machine. You take a pile of dirty clothes, as soiled as you wish, place them into the opening, close the door, add some powder and press this button. One hour later, the clothes are as clean as new. This box next to it is a dish-washer. Simply take all the food-encrusted plates, pots, cutlery of a whole *Shabbos*, pop them into the box, add a little powder, press the button, come back 45 minutes later and they will all be sparklingly clean. Can't think how we ever managed without it. Over here is our freezer. You can cook *Shabbos* on Sunday, prepare for the *Sheva Brochos* straight after the engagement, buy in bulk, bake in bulk, and pop it all into the freezer, where it will all remain fresh and frozen for months."

As the narration went on, the visitor felt weak at the knees. He was thinking how his own family had to wash their clothes at the village stream, wash their few wooden dishes with water drawn from the well; and as for freezing their food — perhaps in the polar regions! His amazement increased as he was shown the mixer, (no need to knead), the microwave, the fridge, the toaster, the sandwich maker, the drier and the frier. And of course, the all-important tape recorder, for constant Jewish music. Not to mention the popular Fax and the ringing Phone. It was almost too much for him to absorb in one session, but before he articulated his great wonder (you say that this is a SIMPLE home?) he just had to ask one very important question.

"Tell me," he said, "how do all these wonderful machines do what they do — how do they work?!"

Almost with a hint of condescension, the host said.

"Why, by electricity of course."

"And what, if I may be so bold as to ask, is electricity?"

The host paused for a moment, caught off guard, and then said.

"Oh! that's simple. It is a form of energy that comes out of the wall.

"That might be so," insisted the inquisitive visitor, "but what does this electricity actually consist of?"

The guide fell silent, unable to supply the solution to the mystery.

Well might the visitor from the past have asked, for the number of electrical appliances with which modern life is blessed is almost limitless, and yet, for the most part, we remain relatively ignorant of the precise nature of electricity. Although the existence of static electricity was known to the Greeks, it was not until the beginning of the 19th century that an Italian gentleman (Mr Volta) was able to produce an electric current. What he discovered was that all matter is composed of atoms, and around each atom there are even tinier particles called protons and electrons. Certain chemical reactions cause these tiny electrons to move around, and the movement of the electrons is called an electric current. If the electrons pass along a very fine wire, they keep bumping into atoms, causing the atoms to vibrate more and more, becoming hotter and hotter until the wire glows with the 'white heat' which we see as light. Once this knowledge was known, it was not long before Michael Faraday of England (of course) invented the first electric motor in 1821. He simply (!) placed a current-carrying wire between the poles of a magnet, and when the two magnetic fields met, they produced a force which turned the wire round. The rest is history!

Clever men! They applied their knowledge and wisdom to produce an invention which is of enormous benefit to mankind, to the extent that we could not imagine a world without electricity (although we would like to imagine a world without electricity bills!). Clever men, who utilised their intelligence to design a portable chemical source which can produce an electric current — called a BATTERY. Campers use them to read after lights-out, car owners depend on them to start the engine, heat the car, turn the windscreen wipers, illuminate the dark road and power the powered steering. Clever men.

And clever fish. Did you say fish? For sure — let me introduce you to the electric eel. Long before either Messrs. Faraday or Volta produced their invention, the unassuming eel, most common in South America (to the great relief of those living elsewhere!) can grow up to six feet in length, and can happily discharge up to 550 volts to anyone unfortunate enough to come into contact with it. That strength of electricity is twice the power that comes out of an electric socket, and is sufficient to stun a horse. The obvious question is, where does it obtain the power to produce such a shocking effect? The answer is amazing. About seven eighths of this fish is tail, with the internal organs crowded into a small space behind the head. The tail contains the electric organs, made up of between five and six thousand electroplates (elements) arranged like the cells in a dry battery. In reality, it has three batteries, two smaller ones and one main battery. One of the smaller batteries is at work continuously, sending out electric impulses at the rate of fifty per second. These impulses are used for direction-finding! The second small battery fires the larger battery, which gives out the high voltage discharges which make this eel so lethal. There you have it — the complete electronic fish. You will have noticed that this clever eel does not electrocute itself — obviously the electric organs are sufficiently insulated to cause the carrier no harm.

When the electric light was invented about one hundred years ago, it was hailed as a major advance in technology, and indeed it was. Now, night could be day, as light and as bright as a summer's day at noon. For us humans, it was significant advance indeed. However, the fish had them already! Some species of fish have been equipped with lights for attack, some for defence. The deep-sea Anglerfish has razor sharp teeth. Dangling over these charming teeth is a 'fishing rod', extending from the back of the fish with a light at the end of the rod. In the darkness of the lower regions, tempting prey are attracted by the shining light, like moths to a headlight, and by the time they come close it is too late to escape. Think of the technology that would be involved in coal-miners growing light bulbs out of their foreheads when going down the pits, and you have an idea of the complex design — way beyond human capability — that enables this almost mindless little fish to be a marine version of the Lady with the Lamp.

There is another harmless fish called the flashlight fish, so called because it has two light organs just beneath its eyes, like two headlamps. It only appears at night, and the lights are used to confuse attackers. When it sees an enemy approaching, the Flashlight fish swims in a straight line for a second, then switches off its light. At the same time, it changes direction and rushes away! During the 1967 Arab-Israeli war, the flashing lights of a group of these fish were mistaken for enemy frogmen, and were dynamited out of the water!

Clever are the men who discovered the power of electricity, and its numerous applications which benefit so many people. Fish, which are endowed with such sophisticated electronic machinery, yet know of nothing, are not clever, but clearly demonstrate brilliant design, and a brilliant Designer!

29

ℬ 'BY YOUR BLOOD YOU ℛ

ℬ SHALL LIVE' ℛ

Panic. *Pesach* was just a few days away, and the poor lady had omitted to order any *Matzos*. No ordinary *Matzos* would suffice, for her family were most particular and would eat only hand-baked *Matzos* produced in the big city far far away. No *Matzoh* bakery yet existed in their small town; all of the precious commodity had to be imported. The lady ran to the town's shop and asked the proprietor if he could help her in her hour of need. She was desperate! Listening patiently to her tale of woe, and blessed with a kind heart, he tried to sound sympathetic.

"I can try to contact the manufacturer and ask him to send some up, if you like."

The lady was immensely relieved.

"That's wonderful," she sighed. "When will it be here?"

The shopkeeper, famous for his ability to be always optimistic and cheerful, did not quite know how to break the news to the lady. He paused, reflecting on the likely reaction, and decided that in this instance, the stark truth was the only option.

"Approximately eight weeks Madam."

The lady looked dazed. Her face turned a delicate shade of very pale white, and she suddenly felt a great need to prop up the wall. She envisaged her family's delight in receiving *Matzos* shortly after *Shevuos* in contrast to their disappointment in not having any for *Pesach*, and shrieked:

"Eight weeks — why so long!"

The ever-patient shopkeeper, in his most amiable manner, began to explain.

"Well," he began, "The situation is like this. For a start, we have to find someone to take your message down to the big city. 280 miles is a long way when you have to walk. Even at twenty miles a day, that can take two weeks. And who knows what condition the fields will be in! It may be very muddy, not to mention the detours if there are bulls in the field. Then think of the way back. The journey from the big city to our village can be very arduous when you are pushing a wheelbarrow piled high with hand-baked *Matzos*. Much of the way is uphill, there are forests and hedges to negotiate, not to mention the wild animals of every description which might be lying in wait. Difficult and hazardous. I think quite honestly that eight weeks is quick!"

In case you think that the above description is exaggerated, it is not. Outdated yes, exaggerated not. That is the way it used to be some time ago. Before the age of the road, and later of the railway, few people ventured far from their village. Towns and villages had to supply most of their own food, clothes — and *Matzos*. Railways and improved road building changed all that. Uninhabited interiors of large continents were opened up, allowing new settlers to build farms. Towns grew larger and factories opened, as raw materials could be easily and speedily supplied, and even news travelled much faster because letters and newspapers now went by train. Think of the transport system now and your mind's eye will picture motorways with heavy lorries, transporters, articulated trucks, private cars and coaches hurrying along, each confident of reaching their destination in speed and comfort. In today's modern world, there is barely a location in the world that is not accessible by air and road.

"Madam — your *Matzos* will be here tomorrow!"

Indeed, a magnificent and efficient system.

Almost. Without wishing to be deprecatory, the whole transport system of the country is Lilliputian and archaic in comparison with that of the human body. When you are talking about the bloodstream, prepare to talk big! In each person's body, there are some 75,000 miles of route — more miles than there are rail tracks in

Great Britain, and more miles of route than a global airline — miles upon miles of tiny capillaries allowing the blood to deliver vital supplies to each and every one of the body's 60 trillion cells. (That is just 17,000 times the number of people there are on earth!) Apart from the hair, nails, outer layer of skin, (and the corneas of the eyes), there is no part of the body that is not served by the bloodstream.

Stand on a bridge which spans a busy motorway, and watch with fascination at the thousands of vehicles of all shapes and models whizzing along beneath you, each one travelling to a specific destination. It is a picture of organised movement, crowd and speed with a purpose, structured and disciplined, obeying the rules that have been enacted for the mutual safety and efficiency of all participants. The blood surging along the body's motorway system carries oxygen to the tissues, where the oxygen is used in energy-producing chemical processes. At the same time, the waste products of these processes are picked up by the blood and returned to the lungs to be breathed out. (The blood acts as delivery boy and refuse collector simultaneously. Could you imagine your refuse collector delivering your groceries and milk, or your postman emptying your dustbin into his spare sack?) But the variety of other merchandise delivered to the tissues is simply amazing, for the needs of each individual tissue or organ cell is different. One cell will require a minute quantity of cobalt, others will call for minerals, whilst others will need glucose, or fats, or amino acids — or simply a drink of water! The blood will carry hormones from the glands which produce them to the organs which use them, and distribute body heat evenly. The blood supply will faithfully deliver every individual cell its specific needs, even if under great pressure. After exercising, the cell requirement for just about everything increases enormously. Your skin will be flushed and red, indicating that the tiny capillaries are operating at full capacity. On the other hand, when you go to sleep, the food requirements of the cells becomes minimal, and over 90% of the capillaries close down for the night.

It is quite surprising that the total amount of blood required to service so many cells through such a huge amount of pipework is just about 9 pints for a man, and 8 pints for a woman. As the heart pumps, the blood surges through the arteries on their outward journey. The walls of the arteries are relatively thick to withstand the comparatively high pressure of the pumping action, and muscles built into the walls of the arteries (arterial muscles) contract and relax to control the flow of blood through them, ensuring that the blood arrives as a steady stream to all parts of the body. (Imagine a system built into the surface of motorways which automatically reduces the sped of vehicles travelling too fast — perhaps by emitting liquid glue!) By the time the blood enters the veins for the return journey to the heart, it is fairly sluggish and under less pressure. Accordingly, the walls of the veins are thinner than those of the arteries. Amazingly, some veins, particularly those in the lower limbs, have specially designed cup-shaped valves that close after each heartbeat, to prevent blood from flowing backwards. (The great height of the giraffe is very exciting to behold. It also demands an extremely high blood pressure to drive the blood up to the lofty head. On the other hand, when the animal drinks, its head is lowered seven feet below the level of its heart; a few seconds later it may again be lifted nearly 20 feet in the air. The blood supply is instantly controlled by a valve to prevent brain haemorrhage when the head is lowered, or sudden drain of blood when the head is rapidly raised. Special valve — special design — present also in humans!)

Blood — the wonder liquid — is composed of plasma and a mass of red and white blood cells and platelets. The plasma, a clear,

In your body there are 75,000 miles of capilleries, more miles than all the rail tracks in Britain!

amber liquid, makes up over 55% of blood, the cells and platelets make up the rest. A red cell is shaped like a round pillow, dented on each side. Red cells wear out in about 120 days. In the second that it takes you to blink, 1.2 million red cells will have reached the end of their 120 day span, and perish. In that same second, your marrow, mostly in your ribs, skull and vertebrae, produce an equal number of new cells. The red colour of the blood cells comes from a pigment called HAEMOGLOBIN. In the lungs, the blood picks up oxygen from the air breathed in, by forming a chemical compound between the oxygen and the haemoglobin. (In the human body nothing, but nothing, is simple!!) The haemoglobin is then responsible for transporting the oxygen to all the cells. These red cells then pick up the carbon dioxide and return the unwanted gas to the lungs for expulsion.

White blood cells are the body's defence forces, the 'fighting cells', and they defend the body against attacks by bacteria and other foreign substances. The road not only transports vital food materials, it carries the army as well! The tiny blood platelets are about a quarter the size of red blood cells, and have no colour. Platelets have the ability to clump together and release the miracle substance which makes the blood begin to clot. In this way they help the blood seal any tear which might occur in small blood vessels or in capillaries. Inside each individual, in constant movement around the advanced transport system long enough to stretch many times around the world, are an impressive array of food suppliers, waste disposers, armed forces trained to repel invaders, instant road repairers and conveyors of warmth — just a few of the incredible qualities of the wonder liquid — the liquid of life.

30

ᛋᚩ COUNTER-ESPIONAGE ᚳᚱ

They are everywhere, but you never know who they are. At this very moment they might be sitting in your own home, or in your office, or next to you on the bus. You never know, and their job is to ensure that you never will know. They look just like everyone else, innocent, unassuming and ordinary. And because they look so very ordinary, they are so perilous; pretending to be your good friend, your close associate, whilst all the time absorbing the vital information that you unwittingly divulge. Who are they? The spies in our midst.

Every country has them, every country denies having them, but they are everywhere. In your mind's eye you visualise a spy as being a surreptitious and furtive figure, with a floppy hat pulled down over his eyes and wearing a dirty raincoat with the lapels shadowing his face. In your innocence, you imagine that he is called Boris or Vladimir, and he does strange things like walk up to a letter-box, mutter some words into the opening in a strange tongue, after which a hand (foreign of course) reaches out of the letter-box, takes hold of the secret messages written in invisible ink, and disappears back into the box. You think that spies give themselves away by revealing their country of origin, like pouring vodka over their cornflakes, or wearing a heavy fur hat in the middle of August, or at the very least by trying to speak the local dialect in a thick East-European accent. That is what you imagine. The reality is of course that the most effective spies are those who are natives of the country whose secrets they seek to purloin. England, for example, has had its fair share of espionage agents, employed by foreign powers, who were born and bred in the British Isles, educated in the very best private schools, served in the armed forces and spoke with the most cultured accent that you could ever expect from a bowler-hatted brolly-carrying English gentleman. They were trusted and impeccably behaved, yet they were spies, traitors to their country.

Imagine that you are in charge of your country's counter-espionage operations, and it is your responsibility to detect and eliminate these foreign agents. How do you do it? You cannot go around suspecting everyone, you will soon have no friends! Where do you begin to look, who do you investigate, how do you know that at this very moment a nasty spy is not sitting in his basement, huddled under the table, broadcasting the country's most vital secrets into his transmitter! You have to find him — and quickly — HELP!

Look at the air around you. It looks empty enough, but looks are deceptive. In reality the air is swarming. Sound waves, radio waves, and millions of particles of dust fill the air, together with viruses, bacteria and germs. These unpleasant characters are constantly attempting to invade our own very personal country, our bodies, and make a take-over bid. No-one wants to scare you, but there are viruses (minute structures which are much less than a thousandth of a millimetre across, and invisible to the eye, they have no independent life and can only live in the cells that they infect); bacteria (microscopic single-celled organisms); fungi (minute plants which do not contain the green pigment which is present in leafy vegetation); and parasitic worms, (no details please!) — all of which are present all around us, and which are only too pleased to invade. Can you avoid these unpleasant guests? It is not so easy. In crowded places, people readily infect one another with their germs. When someone in a room sneezes, and omits to cover his sneeze with a handkerchief, thousands of droplets of moisture containing germs, shoot out of the man's mouth and nose. These droplets may travel up to 70 miles an hour, to a very wide radius. (The irony is that we then wish him a hearty 'Bless you' or *'Gesundheit'*. After kindly donating his germs far and wide, he should be wishing us!) A fly lands on a piece of food, and feeds for a few seconds. Before it feeds, it squirts saliva onto the food, which is likely to contain germs, besides the germs on the fly's feet. (They do not wash their feet before landing). A hygiene expert commented that if you would accompany a fly for a day, you would not eat food for a week! Infections (such as Athlete's foot) can be picked up from the floors of bathrooms and showers, and a host of germs can enter the skin simply as the result

212 / Designer World

of a scratch on the skin, or a fall on the ground. How do we detect these foreign invaders, and how do we combat the enemies in our midst!

Every country relies on a well-organised and efficiently run armed services. Professionals, people who know their job, and through their dedication and selflessness, allow the citizens of their country to live in peace and security. The armed services are highly trained, skilled, and recognise their enemies, and using the most advanced methods of communication, detection and sophisticated weaponry,

Brave soldier defending his country – but who will defend him from the dreaded invader – bacteria?

locate and eliminate the enemies from within. That takes some organisation, and the good citizens of the country fortunate enough to have such a force are rightly proud of their well-organised and well-trained troops. If so, every human being can be even more proud and impressed with the array of defence mechanisms with which his body has been provided, whose sophistication and wizardry makes the combined forces of all the major Super Powers seem like a posse of primitives in comparison!

Let us begin with the first line of defence — the skin. Think of germs as invaders, who try to colonise the land they have invaded. If the land on which they try to settle is constantly eroding and disappearing, and acidic as well, they would soon give up and go home. So it is that the skin provides the body's main protection against diseases. Because it is dry and slightly acidic, and its surface is constantly being replaced, invaders can rarely colonise the outer surface of the skin.

Before the 1860's, any operation, however minor, was a life-threatening experience. Many patients who had operations developed bacterial infections in their wounds, with the most severe consequences. In 1867, an English surgeon, Joseph Lister, discovered that if he sprayed the patient's wound with carbolic acid, it did not go septic, vastly reducing the numbers of casualties of operations. Antiseptics had arrived.

There is one area of the body that needs to be constantly clean — the eye. For that reason the eyelid has been designed to blink every few seconds at great speed, in order not to interfere with vision, and the lachrymal glands above each eye secrete tears which wash dust and dirt from the eyes. These tears contain an enzyme called lysozyme, which like all good antiseptics, destroys bacteria.

Every few seconds, without any conscious effort, and even against our will (see how long you can avoid blinking!) our eyes are bathed and cleansed with antiseptic fluid specially manufactured (again, without any conscious effort) by specialised factories which pump the precious fluid to the site (sight?) just millimetres away. And we think that antiseptic is a modern invention!

It is possible that the food that we take into our mouths can be contaminated with bacteria. Who will come to our assistance? Just thinking about food will 'make your mouth water'. That water is saliva, produced by specially designed salivary glands that are situated in the cheeks and under the tongue. (There are factories and pumps in your cheeks producing 1.5 litres of fluid per day? — yes indeed!) Besides water, saliva contains mucus (to make the food slippery so that it slides easily down the throat), amylase (an enzyme that begins to convert starch into sugar) and — most importantly in our context — a chemical which kills many germs, preventing them passing into the stomach. And we thought that antiseptic was a modern invention! If those germs managed to survive, once they arrive in the stomach they are immediately set upon by the acidic digestive juices (hydrochloric acid) which help to sterilise the food intake.

What about the bacteria which try to invade your nose and mouth — after all, it is difficult to control what you breath in. Be grateful for the very humble, but O so valiant mucous membrane. This is the soft moist tissue that lines the body openings and passages, such as the nose and the throat. It secretes mucus, a sticky fluid which provides protection against some bacteria. In the nasal cavities, the mucous membrane also catches germs and dust. In the vastly complicated wonderful machine called the human body, nothing is accidental! Next in the line of defence are the once much-maligned adenoids and tonsils, which stand like sentries at the entrance of the throat — they act as barriers to bacteria and viruses. Can you believe that doctors used to remove tonsils thinking them useless organs! Would you give your car to a mechanic who throws out bits of the engine because he does not understand their function?

What an impressive array of defence mechanisms, all of them co-ordinated and sophisticated and brilliantly designed. But is that all — what of the immunity systems and antibodies which we produce — wait, the story is just beginning.....

31

௸ THE QUEEN OF FRUITS ௸

This was the test. Until now it had been easy, with a scrumptious *Sheva Brochos* meal each evening. If only that week — with its carefully laid tables, co-ordinated serviettes and delicious food — could have lasted forever, but that magic week was over and it was now the moment of truth. It was the very first meal that the new *Kalloh* had to cook for her *Chosson*. He would be home that dinner time, expecting a grand meal from the grand cook he knew his wife to be. That's what he thought!

With feelings approaching panic, she unwrapped the many cookery books that she had received as wedding presents and spread them out in front of her. With pen in hand, she began to make notes. Remembering the Domestic Science lessons from her school days, she made three columns. Protein, Fats and Carbohydrates. Nervously, she added in brackets (water, vitamins & minerals). What was she going to give for protein — should it be sugar, and would brown be better than white, or perhaps bread would be preferable, but then she would have the same colour problem. And then there was the fats. Fats give energy, and it was now her onerous responsibility to choose the correct food. Should it be butter, or margarine. And if so,

"What shall I choose for his supper?"

would saturated be healthier than unsaturated. Oh dear — then there were the minerals to consider — sodium, calcium, phosphorus, iron, iodine, not to mention flourine — and she had to provide them and quickly! The paper in front of her was soon full of ideas, crossed out, corrected, with as many arrows as a stretch of roadworks on a motorway. The cookery books were strewn all over the table, and she looked like a pressurised professor about to complete a thesis.

Glancing nervously at the clock, she clutched her cluttered paper, and dashed to the shops. Whatever she wanted, "Sorry, we're waiting for it to come", and whatever she did not want was present in super-abundance. Time was pushing on, he would soon be home. Desperately dashing around the shelves, clutching a wire basket in one hand and her copious notes in the other, she made her harassed choice and hurried home. Soon the table was cleared, the cutlery set, and the flowers carefully placed in the vase. The great moment came, her husband arrived, and the meal was ceremoniously served. After the meal, the young man complimented his wife on the delicious repast, assuring her that he had never tasted such delicious baked beans and fried eggs in his life!

All her worrying was for nothing. She could so easily have chosen a single food, that contained all the nutrients essential for good health, a food that is readily available throughout the world (and nowadays throughout the year), a food which requires absolutely no preparation or problems of presentation, a single food which contained the very best of all solids and liquids, — the young wife should have gone out and bought a big bunch of grapes!

There are certain foods which are famous for their remarkable nutritional value. Most people would place milk on top of any list of such foods, and for good reason. Babies all look extremely contented, gurgling happily, and never complain of boredom, even though their diet is singularly milky. For months if not years, this wonder liquid sustains them and gives them all the nourishment that they require in a well-balanced regime. What surprises many people is that, what milk is to liquids, grapes are to solids; what milk is to babies, grapes are to adults. It has been claimed, (and tried and tested), that a person can live on a diet of fresh, well-washed ripe and sweet grapes, without additional food of any description, for several weeks, and not only be perfectly healthy, but actually be in a much better state of health than he was before.

When you look at a grape, all you see is a rather large berry. There is nothing in its appearance to indicate that it contains a long list of beneficial nutrients, together with enough kindly chemicals to fill a shelf in the chemist shop. These chemicals are a perfect solvent, and the fruit must be regarded for what it is — a medicine! They will dissolve all foreign matter in the body without harming healthy tissue. Secondly, the chemicals act as an eliminator. Provided that most of the skins and some of the pips are eaten, constipation is almost impossible. Thirdly, these chemicals are an antiseptic. This has been proved when pure fresh grape juice was diluted with 50% boiled water, and applied to an open wound. Cleansing and healing was far quicker than most remedies. As the grape chemicals destroy foreign matter in the body, they also heal wounds.

If you would ask why it should be that the grape has such remarkable healing powers, the answer would be that there is no other fruit which has such a concentration of elements with such nutritive value and therapeutic action. Perhaps it is no coincidence that the very first act that every Jewish person performs when *Shabbos* arrives, is to take a cup of the juice of grapes, and testify that *Hashem Yisborach* created the world. *Shabbos* is the day of the week that purifies its observer, and through its therapeutic value, eliminates any impurities that six days of weekday might have absorbed. The day that purifies and rejuvenates is introduced by the very liquid (perhaps the only liquid) that has those identical properties. Quite something!

Hikers and climbers are always urged to include chocolate amongst their emergency supplies, because chocolate, with its high sugar content is an ideal source of energy. Look at the grape — its nutritive power is due to the presence of sugars, in a higher percentage than in any other fruit. These sugars (glucose and fructose) are easily assimilated and burn rapidly, giving a speedy source of energy, and vitality to exhausted organisms. We haven't finished yet! No less important than the sugar are the therapeutic properties of other components of the grape — which include all the vitamins from A to C (Vitamin A, Thiamin, Riboflavin, Vitamin C, B1, B6, B12). Add to this the presence of potassium, sodium calcium, phosphorus and iron, besides the beneficial action that the ferments have on the regularity of digestive functions, and you begin to understand what there is to get excited about. It is claimed that the grape is the perfect aid to healing, and certainly one of the purest foods that you can eat, enabling the body gradually to purify and heal through its own automatic mechanism. So pure and perfectly balanced are the chemicals in the grape, that it is impossible for the fruit to go bad. This chemical reaction just cannot take place! Instead, it dehydrates and becomes a raisin, which will keep for unlimited periods. It is only when the tough skin is punctured that fermentation takes place, and the fruit looks mildewed.

Just look at a bunch of grapes. Black, glistening, each grape a handy-size to pop in and swallow, refreshing, juicy, satisfying and nutritious. They are conveniently packed, of ideal size, last for days

The Queen of Fruits / 221

Just a bunch of grapes – but it contains enough kindly chemicals to fill a shelf in the Chemist shop.

(no 'best by' date necessary) and can be eaten with the packaging on. When you want some more, just take a pip, plant it in the ground and grow hundreds more of the precious fruit at no expense. Imagine that when your car begins to grow old, and wheezingly and rustingly shows signs of its age, you could open the bonnet, remove one of its oil-stained spark plugs and plant it in the ground. Return in about six months, and there in front of your very eyes is a field of Land-Rovers growing in your vineyard. Extraordinary? Why, it happens all the time to the grape, as with all fruits. Take another look, how this bundle of gold just pours out of the slenderest of stems.

Perhaps the most amazing aspect of the grape (and all of its many relations) is the fact that the ingredients of this wonder fruit are the very humble soil, sun and rain. Would you, or could you, for today's project take some earth, add a measure of rain and sunshine, and produce the most beneficial food, pleasing to the eye, the palate, and simply saturated with pure goodness! That is indeed some design!

In case all of that was not sufficient, we also know that the skins of grapes contain natural yeast, which react with the sugars of the fruit (yeasts — microscopic fungi which grow naturally on the grape skins — convert the sugar content of the juice into alcohol and carbon dioxide gas, which is given off as bubbles) to produce a liquid which is guaranteed to gladden the heart. This most nutritious of foods can be converted into liquid form which can consecrate, sanctify, add lustre to any grand occasion, accompany every happy event, and is available in different colours and flavours, and improves in flavour as it increases in age.

You don't have to be a *Kalloh* — anyone who wishes to benefit from the most precious of pure and natural foods, turn to the Queen of Fruits, *Hashem*'s gift to mankind.

32

෨ LONG MAY SHE RAIN ര

Poor mother had a problem. She was an accomplished cook, a loving parent, adept in presenting tasty and delectable meals, but junior refused to eat. Fussy was just not the word. It was more like a major battle each meal-time to induce him, beg and implore him, to ingest some nourishment. The strange thing was that he constantly complained of being starving — "Mum, I'm starving!" — but when she eagerly sought to satisfy his hunger, his stubborn streak overcame him. He liked nothing, and the little that he took was eaten begrudgingly with the greatest reluctance. Mother was worried, and with good reason. If he didn't eat he would not grow, to be strong and healthy. Mothers know best — he just had to eat! By dint of her tenacious efforts and insistence, he grew, and as he grew bigger and older he gained sense and appetite. Once, in an honest moment, he confessed that the reason he had demonstrated such revulsion to food as a child was perfectly simple. He hated the inconvenience of eating! Eating meant sitting, and sitting meant no play and no fun, so it was easier to refuse food!

People are funny. Can you imagine loving someone very much, and wanting to give them a present. The present that you have in mind is no ordinary present, not a bunch of flowers or yet another box of chocolates. The present that you are desirous of giving is one which will sustain them and revitalise them, nourish them and refresh them. It is the most valuable commodity known to man, and in the greatest demand. Yet when you give it to them, they spurn it and reject it, abuse it and insult it. Instead of thanking you profusely, they ridicule it and revile it. If they had none of it, they would begrudgingly admit, just about, that they could do with some, but soon after receiving it they would again begin to insult it, calling it nasty, bad, terrible and rotten. What is this great present — RAIN!

What is it that makes perfectly intelligent people behave like spoilt little children? Our Parent and loving Guardian wishes us to live, grow and flourish. He wants to bestow His nourishment and refreshing sustenance upon us — and just because it is wet, we behave like the above-mentioned precocious horror who sulks and throws himself on the floor, kicks the furniture and beats his tiny fists on the lino. "Don't like rain, I don't want rain, why can't the sun shine all the time!" And our weather forecasters reinforce this prejudiced manner of thinking by announcing in a cheerful voice that the south should receive the best of the weather (sunshine), but, (noticeable downturn in voice intonation) rain will spread to all parts by nightfall. 'Bad weather' is synonymous with rain, 'Nasty day' means it is raining, 'The weather was terrible' means it rained, and 'What a rotten summer' means a summer which was blessed with an abundance of rain. Why is this the normal reaction? Perhaps it is because people do not understand what rain precisely is, and the wonder of its blessing. Or perhaps it is because it is wet!

The fact that we are able to have a bath, wash the car, drink lemonade, wear clean clothes, boil an egg, cook food, sprinkle the lawn, irrigate the fields, and wash *Negel Wasser* (not to mention *Mayim Acharonim*) and a myriad of activities vital to life is based on an amazing fact. The oceans of the world hold ninety-seven per cent of the world's water. Two per cent is frozen in the polar ice caps. The remaining one per cent not only provides all the water that we use, but also includes all the lakes and rivers in the world, all the water in the atmosphere and all the water in the ground! We depend on the constant re-cycling of that one per cent of water to meet all our needs. Perhaps even more shocking is the knowledge that all the water in the world's atmosphere only equals about ten day's normal rainfall. You can imagine that if water was something we used up like gas or oil, then the world would run dry very quickly indeed. Thanks to the water cycle, water does not get used up, it simply goes round and round.

'Simply' is perhaps the wrong word, for the rain cycle, like everything in the designed and created world on which life depends, is far from simple. The oceans of the world cover over seventy per cent of our planet's surface. When the sun shines on this vast surface, it turns some of it into water vapour, which rises into the sky to form clouds. There you are, isn't that simple? Not when you realise

Who said rain was nasty?

what exactly a cloud is! Why should water vapour suddenly turn into a cloud? The interesting answer is that air contains millions of microscopic particles of dust. When moist air rises, expands and cools, any water vapour it contains condenses (turns back into a liquid) onto the surface of those dust particles. This forms minute water particles which group together to make clouds. Remember — when you drink a glass of ice-cold water, you are really drinking a cloud! Take a look out of the window, peer at the clouds and thank *Hashem Yisborach* for dust! As the tiny droplets in the cloud collide, they join together, forming large droplets. Gradually the droplets increase in size until they are too heavy to be kept up in the cloud by air currents, and they then fall as raindrops. Each drop is a wonder, and every puddle is a blessing.

When the clouds blow across the land, and the temperature falls, the vapour forms into water droplets, which fall as rain. But why should the clouds which are formed above the oceans move at all? Why don't they all empty out directly above the place where they were formed — what makes those clouds move? Again, we turn to a wonder of creation. The earth is constantly spinning on its axis, and this spin guarantees that the air around the world is on the move all the time. The wavy paths and uneven speeds of the winds disrupts the air around and below them, creating areas of low and high pressure, which in turn causes movement of air from areas of high pressure to low pressure. Blow along, you clouds, evidence of the great driving force of wind, without which we would have no water, and no water means no life. Clouds — wind — water — life!

And water, precious water, is a remarkable liquid. Water is a combination of two atoms of hydrogen and one atom of oxygen. Each of those two gases cannot alone sustain or feed us, yet, remarkably they combine together to form the wonder-liquid. Water is the only substance we know which can be a solid, a liquid, and a gas all under normal conditions of temperature and pressure. Would this not be so, the water vapour in the air would never condense to form clouds, snow would not fall in the winter, and even if it snowed, it would never melt. The fact that we enjoy rain in all seasons, is a blessing not to be ignored. Although the oceans are full of salty water which is undrinkable, remarkably the water which vaporises into the atmosphere is pure. It has no colour and no smell, and is the perfect cooking companion to hundreds of food products. (Imagine a *Shabbos* without water. You could not make *Gefillte* fish, chicken soup, boiled chicken, *kugel*, *tzimmes*, meat, ice-cream, egg & onion, *cholent*, potato-salad, not to mention *challoh* and wine; and without a *Shabbos* urn, no revitalising cup of coffee or a glass of tea.) We cook with it, bathe in it, two-thirds of us is composed of it, it regulates our body temperature, it moves waste products out, it carries oxygen to body parts, it helps to digest our food, and lubricates our joints. Without water we would have no clothes to wear, books to read, or beds to sleep in. Cows depend on it (your average Miss Daisy drinks 90 litres of water each day) cars depend on it (the production of one car requires 15 cubic metres of water, and that is before you fill the radiator and the windscreen wash) and every aspect of industry relies thirstily on it. (In Britain alone, industry uses over 1,000 million gallons of the wonder liquid EACH DAY!) And then when we have finished with it, we perform the ultimate wonder of pouring it down the drain where it dutifully returns to the sea to begin the cycle once again! And people call rain nasty??

Perhaps the greatest wonder of all occurs every winter. Everyone who ever feels the top of the hot water-tank to ascertain if there is sufficient water for a bath knows that warm water rises. If so, in all lakes, the warm water should rise to the surface, whilst the colder water should sink to the depths. This in fact happens. Logically therefore, as the temperature reaches freezing point, ice should form from below. If water followed the laws of logic, all lakes would freeze from beneath, gradually forcing the fish to swim in an ever-decreasing volume of non-frozen water above, until the lake was frozen solid, and the fish would become ice-skaters. Result — end of the fish population. Fortunately for them, the water follows the laws of the Creator, who commanded the life-saving law that at 4 degrees Centigrade everything goes into reverse. As the water dips beneath that critical temperature, it becomes less dense, causing it to rise. The cold water is now at the surface of the lake, and the warmer water below. This remarkable fact ensures that ice forms at the surface of the lake, leaving the water below a running liquid, well-insulated, and swimmable. The fish can live!

The Designer of our world wants us to enjoy water, and have an abundance of it. We have been given springs, rivers, bore holes (underground porous rock, which like giant sponges, fill up with water), and wells, all of which are the natural vessels to hold that most precious of all liquids, the liquid sunshine which will never again be taken for granted, the magnificent gift of rain.

33

ಬ UNDERNEATH ಜ

ಬ THE ARCHES ಜ

The atmosphere was relaxed. The wedding guests had eaten well, the food had been delicious and plentiful, and the band, together with the dancing had been both musical and lively. *Chosson* and *Kalloh* looked happy and pleasantness pervaded the hall. The chairman of the evening, the gentleman whose responsibility it was to set the tone and introduce the speakers, rose to speak. Discreet tapping on the glass with a fork soon brought the guests to a respectful (?) silence. Mindful of his great responsibilities of having to please everyone and offend no-one, the chairman began by explaining why he had been chosen for such an awesome task. Having now justified his existence, he then explained that the *Baal Simchoh* had asked him to thank various people for their invaluable contribution to the night's big *Simchoh*. Although it would be totally wrong to mention people by name, it would nevertheless be totally remiss of him not to mention certain people by name! He thanked the uncles and aunts who had made the great effort to travel long distances to be at the *Simchoh*, the friends and relations who had given up an evening to participate in the *Mitzvoh* of making *Chosson* and *Kalloh* happy; he thanked the caterer for the beautiful presentation and delectable food; the band for their talented performance. With a flourish, he then said:

"With your permission I would like to thank someone who very rarely receives thanks or recognition, but without whom tonight's *Simchoh* could not have taken place."

People's attention was aroused. Who could it possibly be? The Chairman paused for dramatic effect, and said,

"I would like to express our most grateful thanks to Messrs. Smith and Peabody, the firm who designed and built this hall, without whom we would not be sitting here tonight."

The reaction was mixed. Some people laughed, some looked blank, and the vast majority thought that they had not understood the joke.

Had he been joking? Imagine that someone was proposing a vote of thanks for the various parts of the body which help us in life.

The important organs would be obvious, and the thanks profound. If the man would say "I would now like to offer my sincerest thanks for a part of the body which is often overlooked, shamelessly neglected, but without which I would not be standing here today — I am referring of course to my feet!" — would you think he was being funny? Nothing could be more serious, or the thanks more deserved. Let us see why.

Everyone remembers a childhood favourite toy — the spinning top. A large circular sphere with a metallic rod running through the middle, which slumped ungainly to one side when at rest, gained poise and majesty when made to spin around. Balanced on a small piece of metal, it whirled round to the accompaniment of a pleasant musical hum. When the momentum dissipated, the spinning top once again toppled to one side. Why is the spinning top unable to remain erect and stable whilst at rest, or a pear unable to stand upside down on a table, whereas a man, of not dissimilar shape, is perfectly capable of standing on his own two little feet with the greatest of ease? Nothing could be more erroneous than to imagine that balancing a six-foot 180 pound pile of flesh and bone on two size-ten soles is a simple matter. Each foot is a highly complex piece of machinery, and an anatomical wonder, containing no less than 26 bones (one quarter of all your bones are to be found in your feet) together with 107 ligaments and 19 muscles. Are you impressed by jigsaw puzzles? Do you admire the design, the pretty pictures and the skill of the person who fitted the many pieces together? Here you have a jigsaw, composed of many tiny pieces, which fit beautifully together, but does not sit on a table gathering dust, but which actually works, moves, flexes and supports. You cannot go too far in life without your feet, and they are deserving of the greatest admiration.

The structure of the foot is a technical masterpiece. The shape of an arch is ideal for supporting weight. When force, or weight is applied, the rounded shape transmits that force in all directions away from the point of contact. For that reason, the arch is so frequently utilised in supporting roads, bridges, and in the construction of dams. (The Hoover Dam on the Colorado River is 577 feet high and relies on its weight and its arched-shape to hold back some 38 billion tons of water.) In precisely the same way, each foot is constructed in the shape of a three-dimensional arch with the three main points of support at the heel, the base of the big toe and the base of the little toe. (Have a look at your wet footprint in the bathroom and you will see the evidence.) The arches of the foot are formed by the shape of the bones, by the ligaments which hold them together, and by muscle action. By all means, go ahead and admire the Hoover Dam — it's a pretty good analogy of the design and Designer of the foot. But the foot goes further. The shape of the dam and the arched-bridge is solid and inflexible. Not so the foot! In the standing position, the weight of the body locks the bones of the foot together and the ligaments which connect them are under pressure. The foot is then a solid arch. When you walk and run, the weight is suddenly released from the arches, the bones unlock, and the foot becomes a flexible, active spring, which absorbs shocks and adapts to uneven ground.

And what shocks! Each person walks something like 65,000 miles during his lifetime. Let us imagine that you are walking down the road at a comfortable 100-steps-a-minute pace. That means that your foot is hitting the cement with a 180 pound jolt 50 times each minute, and your other foot is doing the same. That means tens of millions of bangs on the foot — the great wonder is that the foot does not collapse entirely. Have you ever watched a pneumatic drill? It hammers into the ground with infernal noise and power, and were it not for the powerful thick springs which absorb the shuddering shocks, the machine would break into pieces. Such is the amazing construction of the foot — weight-lifter and shock-absorber extraordinary. Experts in the field strongly advocate walking barefoot (wherever possible) as the biggest favour you can do to your feet, certainly to allow babies to be barefoot for as long as possible. In quite the same way, they recommend buying shoes that are sensible and fit the foot rather than the fashion. They really work up a lot of steam when describing the folly of females who strut around on much-too-high heeled shoes, pitching the weight forward where it does not belong, throwing the spine out of balance, shortening the calf muscles, deforming the tendons and making it difficult and painful to stand even barefoot!

Those who take an interest in car design cannot have failed to notice the increasing popularity of four-wheel-drive vehicles. Sturdy, sporty, with strong but rugged contours, they are the ideal vehicles for those who have to drive through rough terrain, (or for those who wish to give the impression that they are, like their cars, sturdy, sporty, strong and rugged!) Go anywhere, be independent, they are the embodiment of modern man. And your feet, do they not do the same? Does the wonderful gift of walking not deserve the greatest respect? The profound skill involved in walking is perhaps best illustrated by the amount of time it takes a young child to master the art. And for good reason. Every time you take a step, you are actually thrusting yourself forward out of balance. Vulnerable as you are on one foot, and toppling forward, there is no reason why you should not fall on your face, were it not for the fact that you have quickly positioned your moving foot to halt the falling motion, and so it continues. When your walk breaks into a run, you are actually performing mini-leaps into thin air before a foot is placed onto the ground to provide the impetus for another leap. Every single step demands precise co-ordination between the eyes (to know where to go) the brain (to send the messages through the nervous system) the muscles (to move the legs, ankles and feet) the balance mechanism (to maintain the body in an upright position) — and each component in turn is composed of millions of individual parts whose sophistication is beyond our comprehension. Messages fly back and forth from the brain. Sensor spots in your soles report on the pressure situation — orders come back — tighten this muscle, relax that one, flex the toes, relax the toes, push this leg forward, that one back... running, strolling, hopping, skipping, jumping, climbing,

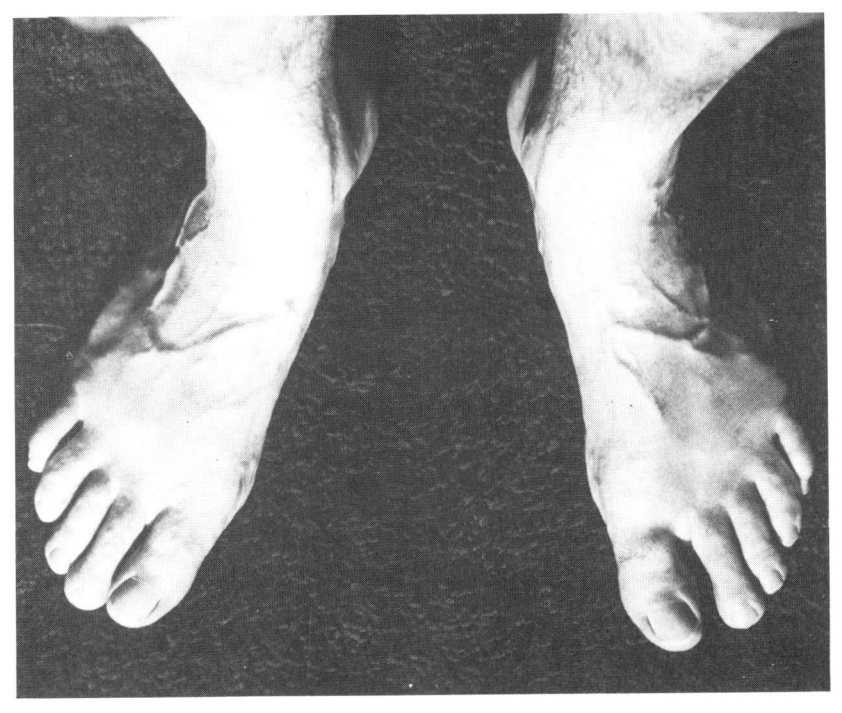

"Go anywhere, rugged, strong, runs on any fuel, never goes rusty – your trusty feet."

chasing, racing, pacing... each in turn is a skill which embodies wonders beyond belief. Go anywhere, be independent, rugged, strong, runs on any fuel, never goes rusty, reaches places that no four-wheel drive could ever go (like up the stairs in your own home) — that's your feet!

If you ever have trouble wondering what to be grateful for, just run up and down the stairs, that should give you enough to think and thank about for a few years! By all means, Mr Chairman, stand up and offer your thanks for the design and construction of the hall. It might sound strange, but that does not matter — and let us all in turn offer our sincerest thanks for something that we should never take for granted — our own two feet.

34

๛ THE REAL FACTS ༄

A visit by Great-Grandpa was always eagerly awaited. A man of wisdom and enriched by a life's experiences, he would never fail to fascinate the children with his tales of, what to them sounded like events from the Middle Ages. The children, on the other hand, greatly enjoyed observing his reaction, ranging from amazement to disbelief, to the modern appliances which filled their home. It was evident that he had only recently been introduced to the modern world and its inventions, so archaic was his conception of technology. (Such things are not so unlikely. A 101-year old lady recently flew by plane for the very first time. She was travelling by Concorde from England to Canada to see her great-grandchildren. Her reaction was, as expected, incredulous. When she was born, it was four years before Orville Wright made the first powered flight, in a machine made from canvas and wire, flying a distance of 852 feet. Now, in her hinge-nosed supersonic airliner, she was whistling through the air at more than 1,000 mph, crossing the Atlantic in under three hours. Her reaction? "If only my mother and father could see me now...")

No sooner had the illustrious visitor arrived and was comfortably seated in the armchair, than the telephone rang. Great-grandchild picked up the cordless phone and walked around the room chatting happily to her brother. The senior gentleman watched, transfixed. The conversation at an end, she pressed the appropriate button and returned the telephone to its cradle.

"Do you often speak to yourself?" he asked her.

"Of course not, great-grandpa, I was talking to my brother."

"You were talking to your brother through a piece of plastic?" he asked with rising disbelief, "Where does he live?"

She laughed:

"Don't you remember — he lives in *Eretz Yisroel*!"

The revered gentleman sat, silent. Here was a child, standing in the middle of her living room in England, clutching a piece of plastic in one hand with absolutely no wires attached, not even very thin ones, and holding a conversation with her brother who was at that very moment in *Eretz Yisroel*! He felt faint at the thought. Looking around, he saw another of his young relatives writing a letter, to the same brother. Letters, now that was something he understood. After all, the postal system was as old as the hills. After a while, the letter was completed, and the young writer stood up.

"Are you going out to post the letter now, young lad?" asked great-grandpa.

"Oh great-grandpa — you are so funny! we don't post letters any more, we send them by fax!"

Elter Zeide slumped in his chair.

"Fax? Who is he?"

The child understood the problem, and said,

"Come on, I'll show you how we send letters through the fax machine."

In a daze of disbelief, but prepared for anything, he accompanied his young charge to the slim plastic box with the buttons on, which lay so innocuously on the sideboard.

With rapt fascination, he watched how the paper was fed into the machine, buttons pressed, interesting sounds emitted, and how the paper entered the machine from above and exited from below. With a flourish, the boy extracted the paper and declared to his mesmerised observer that his brother now had the letter.

"But that's impossible — you're holding it in your hand!"

He really did not believe this. He was accustomed to a letter to *Eretz Yisroel* taking a week at the very least, and here was someone holding a letter which he had just written, telling him that the letter was already in Israel!! What was this amazing machine that could perform such wonders! The young boy began to explain.

240 / Designer World

First of all, the fax (facsimile transmission) machine is not all that new. In 1907 a photo from Paris was wired to a London newspaper. What happens is quite simple. As you feed the document into the machine, it moves across a light source, usually a fluorescent tube. Light from the tube is reflected off the document, and passed by mirrors through a lens onto a device which is made up of thousands of tiny cells that convert the light into electric currents. The voltage of the current varies according to the light that each cell detects. These varying voltages are converted into digital signals which are sent along the telephone wires. When the signals arrive at their destination, they are separated from the general electric current, and

"What is this machine that can perform such wonders?"

fed to a printer that re-creates the document in a chain of dots built into lines. It's as simple as that!

"Simple?" said the venerable sage, "You call that simple — I have never heard of anything so remarkable in all my life!"

The boy was right. The fascinating fax, brilliantly designed and remarkable though it may be, is simple when compared to the system of communication that exists in the human body in the form of the nervous system. The main job of the nervous system is to carry messages from one part of the body to the other. Every single action that a person takes, that is either voluntary, such as walking, talking, eating; or involuntary, such as the heartbeat, the digestive system or breathing, is only possible because of a chain of reactions in the body and the nervous system. Although we are not aware of it, every movement of the legs in walking, each movement of the fingers to grasp a pencil, needs specific instructions from the brain to the nerves in the area concerned.

Let us take an everyday example, a man wishes to lift up a glass of water to take a drink. First, the eyes provide the brain with a visual impression of the glass. The motor part of the brain instructs the body to move forward towards the table. The motor area positions the hand and the arm, and shifts the rest of the body to maintain balance. Messages have been flashing from the brain down the spinal cord to subsidiary nerve centres serving the arms, and from there the message is transmitted along a series of nerves to the fingertips. On the way to the fingertips, the signal triggers off other actions in the arm and wrist. The arm lifts and reaches out, the wrist turns and the fingers close round the glass and grip it. As the fingertips touch the glass, information is sent back to the sensory area of the brain. When the fingers have exerted enough pressure to hold the glass (this information has been gained from previous experience and is stored in the memory bank. Without this memory a person would simply continue to exert pressure on the glass until it smashed!) — a message flashes to the brain saying that the hand is ready to lift. Within thousandths of a second, another message from the brain shoots down the nerve pathways of the arm and hand, instructing the hand to lift the glass to the mouth. Eyes and fingers tell the brain that the glass is tilting, and the brain instructs the wrist to correct this. Sense receptors in the lips and previous experience tell the brain when the glass reaches the mouth, and the brain sends a message back post haste, telling the mouth to open and the head to tilt back. (The water descends the food pipe. It is important that it does not enter the windpipe. This is prevented by the epiglottis, a small flap of skin stiffened with gristle. When we swallow, the epiglottis descends to close off the wind pipe. Just a small feature of special design, powered by the nervous system, without which we could not survive the very first meal.)

Just picture the fastest *Ba'al Koreh* you know *leining* through *Sefer D'vorim* on the night of *Hoshanoh Rabboh*. As your eyes skim along the page, trying to keep up with him, you calculate that he must be saying several words per second. His eyes are relating the visual information of the *Sefer Torah* to his brain which in turn is flashing messages by the thousand through the nervous system to the various muscles controlling his eyes (flicking from side to side, each eye controlled by six separate muscles, yet both eyes working together to focus on the same object!) tongue, palate, vocal cords, (just think of the acrobatics which these organs perform in order to change shape several times each second — each single movement the result of a specific message from the brain, through the nervous system to a specific muscle) breathing mechanism, all of which have to work in perfect co-ordination to ensure that he will be asked the next year!

And if you think that the passing of messages (or impulses) through the nerves is as simple as passing an electric current through a wire, consider this. Nerve fibres, (the wires) are composed of cell membranes. When the cells are inactive, they act as an insulation barrier between two groups of electrically charged atoms, or ions, — potassium ions in the nerve fibre, and sodium ions in the fluid outside it. When a nerve cell is stimulated, the structure of the cell membrane changes and allows potassium ions to flow out of the cell and sodium ions to flow in. This movement of ions sets up a tiny electrical current, which is the nerve impulse. The current builds up at the nerve endings, and when there is enough current, it fires the next cell, then the next, until the signal reaches the brain. A single nerve fibre can transmit about 1000 separate impulses each second, with a pause between each. That means that each second the nerve cell is changing its structure, with potassium and sodium flowing in and out, one thousand times!

We have not begun to comprehend the complexity of the nervous system. The little that we have looked at is a series of electro-chemical wonders that are essential for every action big or small. Great-grandpa was right — the fax is truly amazing, but let us understand our very own facts, and understand how great are the works of *Hashem Yisborach*.

35

ॐ SMALL IS BEAUTIFUL ॐ

Have you ever looked at an old family photograph? Although every family group is different, in one respect they are virtually the same. No-one smiles. Many interesting theories have been postulated for the seriousness of the people posing. One theory speculates that life one century ago was indeed much more serious, and people simply did not smile so readily. Perhaps, and perhaps not. Another, more plausible suggestion is that whereas in our age a camera is an everyday possession, and photographs are taken of every age and stage of life, in previous times a family photograph was a rare — perhaps once in a lifetime-event, certainly not to be taken flippantly. The portrait for posterity had to be dignified and formal. The third and most likely possibility for the seriousness of the pose can only be understood when you know how photographs were taken in those early days. Perhaps you remember? Cumbersome, massive, black structures were placed on heavy tripods, and intricate preparations had to be performed, with heavy photographic plates carefully inserted, before the intrepid operator disappeared beneath his black cloth calling out muffled instructions to remain immobile until the given signal, which was either a little birdie calling cuckoo, or a terrifying flash accompanied by bellowing yellow smoke, causing the immobilised (more likely petrified) customers to wonder if they would ever see the photographer again. Bearing in mind the length of time and the element of the unexpected in their ordeal, is it any wonder that smiling was the last thing on their agenda?

Some idea of the size of cameras in those days can be gained from the Chicago Railway Company in the USA, which wanted to photograph a luxury train in the year 1900. The camera they used was twelve feet (four metres) in length, travelled in its own railway carriage, and required six men to operate it. Today, anyone can go into a camera shop, and purchase a video-recorder which can do anything except make a cup of tea, and which will fit snugly into your pocket. (The camera, not the tea.)

Technology has advanced so rapidly that very little surprises us. Do you have a digital watch, a washing machine, or an electronic calculator — perhaps as an integral part of your watch? All of them owe their phenomenal capabilities to the advent of the silicon chip. Within an area no bigger than a shirt button, a microchip can hold as many as 450,000 electronic components. These are linked into electric circuits and are visible only under the microscope. Tiny microchips have transformed modern life, and have enabled some of the science fiction of the past to become reality. They regulate digital watches, and set programs on washing machines. Have you ever heard of 'Killer bees' of Brazil who migrate north and destroy domestic honeybees? Scientists have captured some of these bees and glued microchips with infra-red transmitters to their backs, in order to study the bees' movements to try and control migration. And the same microchips fit into cameras, enabling the computerised machines to focus themselves, set their own controls, and wind on the film after each shot. No fuss, no mess, and everyone smiles.

And why should we not smile? Everything these days is so well-designed, efficient, and a technological marvel. Computers that used to fill a room now sit on your lap. Everything is compact and marvellous. Just like insects have always been. Insects? Did you say insects? Keep those things away! Just wait a moment — the next time a tiny insect lands on the table in front of you, before you chase it away, have a look, and a think about what is before your very eyes. It is true that some insects are very large (tropical stick insects are up to thirty-three cms — that is more than twelve inches — from end to end) but must insects are tiny (the average length of fairyflies is as little as 0.21 mm). It is true that some insects are heavy, very heavy (the massively armoured Goliath Beetle of Africa is the heaviest beetle in the world and one of the largest flying insects. They come at six inches long and weigh up to 100 g. which is 3.4 ozs and good enough reason never to go to Africa) but most insects are as light as air. It is true that some spiders would happily cover a dinner place (no details, please!) but most are tiny little scampering things. And every single insect, from small to minute, are masterpieces of technological design and equipment. They certainly deserve a closer look.

We tend to think of our eyes as wonderfully efficient cameras, and indeed they are. But our eyes are simple when compared to the compound eyes of insects. Insect eyes are called compound because each is made up of thousands of tiny simple eyes. Dragonflies, for example, strike with deadly accuracy, guided by enormous compound eyes, each containing as many as 30,000 separate lenses. Each single lens is six-sided, and consists of two lenses, one on the surface, the second conical lens inside. These focus the light down a central structure, which is connected directly to the optic nerve and the brain. Every single one of those lenses reflects a slightly different view of the world, allowing the little flying machine to accurately detect even the tiniest movements, making it extremely difficult to catch. At night, bright lights attract many insects. It seems that night-flying insects navigate by keeping the natural light of the moon at a constant angle to their eyes. An artificial light is treated in the same way; the insects fly towards the light in a straight line, but when they reach it they circle it continuously. The eyes of many insects register things that human cannot see. We see in natural light, but not in ultra-violet light. What we see as yellow, an insect may see as grey. Many insect-pollinated flowers rely on ultraviolet vision to attract pollinating bees. The position of the nectar within the flowers is indicated by lines called 'honey guides' (like landing lights on an airport runway) which are visible only in ultraviolet light. It is when you begin to investigate that you see the spectacular design.

Although most insects have eyes, sight is often less important to them than smells and tastes in understanding the world around them. Ants lay down a chemical trail, and constantly touch each other to pass on the odour. This insect world of smells and tastes also includes vibrations and sounds undetected by humans. Such vibrations can be detected either by well-formed ears (the front legs of crickets have a small swelling just beneath their knee, this is their ear, and like the human eardrum, is extremely sensitive to sound vibrations) or through their antennae. Do not under-estimate the wonder of these long slender hair-like antennae which protrude from the front of insects — they are too wonderful for words. Could you imagine possessing a sense of smell so sensitive that on *Shabbos Kodesh* you could detect a good *Cholent* cooking one hundred miles away? The Emperor Moth (male version) has antennae which are so sensitive that they can detect the special chemical scent that is produced by the female at a distance of several miles! If you examine the magnified antennae of a butterfly, you will see that the surface is covered with intricate patterns containing thousands of scent-sensitive hairs. A scent-sensitive hair — you try and make one of those! Even the hairs on an insect's body are anything but simple. Each hair from around the mouth of a carpet beetle larva has its own 'ball and socket' joint at the base (like an arm in a shoulder) and ridged sides, making them extremely sensitive to vibrations!

How does a fly land on a vertical surface, or even upside down? (No plane has yet been invented that can do that). Why do flies always seem to be cleaning themselves with their feet? The answer is that flies are covered in hairs which must be cleaned and groomed regularly if the insect is to fly effectively. The feet of the housefly have special sucker-like pads between their claws like plastic cling-film which enable the insect to walk upside-down on smooth surfaces. (I wonder how they managed to survive the terrible falls they must have suffered during the countless aeons that 'the world' claims it took the flies to develop their suction pads! The next time you need to change a light bulb, try walking up the wall and along the ceiling — you might begin growing suction pads between your toes!) There is an interesting creature called a desert-dwelling cricket which has feet shaped like propellers. This amazing shape is specifically designed to allow it to dig a hole in the sand directly beneath it and

A dragonfly's enormous compound eyes, each containing as many as 30,000 separate lenses

disappear in a matter of seconds — straight down. The wings of this disappearing insect are kept coiled like a spring to keep them out of the way whilst descending. Another little beetle, the rove beetle, can zoom across the surface of water in an emergency. Special glands at the tip of its abdomen release a liquid that lowers the surface tension of the water. The beetle is pulled forward by the greater surface tension of the water in front of it.

The list of wonders has barely been touched, the flying capability, the digestive system, legs no wider that cotton threads containing muscles (the leg muscles of locusts are about 1,000 times more powerful than the equivalent human muscles), the defence mechanisms of camouflage and disguise... just take the time to look, think, and be amazed at the work of the Designer.

36

℘ HEAVEN SCENT ℘

There are two types of people in this world. One is called organised, the other, disorganised. Organised people are a pleasure to live with. They get up on time, know precisely when *Sof Z'man Krias Shema* is according to the two opinions, will tell you how long it is since their suit (weekday) was cleaned, and when it will next be cleaned, always know where the phone book is, and never run out of *Shabbos* candles. Recipes are kept in a plastic folder marked 'Recipes' (and the folder is kept clean with a damp blue cloth which is kept just next to the milky tap (right hand side), and no-one ever shouts "Where is the shoe polish" ten minutes before *Shabbos,* because everyone knows that it is in the under-stair cupboard, second shelf down, with two *Shmattes,* brown and black, folded next to it. In a world of contrasts, there are disorganised people. How they actually survive and progress in life remains something of a mystery. They never know where anything is, and are in a constant state of wonder that their possessions are not where they are sure they placed them. Their kitchen drawers contain everything from dessert knives to biro refills, wedding reply cards (whose celebrants are grandparents already) and shoe-laces. You usually cannot open the said drawer because the phone book is jammed inside ("Who put it there!") and bills are paid on the day before the bailiffs arrive. These people are usually carefree and happy, and their redeeming characteristics make it possible to live with them. Fine though they may be — never allow them to run an airport.

Go to an airport on a busy day, and just watch. Queues of travellers snake around the counters, each with their many items of luggage and members of family. Suitcases are weighed, labelled, placed on the conveyor belt and then disappear through the rubber flaps. Where do they go? Planes land every few seconds, each one knows exactly at which gate to stop, and which yellow line to follow. As soon as it comes to a halt, the plane is surrounded by busy service personnel, as a flower is by bees. Catering vans (who know that on the outgoing flight Mrs Cohen has ordered 'Special Kosher'), fuel tankers, luggage transporters, stair removers and cleaning staff each go to their allotted places and perform their specialised tasks. Each knows exactly where to go and what to do. Just think of the organisation! Chicago's O'Hare airport (the world's busiest) is used by 50 commercial airlines. It handles 55 million people a year (6700 every hour!) and 2,200 aircraft pass through O'Hare each day. In the baggage area (the size of six football fields) computer-coded baggage tags are read by laser, and automatic baggage sorters process 480 pieces of luggage each minute. Each terminal resembles a small city, with its own army of baggage handlers, nursing staff, cleaners and maintenance men. The size of airports is huge — the world's biggest, the King Khalid International Airport in Saudi Arabia is more than four times the size of Bermuda! Then think of the organisation required to ensure that the planes land and take off safely, each with its individual flight path and air corridor. It is when things sometimes go wrong, when a suitcase is misplaced, or a conveyor belt breaks down, or the air traffic controllers work to rule, that one begins to appreciate the tremendous organisation that is required to keep the planes and passengers moving smoothly. You know something — it is nearly as complicated as your nose!

It is underestimated and often unappreciated. Many people consider it simply as a place on which to deposit spectacles, and to wipe every so often — but it houses one of the most amazing machines that we possess. The humble nose has the capacity to process and identify the millions of molecules that constantly fly through the air in a manner which would put any airport to shame. How does it all work?

The sense of smell is a vital necessity. It gives pleasure (the wafting aroma of *Cholent* on *Shabbos* morning), it gives warning (sour chicken soup, eggs past their prime, the smell of smoke or gas) and it evokes emotion (freshly mown grass, polished wooden floors, a pine forest). Everything is composed of minute particles called molecules. These molecules are constantly departing from substances and flying through the air. The warmer the substance, the more molecules it gives off. Put your hand close to the molecules, place the molecules near your right knee, and you will detect nothing.

254 / Designer World

"A Schmeck Tabak" registered by the Olefactory Organs, interpreted by the brain.

There is no receiving station! But place your nose close to an object, take a surreptitious sniff, and instantly you know the identity of the object, its age, quality and desirability.

How does it work? On the roof of each nasal cavity (we have two) there is a patch of yellow-brown tissue smaller than a postage stamp. On each patch there are receptor cells, with each cell containing 6-8 tiny sensory hairs that project from it. Each cell is connected to the brain approximately one inch away. A molecule (let us say of bread in the oven) floats through the air, and is inhaled up the nose. The molecule dissolves in the mucus covering the tiny cells with their tinier hairs. The molecule then reacts chemically with the receptor cell, causing a minute amount of electricity to be generated, and passed along the nervous system to the brain. In a fraction of a second, the message is decoded and the information released — baking bread. Automatically, a message is transmitted to the salivary glands telling them to begin production, (food on the way), the hunger impulse is activated (where is that kept?), especially if it is a fast day, and the brain registers a pleasurable sensation. Each single receptor cell residing on the little square patch is a machine of phenomenal complexity and efficiency, so complicated that we do not know precisely how it is able to react differently (and chemically) to each type of molecule. How many of these wonder-machines do you think you possess in each nostril? Just ten million!! Ten million advanced computers sitting quietly and modestly at the top of the nose.

The sense of smell is incredibly keen. Our smell receptors (official name — olfactory organs) can detect as little as two-thousandth of a milligram of artificial musk in a litre of air (equivalent to one drop of this substance diffused through the air in a room the size of a large concert hall). There is evidence that the direction from which the smell comes can be detected by the slight difference in time of the arrival of the odorous molecules in the two nostrils. Other refinements include warning systems, which are composed of naked endings of pain fibres which are housed in the olfactory mucus membranes, which are stimulated by irritating odours, e.g. onions. Urgent messages of distress are sent to the brain, which instructs the tear ducts to pour water into the eyes to dilute the effect of the stinging vapour, potentially dangerous to the super-sensitive eyes. Hence, crying when peeling onions is an illustration of a chain of events of tremendous design.

In just the same way that the brain can block out sounds which are monotonous or unwanted, a similar block-out mechanism exists for odours. If you are overwhelmed by a particular odour, after a while you cannot detect it. This makes it possible for someone to tolerate an unpleasant odour after overcoming his initial aversion to it. However, the sensitivity of the olfactory organs remains. Even in the stench of a tannery, a rose smells as sweet as ever. The sense of smell does not work in isolation. It is backed up by an excellent memory. Every odour that is recorded by the brain is stored away in the memory bank. (Imagine that you are a librarian. A gentleman comes to you one day and asks you to file away the smell of smouldering wood. The next day, another customer comes to your library and asks if he can borrow the smell of a newborn baby. How would you satisfy your customers! It is practically impossible to describe a smell, let alone store it.) It will remain there forever, ready for instant recall. There are smells of childhood, smells of countries and smells of seasons, smells of trains, new cars, planes, shops, gardens, clothes, besides the more obvious foods, flowers, herbs, and spices. Each and every one of the thousands of different odours is faithfully filed away in a manner that no-one can explain.

The ability to detect odours is a great kindness. We appreciate this most of all if we lose our sense of smell for a short while when suffering from a cold, causing a blockage in the nose, and preventing the scent particles from reaching the receptors. The sense of smell helps us to enjoy our food and keeps us away from danger. The fact that there is such a variety of odours in fruit and vegetables, each more pleasant than the next, is no accident, and is indicative of a great plan and design. What we must never take for granted is the complexity of the millions of wonder machines that work so faithfully and humbly at the top of our nose. Millions of molecules go flying through the air, they are monitored, identified, classified and stored carefully in a manner that can compare most favourably with any international airport. You cannot run an airport without organisation — and you cannot operate olfactory organs without design — brilliant design!

37

ஐ BIGGEST IS BEST ௸

You must have been in traffic jams. You crawl along, bumper to bumper, frustration rising together with the heat of the radiator, the joys of driving non-existent. Sometimes the cause of the delay is known; and when you see a solid phalanx of traffic in front of you, with road signs cheerfully announcing that there are road works five miles ahead, and delays can be expected, then at least you know what to expect. On other occasions, however, you might be driving along the motorway at a cracking pace, and without any warning the speed of the traffic slows, and you find yourself locked in a tangle of vehicles all of which are moving at half speed. You look ahead, and the traffic looks solid. You look around for a cause for the blockage, and find nothing. This can continue for miles and the enigma grows. Eventually, far ahead, you see flashing blue lights. Could be an accident. As you approach, you suddenly understand the cause of the monumental hold-up. Police outriders are escorting an enormous vehicle, which fills up nearly three lanes of the motorway, allowing a trickle of cars to pass in single file. As you gingerly pass the monster, with the happy anticipation of normal driving just yards away, you cannot help but gape at the slow moving giant by your side.

It is a huge lorry, with an enormous trailer supported by as many wheels as there are legs on a centipede. And on the trailer squats the most enormous earth-moving truck you have ever seen. Each wheel fills the horizon like some bloated balloon, and you imagine that the power contained in that Goliath must be tremendous. Every aspect of that giant truck fills you with awe, and you stare at it with dry-mouthed fascination.

Anything large always evokes a special wonder. In those books which chronicle fascinating facts and extremes, the largest is inevitably more exciting than the smallest. There is something gripping about the fact that the longest car in the world is an incredible 100 feet long, has 26 wheels, lives in California and contains amongst its many features a swimming pool with a diving board. There is a special fascination in the massive. The knowledge that a man from London built and drove a car weighing 21 pounds, powered by a tiny 2.5 cc engine, is interesting; but to know that the massive Terex Titan truck, used in Canada, weighs 548 tons, and hold 1300 gallons of fuel in its tank, grips the imagination. It is just the thought of

"Anything large always evokes a special wonder." This Goliath truck (note the size of the man by the wheel) is no exception.

this monstrous machine, probably as long as the street where you live, crawling along the ground and performing amazing feats of strength with thundering noise and ground-shaking power that seems to mesmerize the onlooker. If you could open the bonnet of that enormous monster, you would see all the pipes, valves and cables, hydraulics, mechanics and cylinders, each built to a huge scale, every one the largest of its kind. Little man, with his clever little head, can build very big machines.

But how delicate are they? How deft or how dextrous? If you placed an artist's brush in the grip of a ten ton bulldozer's teeth, could you expect it to draw a delicate and tiny flower?

How nimble could a locomotive be when it requires about two miles to come to a stop from a top speed of 162 mph? What degree of gentleness could you expect from the world's biggest mechanical shovel which has a grasp capacity of 325 tons! Great power and size do not normally go together with gentleness and refinement. Until you meet the elephant.

In the world of animals, there is nothing bigger. It is a giant among land animals, and dwarfs human beings. Everything about it is on a massive scale. A tiny baby elephant stands (and indeed it does stand just a few minutes after its entry into the world) three feet tall, and weighs about 200 pounds (the weight of a fully-grown man who needs to go on a diet). It continues growing for most of its life, reaching a full height of $10\frac{1}{2}$ feet, and weighing in at almost 6 tons. Even that is diminutive in comparison with the largest elephant, which weighed over 12 tons, and had a circumference of its front foot of some 5 ft 2 ins. Elephants have enormous strength, and can rip the roof off a car with the greatest of ease to reach some food. They carry logs of wood as if they were matchsticks, and their long curved ivory tusks (which are their front teeth, and grow all their life and need to be constantly worn down if they are not to become too heavy even for their owners) are fearsome weapons. In the age before Centurion tanks, elephants were the perfect weapon. In the days of the second *Beis Hamikdosh*, elephants were used in *Eretz Yisroel* by the Greeks, and the famous Hannibal, ruler of Carthage in North Africa, took his elephants from Spain to France, and then over the Alps, to invade Rome.

262 / Designer World

On any visit to the zoo, two areas are always popular. The first is the Reptile House, where people can satisfy their morbid fascination of the horrifying by staring at all the poisonous snakes and man-eating spiders in existence in perfect safety (they hope). The second is the Elephant House, where these great giants of the animal world amble around with their slow and dignified gait, gratefully accepting the humble offerings of the admiring public. The very last thing you would expect an elephant to be is gentle. People would laugh if you told them that an elephant is sensitive. Do you mean to say that the skin of an elephant, which is 1.2 inches thick, and weighs about one ton, is sensitive? Similarly, if you were told

In the world of animals, there is nothing bigger. Yet its trunk is so sensitive and gentle that it can pluck a single leaf off a tree.

that these massive creatures are terrific swimmers, you would think that it was a joke. Prepare for some surprises!

In complete contrast to everyone's expectations, the elephant is not clumsy. It can, and does, step on a coconut with a delicacy that cracks the shell without crushing the meat. There is a record of a train of 79 Asian working elephants crossing tidal stretches of the River Ganges where they had to swim for six hours without touching the bottom. Could you imagine a column of massive tanks charging down the beach at Dover, and swimming at full speed across the English Channel and charging out at Calais, on the French side, stopping for a moment to shake off the water and jellyfish, and then continue on their merry way? Unbelievable for the best of human construction, no problem for the elephant. This greatest of all creatures has an appetite to match. Its daily diet consists of 1000 pounds of leaves and grass, and it must continually search for water, requiring some 30 to 50 gallons each day. To search for and consume this massive quantity takes sixteen hours out of each day. It is therefore no surprise to us to learn that the elephant needs very little sleep, about half as much as a human being. Nothing is without design.

Especially the elephant's trunk. This most versatile instrument, surely the trade-mark of this noble creature, contains some forty thousand muscles (in contrasts, think of your own arm with its two muscles), each of which needs the appropriate orders from the central nervous system to function. And function it certainly can! It is partly lip and partly nose, with two 'fingers' on the tip, it is used as a worker's arm and hand. It has double hoses, one for sucking in, and the other for spraying out water or dust. It can push down trees, or pick off the smallest leaf. It can be as gentle as the most tender arm, greeting, scratching or rubbing, and at the same time it can change into an efficient weapon, strong enough to kill. Perhaps it is its sense of smell which is the most amazing. At the tip of its trunk are tiny little hairs which locate the precise location of a scent in the wind. And an elephant never forgets the scent of man. It has been said that an elephant, using its trunk, can detect the difference between the scent of a white man and an African at a distance of two miles. An elephant had once been hunted, but survived. Thereafter, he trod with the greatest care, veering to the left or the right, but always returning to cross his trail. There he would stop, sniff the ground with his trunk, and if there was no scent, he would move on. If he scented a native foot on his trail, he would back into cover and watch until he was sure all was safe. If he scented a white man, he would trample the ground in a rage, and take off in a straight line for 50 miles or more! He knew what kind of weapons white men carry.

The great elephant, with its enormous ears with which they control their body temperature (by spraying water behind the ears or flapping them in the wind) is as designer-made as the largest man-made machine. Only so much more efficient, versatile and gentle. Stand in awe of titanic machines with their many wheels, and then appreciate all the more the intricacy and design of the greatest of all the animals. Then look at the whole world — with millions of examples of the miracles of design — and again at the vastness of the Universe, and recognize the greatness and wisdom of the One who made it all.

38

৯০ WONDER OF WONDERS ০৪

Harry Houdini, (born Ehrich Weiss in 1874 to a Rov in Budapest), was famous throughout the world for his ability to escape from impossible situations. When he was a child, his family moved from Hungary to the USA, and by the time he was eleven, he was an expert at picking locks and untying ropes. He travelled throughout America and Europe, devising ever more daring escapes which were performed in front of horrified and mesmerised audiences. Underwater escapes featured among his most spectacular stunts, and in rivers from the Hudson in New York to the Mersey in Liverpool, he would allow himself to be handcuffed and shackled in irons, and then placed in a sealed wooden packing case, taken out to mid-river in a tugboat, and lowered by crane into the water. There the crate sank as water poured in through a hole in the bottom. People expected never to see him again, but within seconds he had emerged unscathed from the watery depths. How he did it, no-one knew. Another favourite trick, which was performed on dry land, involved his escape from a milk churn brimming with water. He first performed this trick, billed as 'a death-defying mystery', in 1908 in St. Louis, Missouri. Mr. Houdini would enter a galvanized iron milk churn, which would then be filled with water by three fierce looking gentlemen wearing black cloaks, and the lid then secured by massive locks. Crouched inside it, there seemed to be no way that he could possibly reach the locks on the outside. The curtains were drawn around the churn, and the orchestra played breezily away. Again, Houdini achieved the impossible, and he appeared, dripping with water, to the astounded audience.

There must be easier ways, and certainly more preferable ways, of earning a *Parnosoh*. The fact is, however, that Harry Houdini was never in the slightest danger from all his self-imposed exploits. Every trick had a method, by which the 'master escaper' would effect his release. In his water-filled packing case, secret springs released Houdini's bonds, and he cut the nails in the main plank in the lid with hidden cutters. Within seconds, he would push up the plank, wriggle free, and surface. The milk churn had a separate inner section, into which the magician stepped. The lid and padlocks were only fitted to this inner section, which, by means of sham half-rivets, could be twisted round and released. All that remained was for Reb Houdini to push up the middle section and step out onto dry land.

Like so many things, it is easy once you have learned how to do it. His audiences did not know the tricks, and to them it appeared impossible. Ask yourself the question. How would you like to be in Houdini's situation, in which you have to escape from an enclosed and secured water-filled container, and no-one has taught you the method of escape. Not a single person in their right mind would volunteer. How could you possibly survive! By the time you would have concentrated your mind, it would be too late. It doesn't bear thinking about! You cannot place someone in a totally foreign situation, fraught with danger, absolutely ill-equipped, and expect him to survive. It would be like taking a fish, who is accustomed from birth to live in water and breath through its gills, placing it on dry land, and then saying to it "Come on fishele, learn to breath through your mouth. You have one minute to learn, starting from now...!" Poor little fish, what do you want from it, don't ask the impossible. So would you care to be a Houdini, without his knowledge?

You are. Not only have you performed tricks similar to his without the slightest amount of knowledge, you have achieved even more. What the little fish could never do, you have done. The fact that you are reading this article, is a reasonable indication that you were born. The events surrounding the birth of a person are so amazing (and seemingly impossible) that to this very day, when man can stand on the moon, no-one is too sure how it all works. The cause of the onset of labour remains unknown. But *Boruch Hashem* it happens! The actual process of birth is a series of co-ordinated wonders beyond the scope of this article. It is immediately after birth that a new series of wonder commences. Think for a moment what a little newborn infant has to do. Whilst unborn, it could rely on its mother to carry out its respiratory functions, and to provide it with all its nutritional requirements. It had no need to use its lungs, little need for its

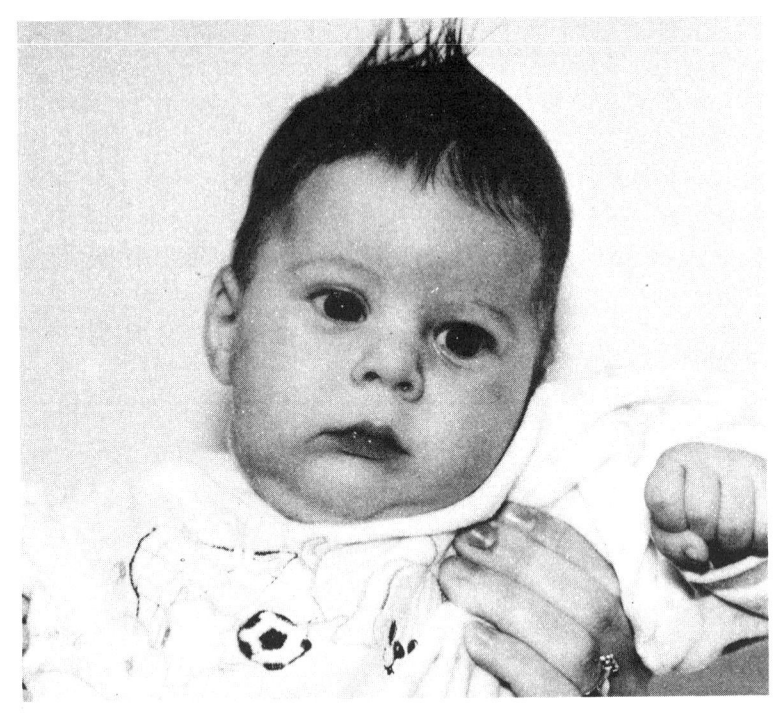

A bundle of joy, a bundle of miracles.

liver function, and its energies were mainly concerned with developing within the womb. In its watery environment, food, oxygen and its every need were provided by a devoted mother.

All of a sudden — with a loud *Mazal Tov* — the child is born. The newborn infant is now dependant for life on its own efforts. It has to begin breathing through its mouth, and use its lungs. It has to alter its circulatory system so that blood is pumped to the lungs (to receive its oxygen supply) instead of the placenta. It has to obtain its own food, and eliminate the waste of its own digestive system. It must maintain its own fluid and electrolyte balance. It must maintain its own body temperature. All of a sudden, it must manufacture its own immunoglobulins (in its blood supply) and mobilize its own defence mechanism to counter any infection. Never has the little baby had any lessons, all these enormous changes and challenges are vital to its life, and they must all be achieved in the shortest possible time. Houdini knew the tricks, and the tricks were relatively simple. The baby knows nothing, and the procedures are staggering in their complexity. There are no tricks, it is all for real, and the baby must succeed within seconds!

One of the most well-known and well documented changes that must take place in the little child is the actual structure of its heart. Every person's heart is in reality two separate pumps. The right side of the heart pumps blood to the lungs where it takes up oxygen. This oxygenated blood is taken back to the left side of the heart, where it is pumped to the rest of the body. As can be imagined, the pressure required in the left side of the heart, which has to pump the blood throughout the many miles (76,000 of them) of blood vessels, is high, much higher than the pressure in the right side, which only has to pump the blood the short distance to the lungs. This difference in pressure is maintained by keeping the two sides of the heart separate, divided by a partition. If there would be any hole or perforation between the two, the pressure would be equalised, with very unhappy results. Before it is born, the baby receives oxygenated blood via the placenta from its mother, and there is no need for the heart to pump blood to the lungs for its oxygen. The pressure in the two sides of its heart can be equal, and indeed they are. This equality is possible because of a small vessel (the DUCTUS ARTERIOSUS) which joins the two sides. Immediately after birth, the little vessel would spell disaster if it remained open, and it must disappear, and fast!

It does, but how it does remains a mystery. The learned books are quite frank. "The mechanism responsible for the obliteration of the ductus arteriosus, like that of the expansion of the lungs, is incompletely understood..." Something tells this little vessel to destroy itself, and it obeys. Within minutes it has closed, and soon afterwards it disappear entirely.

You will notice that the book makes mention of that other mysterious miracle, the first breath. The unborn child does not have to breath. All the oxygen it requires comes through the lifeline. Its lungs are filled with fluid, and lie unused, but ready, waiting for birth and use. Immediately after birth, the amazing chain of events must be initiated. The baby must open its mouth and inhale a good mouthful of air, and the fluid in its lungs must suddenly disappear! Somehow, and it remains the happiest sound known to mankind, the baby is stimulated to cry and gasp for air. With the first gasps, the fluid filling the lung passages is driven into the expanding little sub-branches of the lungs, where it is quickly absorbed into the system. Within fifteen minutes of birth, the fluid (which threatened the very survival of the child) has disappeared, and all the thousands of branches in the lungs have been filled with life-giving air. Another miracle has been achieved! (Hundreds, if not thousands of details exist in the development of the baby, of which we are unaware, and therefore perhaps unappreciative. One detail. Between the 20th and the 24th week of its pre-birth development, a special substance is secreted into the growing lungs. This substance spreads over the surface of the tiny branches, and has the effect of reducing their surface tension. Before birth, this is of no value to the child whatsoever, but it is of vital concern as soon as the child needs to breath — about a second after it enters the world. Thanks to the wonder liquid — a complex of protein and lipids — lung expansion is greatly improved, making breathing so much easier.)

There is no-one alive who does not have an enormous debt of gratitude to the Creator of all, for the stunning events which enabled him to be born, and survive those first crucial moments when such a complex series of changes had to be achieved. Thank you *Hashem*!

39

ᛰ A JOINT EFFORT ᛱ

Driving someone else's car is like having grandchildren. It's all the enjoyment without any of the headaches. If you hear a strange noise coming from under the bonnet — it's not your problem; if a tyre needs replacing, you just tell the owner and walk away smiling. Road tax, insurance, and servicing — all these things are not your worry. There are some responsibilities, however, which even the driver of a borrowed car cannot escape. One of them is the task of keeping the vehicle adequately-fuelled. Neither wishful thinking nor orange juice will enable an internal-combustion engine to combust, and petrol costs money. So, something you have to be prepared to sacrifice for your borrowed convenience. Another is oil. Every driver of a car knows that on four things does a car run — petrol for the tank, air for the tyres, water for the radiator and oil for the engine. Everyone knows where the petrol goes; even a child knows how to inflate a tyre; that the water lives in the radiator at the front of the car is elementary knowledge, but what about the oil!

Someone once borrowed a car. What could be better. He borrowed it for two weeks, during the summer holidays. Better still. It happened to be a foreign car, with the steering wheel on the opposite side. Well, you can accustom yourself to most things, if it means a free car. Now the law of etiquette declares that if you borrow a car to collect mother-in-law from the station, you do not have to check the oil. The journey is simply too short. If, however, your term of borrowing extends to two weeks, it is understood that the borrower will check the oil at least twice. And that was the problem. Wishing to fulfil his obligation, the driver drove the car into a filling station, and raised the bonnet. He stared into the engine, and in the maze of wires, coils, pistons and manifolds, saw nothing whatsoever that indicated where the dip-stick was hiding, nor a place to pour the oil. The garage attendant, expressing genuine English distrust of anything foreign, was equally unable to help. What to do — it had to be somewhere! In a flash of inspiration, he remembered that every car is provided with a thick book of instructions, in which every function and component of the car is described. With eager anticipation, the driver opened the glove-compartment, extracted the manual, and soon found the appropriate page, which in poetic French described how to check and replenish the oil. Problem solved!

Topping up the oil. Without it, the car would grind to a halt.

He understood, as we all do, that oil is essential for the engine of a car to operate efficiently. In an engine, there are many moving parts, some sliding, others rotating. No matter how smooth a metal surface may seem, there will be 'mountains and valleys', and these irregularities create resistance and friction. The use of oil as a lubricant serves to keep these moving surfaces apart, and reduces friction. The quantity of oil must be carefully regulated, hence the dip-stick, and only specially prepared oil can be used — sunflower oil might be wonderful for preparing mayonnaise, but would not be appreciated by your car-engine. Besides reducing friction, oil has to carry away excess heat, prevent corrosion, and absorb waste products. In addition, the oil must not be too thick when cold, nor too thin when hot. No wonder that its ingredients are so carefully selected, and its price so high. It truly can be described as a wonder liquid — but truly not a patch on the wonder liquid that you carry around with you. What is this wonder liquid? Read on!

If you wish to keep children amused on a rainy day, you can teach them how to make little model people. On a sheet of card you draw the outline of a head, arms, legs and a trunk. You cut them out, and attach them by means of a large pin whose ends can be bent backwards. The little figure is very sweet, but cannot move. The limbs just hang loosely. We understand that to enable limbs — human limbs — to move, they need bones to give them rigidity, and they in turn act as a chassis to which muscles are attached. It is these muscles which allow the body to move, and they are attached to the bones by means of tough elastic tissue called tendons; and it is by means of tendons that they exert their pull. But bones cannot bend! However, where two bones meet, they form a joint, and this allows us to bend, twist or turn our bodies. At a joint, the bones are held together by strong elastic straps called ligaments. It can be well imagined that if the two bones at the joint would have to twist and turn while rubbing against each other, it would be painful in the extreme. Two things can prevent this happening. The first is that the end of each bone is covered with a soft but tough tissue called cartilage, and this prevents the bones from grinding against each other. This type of joint allows limited movement, and is to be found between the bones of the spine, in which the vertebrae are separated from each other by tough discs of cartilage. These discs cushion the body against shock, and allow some movement between the individual vertebrae.

The second type of joint allows for much more varied movement. In this type of joint the cartilages at the end of each bone do not touch each other. Instead, the end of each bone is covered with a smooth layer of pearly white cartilage, and the entire joint is lined with a smooth, thin layer of tissue called the SYNOVIAL MEMBRANE. This produces a small quantity of fluid, which lubricates the joint in exactly the same way that oil lubricates the moving parts of a machine. The two bony surfaces never touch; they are always separated by the thin layer of fluid. This is the wonder fluid!

It all sounds so simple! 'The synovial membrane produces a small quantity of fluid (synovial fluid) which lubricates the joint...' Let me ask you some questions. What is synovial fluid made of? Is it water, is it oil, or is it just some magical mystery fluid? How precisely is it produced? Does it ever go bad? (Apart from wine, most liquids do not improve with age). Does it leak? (Have you ever wondered why it is that when you sit in the bath for a prolonged period your skin becomes wrinkled and shrivelled in appearance — the reason is that when you immerse you hands in water, a process called OSMOSIS causes fluids from your body to percolate through the porous skin into the fluids in the bath.) If it happens to your hands, does it also happen to the synovial fluid?

The answers are remarkable. The synovial membranes are composed of synovial cells which secrete the thick and sticky liquid, which contains proteins, salts and hyaluronic acid. Not only does the synovial fluid lubricate the joint, it actually acts as a nutrient for the joint surfaces. It oils them and feeds them! Here is today's project. Take whatever ingredients you wish, and using your food mixer, food blender, and all your modern appliances, make some synovial fluid. Where would you begin? Yet all the time, despite the fact that your brain does not contain the information (you might never have known that you have any synovial fluid!!), those membranes in your elbow, your knee, your shoulder and your hip are happily producing the wonder liquid which allows everything to move so smoothly. How exactly it produces it, in precisely the correct consistency and quantity, is a clear indication of the profoundness of the design of our bodies. It does not go bad, it does not leak, and no dip-stick is required to check if it needs topping up. It is the perfect liquid for the job, it is ready-enclosed and operational at birth, it grows with the baby into adulthood, and it costs precisely nothing.

When you wish to leave a room via the door, you do not expect to lift the door off its socket and place it next to the gaping aperture

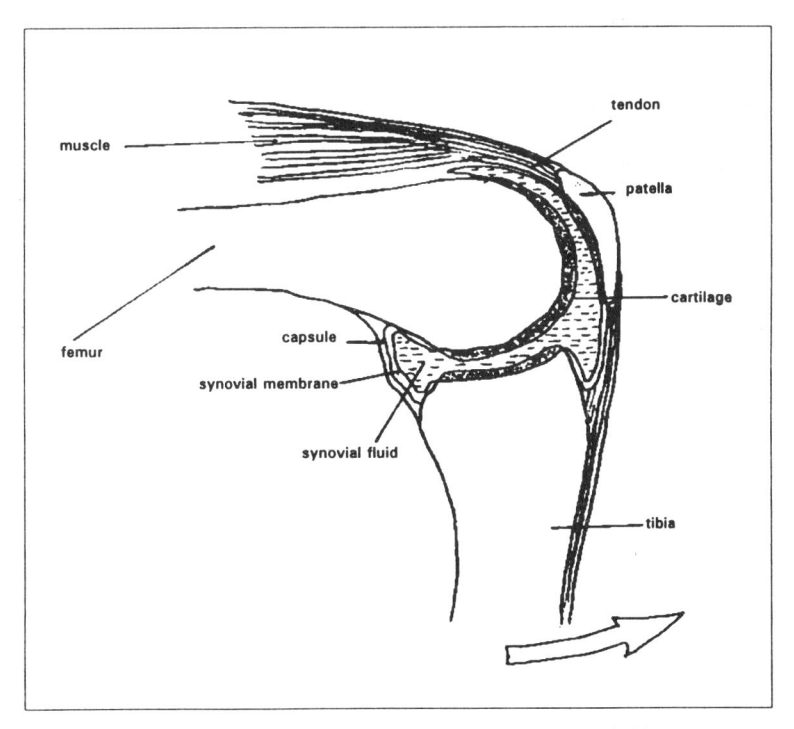

Hinge Joint of the knee, showing the synovial fluid.

— you open it on its hinge, and it swings open. The hinge happened by itself? If it is obvious that it was designed for the job, what did the designer use as a model? When you swing your arm from the elbow, or your leg from the knee, or move the fingers in your hand, you are operating a hinge joint, just like a door opening. When you swing your arm around your head, or 'stretch your legs' by going for a walk, you are using a ball and socket joint, which allows maximum movement at the shoulders and the hips. A pivot joint permits rotary motion with the head that rests on your neck. The elbow is also a rotating joint, allowing the forearm, wrist and hand to turn over; and sliding joints facilitate movement at the wrist and the ankles. Every type of joint is present in the body, each one ideally designed for its precise and specialised function, a harmony of co-ordination between bone, muscle, ligament, cartilage, nerves, blood supply, membrane and lubricating fluid.

Take a look how a car (bought, hired or even borrowed) is made. The ideas, the market research, the design, the models, the testing, the production, assembling and distribution. Engine, moving parts, lubrication, every stage the result of painstaking research and thought — now move your arms up and down, and thank *Hashem Yisborach* for the brilliance of the design of you.

40

ಉ STRIKE A LIGHT ಲ

What would you do if you found yourself stranded in the middle of nowhere, it might be a desert island, and you needed to light a fire. Fire will provide you with heat and light, it will cook raw food and make it edible — but how will you produce that fire? Not being a member of the scouting fraternity, you did not remember to be prepared before becoming stranded, and so you have no emergency pack with you. As you stand, alone, surrounded by the stark land and its elements, you feel at once vulnerable and insecure. Desperately you try and rack your brains for some vaguely remembered information concerning 'How the early peoples lived'. Of course — why did you not remember immediately — they used to rub sticks together to produce a spark. Well, that sounds simple enough. Two likely-looking sticks are produced, and you begin the great rub. Two hours later, you have blisters on your hands, a great deal of sawdust on the ground, and not a single spark to brighten up your deepening gloom. And even if you did manage to produce the elusive spark — what would you do with it? "Stay there, spark, don't move, I'll be right back with some dry grass or paraffin-infused cotton wool!" By the time you return, the spark will long have taken its leave. As you sit, cold, dark and disconsolate, you wonder how people managed to light fires in the olden days.

How indeed did they manage? Until matches were invented, people would carry a tinderbox. This was a metal box containing a flint and a piece of steel. The flint was attached to the side of the box, and the piece of steel hung loose by a string. They would then strike the steel against the flint with a rubbing motion, which produced sparks. (Try it with a metal tipped heel of your shoe on the stone pavement.) These sparks fell into the tinderbox, which was filled with bits of cotton and scorched linen yarn, which readily burst into flame. Interestingly enough, this flint-and-steel principle is still used in most cigarette lighters; and some explorers and hunters still carry old-fashioned flint and steel with them for use in emergencies; but the real fiery revolution took place in 1827.

Enter the match! In that fateful year, John Walker, an English pharmacist invented the first 'lucifer' ('light-bearer'). His matches were not too reliable, and even the improved version, which used phosphorus on the tip of the wooden stick, had a great disadvan-

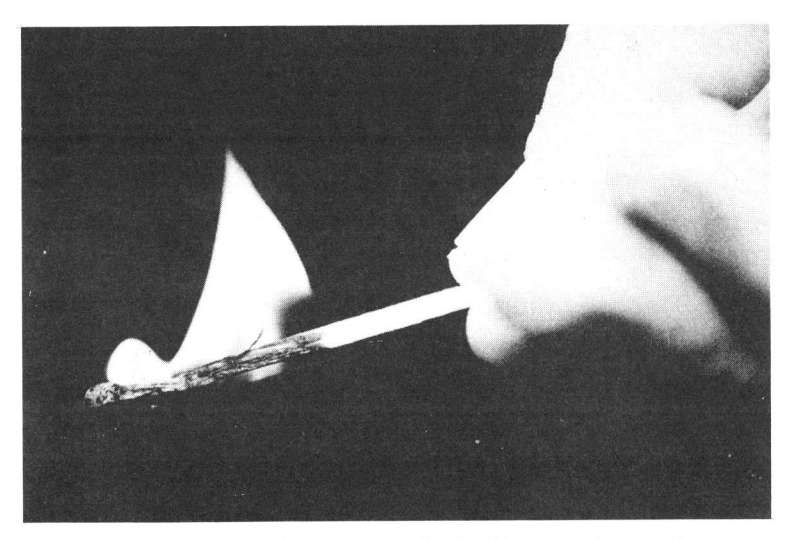

Just an ordinary burning match. Could you produce one?

tage. They could, and often did, kill people! White phosphorus gives off poisonous fumes, prolonged exposure to which caused the jaw-bones to rot. Workers in match factories were affected most, and by the turn of the century, white phosphorus was banned. In modern times we have the improved product, with safety matches that will only light if struck on the side of the box (because they work by the reaction that takes place between chemicals on the match and a chemical in the striking surface on the box), and 'strike anywhere' matches that will ignite if struck against any rough surface. We are blasé enough to accept as a matter of course the information that matches today are made by automatic machines that produce two million matches an hour; and that the stick of the match is soaked in a solution of ammonium phosphate, which is a fire-retardant which ensures that the sticks do not continue to smoulder. We assume as natural the information that the head of the safety match contains sulphur to create the flame, and potassium chlorate to supply oxygen! Well naturally! Although a box of matches is one of the cheapest articles that you can purchase, you expect the greatest degree of design and sophistication from your fire-producing product. Naturally!

If you saw a tiny insect whose light-producing capability not only rivalled the household match, but far surpassed it, would you be impressed? Are there such creatures? Indeed there are. In countries where the temperature is warm and welcoming, when the dusks deepens into night, there you will see the glittering fireflies. In the West Indies, barefoot natives tie the big, brilliant fireflies called 'CUCUYO' to their toes to light a way through the jungle paths. When American troops were fighting Cuba in 1898, the famous Dr William Gorgas was operating on a soldier when his lamp went out. By the light of a bottle-full of cucuyos, he successfully finished the operation (and then put out the fireflies!). If you want to see these fiery little creatures at their best, go to Thailand. During the summer evenings, thousands of the flies cluster on the mangrove trees lining the rivers. Flashing 120 times a minute, they all synchronize to the same interval, so that one instant there is blackness, the next — every tree, every boat on the river is revealed as if by lightening, then blackness, then brilliant light again.

How many people do you know who could produce a box of matches given any chemical they requested and a modern laboratory? Even if they knew anything about chemistry and explosives, you would probably hear the explosion before you saw the matches! Yet here we have a tiny insect that knows nothing about anything, yet is able to produce a sophisticated level of light. How does it do it? The diminutive fireflies (not really flies at all, but beetles,) are greyish or brownish in colour, narrow and flat. There is absolutely nothing striking about these beetles when you see them by day. Yet at night they produce light with almost no heat — perfect illumination, something that men have not yet been able to achieve. (Try touching, or rather don't try touching a light bulb which has been on for just a few minutes.) The firefly is eerily cooler than the air of the summer night which it illuminates.

If you would hold a firefly in your cupped hands, you would notice a continuous subdued glow in the luminous organs situated in the last segments of the abdomen. Then, like a flash from a revolving beacon, the light leaps up brightly, lasts for a fraction of a second, and is renewed again at the precise rhythmic interval. If the firefly is hurt, the interval is shortened, and the flashes become almost continuous, just as our heart beats faster when we are excited. What is the secret? Prepare to be amazed. The luminous organs consist of two layers of tissue. Near the surface is a layer of granules, and on the back of it are a layer of crystal cells which act as reflectors. Those granules are the source of the light. Through them runs a network of air tubes and nerves. It is thought that when the firefly flashes, the air tubes open, oxygen rushes over the granules and they flare up, just as an ember of coal brightens when you blow on it. If you would take those light-producing granules out of the insect and drop them into pure oxygen, they would glow continuously, until 'something' is all used up. That 'something' contains the secret of the light. Chemists who specialise in biology have discovered that the luminous organs contain a combustible substance called LUCIFERIN. However, this substance will only combine with oxygen and glow in the presence of an enzyme called LUCIFERASE, which fortunately is also found in the granules. Here comes the remarkable — this luciferase has a double function. Not only does it assist the luciferin to combine with oxygen and glow, it also deoxidizes it (in the same way that you would unrust rusty iron) so that the luciferin can be used over and over again.

One of the purposes of the flashing beacon is to enable the firefly to find other members of the same species. Flying low above the ground, they flash rhythmically, searching for answering signals. The response, when it comes, is always precisely 2.1 seconds later. Another creature which employs lights is the deep-sea Angler fish, which uses a 'fishing rod' which is baited at the end with a shining light. The light dangles alluringly just in front of its mouth, which contains razor sharp teeth. In the blackness of the deep, unsuspecting little fish are attracted to the light — and then — supper is served! There are even some species of squid that have light organs that shine through their body wall. Again, these lights are complex structures complete with reflectors and lenses. It is the individual patterns of light that allow squid to recognise their own species.

Next time you see a tiny firefly, or the anglerfish, or even an illuminated squid, try having a conversation with it. Ask it what it knows of revolving beacons, lucifering, luciferase, airtubes, and the combustible properties of oxygen. Ask it how it managed to develop a method of producing light which is far more advanced than anything that mankind has yet invented, and how it managed to survive whilst it was developing it! (Fireflies, without their signalling beacon, cannot find a mate with which to propagate their species. They either have their light-producing mechanism, or they cease to exist!) The little fly, and fish, and squid, knows nothing, yet it has always possessed its sophisticated machinery. They, in the good company of every creature, have been provided with all the equipment that they require by the greatest Designer of all. Next time you strike a match, think about it!

41

ଶTHE COMPLETE MEDICINEଓ

What would you do if a child came running to you with a grazed knee, resulting from a fall on the pavement. It is a minor wound, one which anyone could handle. Would you simply apply a bandage to the wounded area, and hope for the best? You do not have to be an expert in First Aid to know that a wound has to be cleaned. So you would clean it, using antiseptic spray, fluid, cream, or the handy antiseptic wipes. When everything was clean and dry, you would then apply the dressing, and with confidence hope for the best. Quite elementary, you would think. It was not always so. Anyone entering hospital before the year 1865 for even the most minor of operations was risking his life. A simple fracture of the bone usually healed well, but a compound fracture, in which the skin was pierced, was very often fatal. Anything more complicated, had a higher risk of fatality. Along came an English surgeon by the name of Joseph Lister, and pulled medical practice into the modern era.

    Joseph Lister's father was someone who sold wine for a living, but enjoyed using a microscope as a hobby. Perhaps it was this family trait in searching for the almost invisible that helped Joseph to discover the existence of thousands of tiny organisms that make their home in the nooks and crannies of the uneven surface of the human skin. (An enormously magnified picture of the surface of human skin shows groups of bacteria, rather like collections of grains of rice, living in the crevices!) Some of those organisms kill harmful germs, and help protect against disease, however others are positively harmful. When the skin is cut, the door is opened to these germs, which then multiply causing the potentially dangerous infections. Mr Lister was determined to kill the organisms on the surface of the wound. He tried various chemicals, but finally selected carbolic acid. In March 1865, he first used his method in the treatment of a compound fracture, and was successful. You can still see the very first antiseptic spray — a glass bottle containing carbolic acid, which was connected to a small water boiler with a spray nozzle. The antiseptic principle was established and widely practised, both on the patients and on the surgical instruments used for operations, and septic disease following operations became a rare exception. Thank you Mr Lister!

Joseph Lister, the man who pulled medical practice into the modern era.

Enter the antiseptic. No home is without some, either in liquid form or in a cream. But it costs money! Would you care for some antiseptic which is dry, can be kept in your pocket, comes in handy dispensable containers, is obtainable anywhere, is completely odourless and which costs pennies, and can even be obtained free of charge? It is yours for the asking. Enter the garlic!

Garlic has been used as a medicine for centuries, and has long been recognized as an antiseptic. During the First World War, the British Government asked for tons of the bulbs, offering one shilling per pound for as much as could be produced. The garlic was used to treat wounds, by squeezing out the raw juice, diluting it with water and then applying it to the affected area. This treatment was successful in preventing the wounds becoming septic, and thousands of lives were saved by its use. What is it about this remarkable plant that it should have such beneficial properties? You have to know what treasures lie within. Garlic contains ALLIIN and ALLICIN, two sulphur compounds with antibiotic activity. Laboratory experiments and experience have shown that garlic juice inhibit a broad variety of micro-organisms, including bacteria, yeast and fungi.

Did you say that garlic is odourless? Everyone knows that the opposite is true! 'An apple a day keeps the doctor away; a garlic a day keeps everyone away' is a saying much quoted by non-enthusiasts of this wonderful plant. The answer to the contradiction is that both statements are true. When you buy a bulb of garlic, and even when you divide it into its 10-12 individual cloves, it emits no smell whatsoever. There is not the slightest hint of the explosion of aroma that will burst forth once the clove is cut. Cut it and there is no escape. It has one of the most powerful odours in the plant world, indeed it is so strong that if a clove of garlic is rubbed on the soles of the feet, the odour will be exhaled by the lungs! The peculiar penetrating odour of garlic is due to a very pungent chemical oil, DIALLYL DISULPHIDE, which is rich in sulphur, but contains no oxygen. One of the properties of garlic is its ability to make you perspire if it is used on a daily basis, and the powerful diallyl disulphide is carried in the perspiration and in the air you exhale, which is why eating garlic makes you smell 'garlicky'. Interestingly enough, heating garlic destroys the chemical that gives it its powerful smell, which is why cooked garlic is so much milder than its raw counterpart. It is truly remarkable that such a potent chemical can be kept locked in and enclosed by a covering as thin and as delicate as the tissue-like skin which covers each individual clove.

Many and varied are the ills and ailments that garlic has been claimed to cure. Everyone has heard of cholesterol, a susbtance which is present in the blood as well as in many foods. What is perhaps not so well known is that there are two types of cholesterol, a so-called 'good' cholesterol, that does not stick to the walls of the arteries, and a 'bad' cholesterol which does adhere to artery walls. It has been demonstrated in laboratory studies that animals which have been given garlic oil show a decrease in blood levels of low-density lipoprotein (the 'bad' cholesterol), and a corresponding increase in blood-levels of high-density lipoprotein, (the 'good' cholesterol). Similar studies of human patients with heart disease have shown some increase in the activity of anticlotting substances in blood when the patients were given ten cloves of garlic a day for one month. Not for nothing is garlic praised as the great blood purifier!

There are two benefits of the use of garlic which you might say are hardly world-shattering. The first is that if you chop a small piece of garlic very finely and add it to the diet of your chickens, they will produce better quality eggs. It is, however, advised that this additive is stopped as soon as they start laying, otherwise the chickens will produce garlic-flavoured eggs! The second is a claim that the wine of garlic, made by soaking three or four bulbs in a quart of spirit, is a good stimulant lotion for baldness of the head! Other claims deserve perhaps more serious attention. It is recorded that during an outbreak of infectious fever in certain poor quarters of London in the last century, the French priests who constantly used garlic in all their dishes, visited the worst cases with complete impunity, whilst their English counterparts caught the infection, and in many cases fell victim to the disease.

Garlic is a powerful and effective expectorant. That means that it helps to expel mucus. As such, syrup of garlic is an invaluable medicine for asthma, hoarseness, coughs, and many disorders of the lungs, particularly chronic bronchitis. It has been proved to relieve whooping-cough if rubbed on the chest and between the shoulderblades. It is claimed that a clove or two of garlic, pounded with honey, and taken two or three nights successively is good for rheumatism. It is considered a very great aid to digestion, keeping the stomach-lining healthy, and the more senior books of medicine state that if sniffed into the nostrils, it will revive anyone suffering from hysteria. The powerfully pungent smell is guaranteed to bring anyone to their senses!

There are few plants which are as effective as the humble garlic in curing or alleviating such a wide variety of ailments. Besides its medicinal properties, it is used as a most effective seasoning, perhaps

Garlic. Raw materials – sunshine, rain and earth, but it prevents infections, cures the sick and gives strength to mankind.

not so much in conservative England, but in the more southern countries of Europe it is a common ingredient in dishes and widely consumed by the population. Jewish people are certainly aware of its positive qualities, and it is widely used, both as a *Segulah* (*Pidyon Haben*) and for its many beneficial properties.

Take a look at the little garlic. It sits inconspicuously on the kitchen vegetable rack, it occupies a humble place in the greengrocer's window, it costs but pennies, or nothing if you grow it yourself, it is diminutive, white, and largely unnoticed. You would not include it in a festive fruit-basket, nor would you send some to your friend for their birthday. Yet in its humbleness lies its greatness! Its is made from the same raw materials as all plants — sunshine, rain and the bare earth — and from the most common, most simple ingredients come a complex compound of chemicals and oils, pungent aromas and flavours, which delight the palate, prevent infections, cure the sick and give strength to mankind. All in the little bulb of garlic!

מה גדלו מעשיך ה'

42

℘ THE GREATEST LIFT ℘

℘ OF ALL ℘

Owning a car has its problems. Very often, the age of the vehicle advances with that of the owner, and its signs are all too noticeable. The door only closes if you lift it as you swing it, and then only with a jarring clunk. There is a residual smell of petrol in the boot, which indicates something nasty in the fuel tank, but if you leave the rear window open a fraction, you can make believe that all is rosy in the rear. The engine might falter and backfire as you attempt to climb a hill, but with perseverance and gritted teeth, you chug-chug to the top. Starting in the morning is always a lesson in trust! In order to lessen the *Nisoyon*, it is beneficial to live on a hill, so that you can park the trusty vehicle facing downhill. Then, in the likely event of the early morning turning-of-the-key producing nothing more inspiring than a reluctant groan, resembling a post-*Purim* hangover, you can simply release the hand-break and sail down the hill, at first with dignified serenity, and then as you engage gear, and the unwilling old thing jerks and jumps into action with billows of blue smoke, at least you will be saved the indignity of pushing it! (There are two indignities that no-one should experience. One is chasing your hat on a windy day on a main road; and the second is heaving and pushing your car on a flat surface!) We shall not mention the windscreen wipers that have a mind of their own, quite unrelated to the control button or the rain, or the window-winder on the passenger's door that comes off when turned too enthusiastically, nor the permanent collection of empty (and not so empty) confectionery packets under the rear seat. It's a *heimishe* car!

Not so the hired car. For the ultimate pleasure in consumerism (a pleasure made even greater if you do not have to pay the bill), hire a car for a day. There, standing in front of your door you will be handed the slim piece of metal which they call a key, the passport to pure travelling pleasure. It is new, and gleamingly clean. The shining piece of technology contains every innovation and advance known to the motoring world. Just sitting inside is an experience. Besides the fact that there are no fossilized apple-cores littering the floor, it smells fresh. The seat can be adjusted forwards, backwards, sideways, up and down. A little more lumbar-support for your back, Sir? Why, certainly, just press this little button. Are the lights which illuminate the controls too glaring, Madam? Why, just turn the little dial and they will dim to suite your convenience. This little catch by your right hand will open the boot, the other will spring open the fuel cap. We understand that turning a winder to open the windows is a most arduous effort (how people managed in the old days is just impossible to imagine — it must have been terrible!) — just press the modestly glowing button and with a soft purr the window will rise or fall. Switch on the engine, and in any weather, the powerful engine will breath to life, eager to release its many horse-powers and

"All praise to the designer of this dream machine"

cylinders, all fed by fuel-injection, to respond instantly to the slightest hint of a command from the accelerator. As if in a dream, the sleek wondrous machine sighs up the harshest incline, and glides along the motorway swallowing the miles as effortlessly as a blue-whale swallows sardines.

From the heated wing-mirrors to the airbag hidden in the steering wheel, from the catalytic converters to the central locking system, all praise to the designers and manufacturers of this dream-machine.

What would you do if you were coming out of *Shul* during the week, expecting (or at least hoping for) a lift home. You would not mind whether the car was new or old, bought or hired, any lift is preferable to having to walk, especially if the weather is bad. If the car cruises past without stopping for you, and your mood is as black as the scudding clouds, take comfort. The lift which the Designer of the Universe is giving you is infinitely more precious, involving machinery much more complex and refined than the most advanced, luxurious, dynamic car yet invented. You are walking!

It is well known that in order to walk (or make any movement) you require muscles. You do not have to be strong to be muscular, for everyone's entire skeleton is covered with muscle. However, muscles by themselves do not produce movement. In order to produce movement in the leg, various muscles have to be commanded to contract, all in the correct sequence, in order to move the bones in the leg in a forward direction. How does that happen? Prepare to be amazed. Let us take a closer look at the type of muscle that is under the conscious control of your brain. This muscle is called a skeletal muscle, and there are a total of 620 of these muscles, varying in shape from broad sheets, such as in the diaphragm, to shin straps or spindles, such as those that make up the muscles of the forearm. Each skeletal muscle consists of bundles of parallel fibres enclosed in a strong membrane. (The number of fibres is greatest in the middle of a muscle, giving it the characteristic bulging appearance — as in strong men flexing their biceps, or ordinary men putting on their *Tefillin Shel Yad*!) Each fibre is composed of a large number of FI-BRILS. Imagine a large telephone cable, containing many separate wires, each wrapped in their own protective sheath, and each wire in turn containing many separate little wires. The cable is the muscle, each wire is the bundle of fibre, and one individual wire is a fibril. Each tiny individual fibril is made up of two types of filaments. There are thick filaments made of a protein called MYOSIN, and thin filaments made up of a protein called ACTIN. When instructed to do so, (by the brain, via the nervous system) the long thin strands of actin slide into spaces between the short, thick strands of myosin. When this happens to thousands of strands, the muscle contracts.

Why is it that when you walk, you do so in a smooth, flowing motion, and not in a jerking, abrupt manner? In reality, this is how it should happen, if all the cells in a muscle would contract at the same time, (and as they in fact do when you snatch your hand away from a hot object). Fortunately, however, muscle cells contract in sequence, allowing the muscle to move smoothly. Thank you O muscle for that useful bit of design! Let us consider one single step. In order to move the leg, we require one muscle to bend it, and another muscle to straighten it. These two muscles obviously produce opposite effects, so they must not contract at the same time, otherwise the leg will not move at all! The nervous system ensures that this does not happen. Each muscle has its own nerve supply (separate wiring) so that when messages are sent to one muscle, telling it to contract, they cease to be sent to the other, and vice-versa. When muscles work in pairs, as they do in the leg and in the arm, they are called antagonistic (an interesting example of '*Ezer Kenegdo*'?). In order to produce that single step, there has to be co-ordination in the limbs, activated by antagonistic muscles contracting and relaxing alternately. Even when you are not moving, some of your muscle fibres have to contract to keep you standing up or sitting down... This is called 'muscle tone' and it keeps the body in its correct position.

If you are not a practical person, and have the greatest difficulty trying to fix a wooden shelf to a brick wall, do not try and imagine how muscles are attached to hard bone. The fact is that muscles taper into strong non-elastic tendons. These attach the mus-

No car yet invented can climb a climbing frame.

cle either to the ends of bones, or to cartilage or ligaments (tough fibres connecting the bones together). The fibrous tissue of the tendons fuses with the bone at one end, and blends into the tissue of the muscle at the other end, enabling muscular contraction to act on the bones and convert into body movement. Do you think it all just happens!

So you want to move forward. How is the message from your brain conveyed to your muscle? Every muscle has a nerve leading to it. When it reaches the muscle, the nerve splits up into branches which supply the individual muscle fibres. The point where the nerve joins the muscle fibre is called the nerve-muscle junction. When the message reaches the end of the nerve, it crosses the nerve-muscle junction and then spreads along the muscle fibre, making it contract. Message received. To make the antagonistic muscle do its work and bring the leg back into its original position, another message needs to be sent to that muscle. And quickly.

So there you go, walking home just using the two muscles? Nonsense! Over 200 different muscles are operated when you walk! Then bring to mind your sense of balance, housed in your inner ear, the sense of sight and hearing, your cooling system which keeps your body at a steady temperature however fast you run, your arms which swing by your side (why do they?), your toes which help to keep you on your feet, think of all the incredible nervous-electrical-chemical (muscles use oxygen to release energy, and use their own store of glucose when oxygen is in short supply) activity which is surging simultaneously through your body, understand that no car yet invented could undertake all that you are doing (do you know any car that can travel on three wheels, as you do when you hop, or can climb stairs, swim and jump) and be grateful that you missed your lift. You have the greatest lift — and the greatest gift — of all!

43

◈ THE CONDUCTOR ◈

Imagine a *Simcha*. It might be the celebration of a *Bris*, a *Bar-Mitzvah*, or a *Sheva Brochos*. The guests come at a time that they think the proceedings will actually begin rather than the time requested by the host. Eventually, everyone is seated, their good mood is accentuated by the tempting hors d'oeuvres ('starters' in English) which they attack with vigour, and an enjoyable time is anticipated. Soon enough, the little plates (hors d'oeuvres are never served on large plates) are empty, and a few enthusiastic guests begin a *Nigun*, which, in the absence of additional food, quickly catches on. The song fades away, a half-hearted attempt at a second round does not succeed, and the guests begin to examine the wallpaper and the design of their plastic forks. Nothing is happening. The host sits at the top table with a serene smile on his face, oblivious to the fact that his guests are becoming bored, tired and hungry. After a long while, he signals for the next course to be brought in, and relief ripples through the hall. No sooner is the steaming chicken soup set before the guests, than the *Baal Simchah* decides to stand up and deliver his address. Good manners demand that the guests do not put spoon to plate during the *Droshoh*, so they anxiously watch their soup drop in temperature, and the *kneidlach* deflate. The *Baal Simchah* is so happy to have the opportunity to say 'a few words' that the term 'endless' is given a new dimension. The soup is cold, the *Kneidlach* sad. Another excruciating wait precedes the main course, which in turn is pounced upon by yet another s.p.e.a.k.e.r... and so it goes on. At the hour when Cinderella turned into a pumpkin, the guests finally are able to leave, feeling like prisoners released from prison with no remission! Not exactly a resounding success.

What went wrong? The answer is one word. Co-ordination. For any event, big or small, to be successful, it must be planned in advance, with co-ordination between the catering staff and the organisers. Besides the planning, there has to be someone who can see what is happening, and have the authority to give the orders to ensure that the speakers and courses dovetail in efficient sequence. When that happens, the *Simcha* is a pleasure.

Everything needs co-ordination. Imagine an orchestra without a conductor! A cacophony of sounds assaults the ears as individual members of the ensemble decide unilaterally in which key to begin, when to begin, and the correct volume at which to play. Even the

"Imagine an orchestra without a conductor!"

pussy cats would block their ears with their paws. Imagine a busy road junction without traffic lights, where every driver thinks he has right of way, and is in a great hurry; imagine (perhaps better not) a teeming airport where some Jumbo-sized planes are seeking to land, and other are trying to take off, and there is no air control....

And imagine the body without a tiny piece of tissue called the PITUITARY GLAND. What the conductor is to the orchestra, this tiny gland is to the body, with one small difference. An orchestra without its conductor will produce disharmony, but will harm no-one; a person without a pituitary gland cannot function. In the complex machinery that is the human being, various functions and rhythms of the body are controlled by hormones. You can tell yourself to reach out for an apple, but you cannot command yourself to grow. You can consciously decide not to blink (for a short while at least) but you cannot consciously control the level of calcium in your blood. Yet all of these acts are under the control of the brain. Instead of responding to messages sent by the brain along the nerve pathways, certain rhythms and changes are responses to messages which are delivered in code — the chemical code of hormones. Hormones are chemical messengers which are produced by glands and discharged directly into the blood stream. Although there are six main sets of glands scattered throughout the body, it is the pituitary gland which effects the working of many of them. It is indeed the conductor of the endocrine (a gland that secretes a hormone directly into the bloodstream) orchestra, and the world's most compact and intricate chemical plant.

How large is this master-conductor? Prepare for a surprise. It is as large as a pea, weighs one fiftieth of an ounce, is composed of 85% water, its total daily output of hormones is less than one millionth of a gram, and is one of the most complex organs in the body! It lives on the underside of the brain, and hangs, like a cherry on a tiny stem, from the part of the brain called the HYPOTHALAMUS. Being such a vitally important organ, it is very well protected inside the bony cradle of the skull, and performs mighty tasks. (It is interesting to note that for centuries scholars thought the pituitary gland was of little importance. At one time it was thought to be the source of nasal mucus! It is only recently, with the advance of modern chemistry, that some of its complex functions have been revealed. Never denigrate that which you do not understand!)

When a baby is born, it begins to grow. The rate of growth is steady, with a sudden acceleration during adolescence after which it tapers off and ceases. The rate of growth of a child is directly affected by the hormone SOMATOTROPHIN which is produced by the front of the pituitary gland. This hormone acts directly to regulate the growth of nearly all bones and tissue. When the young person has grown to adult size, production of the vital hormone ceases. Working as it does through the blood stream, distance is no object. Thus we find that the machine which controls the growth of your big toe lives far away in the pea-sized wonder box that is the pituitary gland.

The baby can thank the pituitary gland for more than just its ability to grow — it can thank it for being born, and for the miraculous events which enable it to feed from its mother. One of the contributory factors in activating the birth process is the release of a special hormone called OXYTOCIN, which starts the contractions of the mother's womb. Approximately fifteen minutes after birth, the mother's rear lobe of the pituitary gland releases more of the hormone oxytocin into the bloodstream, this time designed to cause further contraction of the womb muscles. This forces out the afterbirth, and closes torn and damaged blood vessels. The front section of the pea-sized gland produces PROLACTIN, which in turn stimulates the glands which produce milk — the constituents of which are extracted from blood flowing through the glands.

One of the vital functions of the pituitary gland is to stimulate and control the other glands in the body, ensuring that the correct level of hormone activity is maintained. Let us take one example. No two people seem to have exactly the same amount of energy. One person may be energetic, always on the move, whereas another seems slow and methodical. This is due to the action of the THYROID GLANDS

— which lives on either side of the windpipe — and which control the rate of chemical processes in the body (called metabolism). The thyroid glands themselves produce the hormone THYROXINE. This hormone contains iodine, and is needed by every cell in the body. Now if the thyroid gland is underactive, there will be too little of this vital hormone in the blood. The pituitary — the master gland — registers this and jumps into action. It produces a hormone called THYROTROPHIN which rushes to the thyroid gland via the bloodstream and stimulates it into greater activity. If the level of thyroxine rises above normal, the pituitary's output of the thyroid-stimulating hormone falls.

In hot weather, you perspire a lot, and this evaporation of water through the skin means a drop in the water level of the blood. That is not good! The vigilant pituitary gland notices the lower level, and produces a hormone called vasopressin. This hormone travels through the blood to the kidneys, stimulating the filter units of those wonder machines to absorb more water from the urine (which explains why in the summer we tend to eliminate less water than in winter). Interestingly enough, one of the things that can retard the pituitary's production of vasopressin is alcohol. Too many *l'chaims* or glasses of beer, and the kidneys produce urine very rapidly, which can cause dehydration. If you feel extremely thirsty and crave for liquid on the morning of *Shushan Purim*, you know why. You have interfered with your master gland!

In time of danger or stress, man can become superman. The brain sends a signal to the pituitary gland, which in turn sends a special hormone (adrenotrophin) to the adrenal glands (which live atop the kidneys) to stimulate them into emergency action. Adrenalin pours into the blood, the liver releases stored sugar, instant energy into the bloodstream, the heart speeds up, digestion is halted, blood-clotting time is quickened in case of injury — and he can run faster, jump further or hit harder than he ever thought possible.

Just think. This little pea-sized wonder produces at least eight major hormones, each of which is vital to healthy life. These hormones are amongst the most complex substances known to man. The pituitary gland silently and efficiently co-ordinates the vastly complicated chemical processes of the body into one harmonious symphony. What a tremendous conductor! Just think, therefore, how indescribably great is the wisdom of the Conductor and Co-ordinator who designed and created the precious little conductor within us!

מה גדלו מעשיך ה'